Also by Robson Green

Robson Green: Just the Beginning

Robson Green Extreme Fishing

With Charlotte Reather

SIMON &
SCHUSTER

London · New York · Sydney · Toronto · New Delhi

A CBS COMPANY

First published in Great Britain by Simon & Schuster UK Ltd, 2013
A CBS COMPANY

Copyright © IWC Media Limited (a Zodiak Media Company) 2013

1 3 5 7 9 10 8 6 4 2

Simon & Schuster UK Ltd
1st Floor
222 Gray's Inn Road
London WC1X 8HB

www.simonandschuster.co.uk

Simon & Schuster Australia, Sydney
Simon & Schuster India, New Delhi

A CIP catalogue record for this book
is available from the British Library

Hardback ISBN: 978-1-47112-748-9
Trade Paperback ISBN: 978-1-47112-803-5
Ebook ISBN: 978-1-47112-750-2

Typeset by M Rules
Printed and bound by CPI Group (UK) Ltd, Croydon, CR0 4YY

I dedicate this book to my beautiful son Taylor
and to my Uncle Matheson who gave me everything
I needed to know about Fishing – *Robson*

To my darling High Tower, Mom & Pops,
Mo Granny and Robson – *Charlotte*

Fish Anatomy

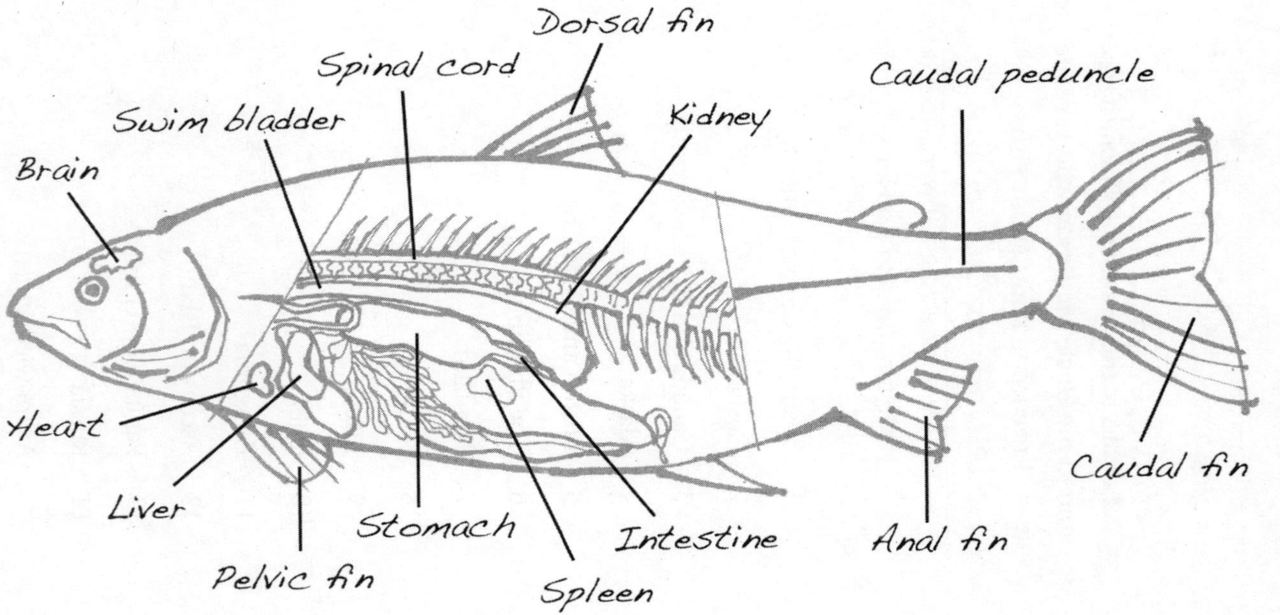

Caudal fin

Caudal fin

Anal fin

Caudal peduncle

Kidney

Dorsal fin

Intestine

Spleen

Spinal cord

Stomach

Swim bladder

Pelvic fin

Brain

Heart

Liver

CONTENTS

Chapter One

SPAIN, THE CANARIES AND THE AZORES

'Don't Go All Scrambled Egg'

May 2008

I'm in the mid-Atlantic, off the coast of the Azores, powering through the waves on a high-tech fishing yacht. South African Captain Ian Carter and shipmate Steve Hall are taking me on a deep-sea adventure in pursuit of the Holy Grail of game fish, the Atlantic blue marlin. The sun is warm, birds are flying high in the sky above, and dolphins are leaping just metres from the boat. Conditions are perfect for catching a billfish and Ian tells me I'm here at exactly the right time, when the Gulf Stream brings the marlin within striking distance.

We've been motoring across the ocean for four and half hours and at last we're approaching our destination. Ian slows down and we put out squid lures at the back of the boat and begin to trawl. The vibrations of the boat should help attract marlin and maybe, just maybe, one will take the bait. We trawl and we trawl but nothing is going for our lures. The hours tick by. Unlike our reels, everyone is at full tension.

Suddenly, Steve tells Ian to change course. He can 'smell fish'. I sniff the air; I can't smell a bloody thing. I sniff again: nope, nothing. Ian swings the boat round and heads west. Steve points at a small slick of oil on the water; we're going to head straight through it. It's a sign that something is feeding on bait fish, possibly sardines or mackerel. We're closing in on our target. I ask Steve for some advice in case I am lucky enough to hook a blue.

He is a man of few words. He says, in his North Carolina drawl, 'I'll be watching from the corner of my eye. I'll say "Go to the chair", and you go. Just take your time and don't go all scrambled egg, do you know what I mean?'

Right, got it. No, actually I haven't. What the hell does that mean?

About twenty minutes later, and with little time left on the clock before we have to return, one of the reels starts making a loud whirring sound, like a primitive yawn. We are in! The line is taken out at high speed, 200 metres or more.

'Hold me glasses. Hold me glasses!' I say, panicking and flapping like the actor I am. My heart is pounding as I click on the harness and take the rod. The fight is immensely powerful. It *must* be a marlin but I'm not certain. I am yanked forward violently and swung round in the chair. I lean back with all my might, release and reel, ten to the dozen. And very slowly I begin to bring the fish closer to the boat. But soon it turns and runs again, stripping the line out another 150 metres.

'Please, please stay on the line. I beg you to stay on the line,' I say.

'Relax,' says Steve, but that is impossible right now.

I wind as fast as I can without letting the line go slack, otherwise I could lose the fish. *Think positive, Robson.* My muscles are burning and my arms feel as if they are going to drop off. Ian is backing up the boat to help me. *I am hard-boiled, not scrambled. Hard!* I shout at myself internally, like a fishing coxswain. *Come on, Robson. Come on!* I fight with all my might for fifty minutes, winding and pulling, when suddenly a 500-pound blue marlin bursts though the crest of a wave, piercing the sky with her spear.

She is the most amazing creature I have ever seen. Her body is midnight blue with a silvery white belly and faint cobalt stripes on her side. I am awe-struck. *Makaira nigricans*, the 'black sword' of the Atlantic (in Latin, *machaera* is a sword and *nigricans* means 'becoming black'). She is the reason we have come here and it's taken only a matter of hours to find her. It took poor old Santiago eighty-five days to catch a marlin in Hemingway's *The Old Man and the Sea*. Our budget just wouldn't stretch to that.

Jaded, I slowly reel in my beautiful fish. She is tired, too. Steve grabs the line and pulls her to the side of the boat. For this to count as a catch, he needs to get hold of the last bit of the filament, called the leader, which connects the line on the rod and reel to the hook. We can't bring the fish on board as the species is not only protected but also seriously dangerous. Steve leans out and grips the leader with his right hand and smiles at me. We have officially caught an Atlantic blue marlin.

We all stand and stare silently at the magnificent fish moving with the waves at the side of the boat. With a gloved hand, Steve carefully 'bills' the fish by firmly grasping her spear so she can't injure anyone. Marlin use their bills to slash and kill schools of fish before they feed and they have been known to spear boats and the odd fisherman, too, including one woman I read about on the Internet who was pierced through the chest when a marlin leapt onto the boat. The only thing that saved her was her breast implant. Perhaps Katie Price should be doing this show instead of me. After all, she is better equipped.

I run my hand across the marlin's back and say goodbye. Steve unhooks her and releases the bill. Capable of swimming at up to 68 m.p.h., she is gone in a matter of seconds. Everyone is pumped with emotion and adrenalin; the marlin was truly astonishing and her magic lingers. We hug and engage in male back-slapping.

'Don't forget to breathe,' says Steve.

We return to shore, the marlin flag upside down to show we've caught and released an Atlantic blue today. I am a hero and this episode is a triumph – except that this is television and our fishing adventure hasn't been quite as clear-cut as it would seem.

In reality, we have just pulled off a miracle at the eleventh hour. The show was on the verge of being cancelled and my career well and truly down the pan. *Extreme Fishing* could have been my second Vietnam, the first being my singing career with Jerome. Director Ian Lilley and I hug each other out of pure relief. He goes back to projectile vomiting off the side of the boat, which he and his assistant, Anna Hassan, have been doing for the past few days. I have done most of the filming myself, by fixing the camera to the side of the boat and talking into it. It's the eighth day of a disastrous trip and we are all exhausted. Catching the blue marlin has pulled us back from the brink and it's all thanks to one extraordinary man, Steve: The Man Who Can Smell Fish.

Rewind to eight days earlier. I've just landed my own fishing show. I am unbearable to my wife, colleagues and peers. What mortal can resist the sensuous mix of exotic travel, hard cash and fish? In every fisherman's eyes I've won the lottery. My mentor and uncle, Matheson Green, who taught me to fish as a boy, is sick as a parrot with envy; he's also very proud. I, however, am smug and heading for a fall, and it comes sooner than I think.

Some people say the anticipatory fear of doing something is far worse than actually doing it. What a load of old cobblers. From the moment I step on to the plane to Madrid I know I have made a terrible mistake. Matters aren't helped at Heathrow when an old woman comes rushing over and says, 'Eeeh, look who it is and I haven't got my teeth in.' She continues, 'I've got your album – I got it free with a chicken at the supermarket.' She thinks she is paying me a compliment, and goes on to tell me she uses the CD cover to stop her fridge from wobbling. The director, Ian, literally has to pick me off the floor, where my ego lies in tatters.

River Ebro

Our first port of call is the River Ebro in Spain. I am supposed to catch a wels catfish today but at the moment I feel I'm more likely to suffer a heart attack. I take my pulse subtly in the van – it's over 100 beats per minute. I need beta blockers. Fishing used to be my stress relief but not anymore. Not only do I have to fish on camera but I also have to present, and I'm not really used to being myself in front of, well, anyone these days. I prefer to dress up, slap on the make-up and pretend to be someone else. Anyone but me.

I swallow hard as I prepare for my first piece to camera. We enter a local drinking hole in Mequinenza, full of rowdy British cat-fishermen. It looks like the bar in *Star Wars*, where Han Solo meets Chewbacca. Talk about an owner looking like his dog; these guys all look like catfish, complete with hairy barbels.

This place is obsessed with catfish and here in Spain they grow to epic proportions. If they're not in the river, they're on the wall. A 150-pound giant protrudes out of the brown wood above the bar, like an ichthyic tumour.

'To me it looks like it's swum past a nuclear power station. It's too big; it's not right,' I say, jabbering at the camera.

Everyone is staring at me. *Just pretend you're Noel Edmonds, Robson*, I think. *He makes the camera his friend; he has a winning formula.* But I don't want to be bloody Noel Edmonds. He's a bit creepy, with too much facial hair, and I don't trust men with beards. Blind panic descends as I look around and see everyone in the bar has a beard. I don't know what the hell I'm doing and they're all staring at me thinking 'You lucky Geordie git – how did *you* get a fishing programme?' And I'm thinking exactly the same thing. I'm racing my words and I'm so tense I sound as if I've had a hit of helium. I'm somewhere between Noel Edmonds and Alan Carr, and that's not a place I'd like to be.

The first take is a disaster and we need to re-shoot the scene. It's not getting any better and my inner voices are now shouting.

Why the hell are you doing this, Robson?

Because I didn't think it through.

You're winging it and dying on your arse. You need a script. You don't even know who you are without a script. Why haven't you got an American series like Hugh Laurie or Damian Lewis?

Because I didn't go to Eton. No, it's because you're fannying around pretending to present a fishing show. Oh God, I'm a fraud. I want to go home.

'And, action!' shouts the director.

I have nothing to give so I waffle. We move outside to meet Birmingham-born contributor Colin Bunn, who is going to help me catch a catfish. Up until this point the biggest fish I have ever caught is a four-pound trout and an eighteen-pound salmon. Colin's nice but I can tell deep down he pities me.

Although I've never landed a wels catfish before, I've thankfully done loads of research. For example, I know that catfish are also known as sheatfish – and that's not a Geordie insult. ('You call this a catfish, bonny lad? I call it a sheat fish!' In fact, it sounds more French: 'Zay are really sheat fish.') I rehearse some lines in my head ready to use on camera. 'The Latin name is *Silurus glanis*, they have good hearing and can live for around thirty years. The species is not indigenous to the area and there are concerns about the ecological impact on the Ebro, including a decimation of the endemic Iberian barbel species.' Colin sets up a couple of rods and I relate the facts to camera like rapid machine-gun fire. It is another total waste of video tape.

I give up talking directly to the camera and instead get some tips from our contributor. Colin, like many other Brits, used to come here fishing on holiday and loved it so much that he moved here permanently. I want to know if these catfish really do live up to their fearsome reputation.

'I can give you an example,' says Colin. 'Put your two hands on the rod.'

I lift the heavy rod as he instructs. Colin gets on the other end of it and yanks me forward, pulling the line up and down sharply.

'That's what they're like, and they shake their heads like this so you get that banging action.'

After the demonstration we crack on with the real thing. Colin's mate, Ashley, rows the bait out into the middle of the river and drops it in. We are using halibut pellets, which are fed to farmed fish. They look a bit like pony nuts, which possibly explains why some of the catfish are the size of Welsh Cobs.

'I've heard they can take egrets off the surface,' I say.

'And swans,' says Colin.

OK, Colin, I see your swan and I raise you. 'And wild boar,' I add.

'Yeah, anything that swims in there that's big enough.'

Anglers have been known to tell a few tall tales in their time but this fish really does have an incredible reputation. In the eighteenth century, it was reported that the body of a woman had been found inside a catfish. Well, I wouldn't mind curling up in one right now, because at least I would be dying in private rather than in full view of the cameras.

One of the sensors starts to bleep. Colin hands me the rod and I pretend to know what I'm doing. The fish packs a punch and I am immediately working hard. It runs, almost pulling me into the water as Colin had demonstrated.

'Just pump and wind,' Colin says. What he means is that I need to lift the rod to pull the fish towards me, then wind it in quickly. If I just try to reel, the reel could break, or burn out the clutch. Either way, I could lose the fish and, after all this effort and anxiety, that's not something I'm prepared to do. Deep down I know I am living the dream; I'm just looking forward to the time I can start enjoying it.

The catfish hoves into view in the shallows. Colin gets hold of it by the lip and passes the large fella to me. This is my chance to share my knowledge of catfish with the viewer, but all I can say is: 'Look at the size of that! Oh, my goodness, what a beautiful creature.' I look down at it again, with its massive mouth and strange fleshy whiskers (barbels); it's certainly not a looker. Beautiful? Why did I say that? It's impressive but not pretty – a bit like Ann Widdecombe.

The fish is weighed and comes in at 33.5 pounds. I carry it back to the river and release it to swim another day. Thank God I didn't fail on the fishing side of things on my first outing: I can't present but at least I can fish. I take a breath as I look across the murky Ebro to the verdant Spanish countryside; it really is lovely here. Right, let's see if I can reel in another. Over the next few hours it's a catfish-fest. I land a dozen fish and my personal best is ninety pounds – the biggest river fish I have ever caught. All together a 400-pound haul isn't bad for a day's work.

I pick up the phone to the producer, Hamish Barbour. I want to talk about my problems in depth. He listens.

'Basically, Hamish, it's all been a big mistake. I can't present to save my life. I might have got lucky with the catfish, but I'm feeling like a total fraud – the only fishing I've done is on some streams in the northeast. Why didn't you choose Paxman? Or Chris Tarrant, an angling ninja and an actual TV *presenter*? Hamish, you've got the wrong man.'

'No, we haven't, Robson. We want you. We believe in you. You have something they don't.'

'What's that? Well, I suppose I am better looking.'

'Exactly. They'll never look as good on camera as you do.'

This is music to every shallow actor's ears – all we want to know is that we look good on camera. Hamish, the TV Svengali and puppet-master, plays me like a carp in a bucket. (No offence to carp fishermen, although they hate me already – but more on that later.) After our chat, my confidence slowly starts to return. I realise I need to embrace the opportunity and stop worrying. Everything is going to be OK.

Later that evening we travel by car to the coast just south of Barcelona. We're all tired but we have to shoot a night fishing sequence. Centuries ago, fishermen used to catch fish by putting flames on the water to attract sardines, rather like moths. Tonight we are using halogen lamps. Without sardines big fish wouldn't exist, and I enthuse about the species on camera. It's going really well.

I am on a boat with director Jeremy Cadle and two guys who don't speak a word of English. My Spanish is also poor. It's pitch black save the lanterns and a few torches, and as the fish come to the surface I say to Jeremy, 'Aren't those a bit big for sardines?'

'No,' he says.

'In fact, are you're sure they're not mackerel?'

'No, Robson, they are sardines,' he says with the utmost authority.

'Oh, OK,' I reply, assuming he must be a marine biologist. He is not.

We film for seven hours, gathering the fish in nets. I do a PTC (piece to camera) about the sardines and the fact that I have never caught so many fish in such a short time. There are thousands of them. I take one in my hands and say, 'If it weren't for sardines, big game fish like marlin wouldn't exist.' One of the Spanish guys lightly taps me on the arm but I ignore him and carry on talking. He coughs loudly. He is ruining my PTC.

'What?' I say indignantly.

'Eh, Señor, no sardine. Mackerel. Mackerel,' he smiles, revealing several missing teeth.

I can hear the blood whooshing around my brain as the pressure increases. I thank our Spanish friend and shoot Jeremy a look that could freeze concrete. *Oh, bloody hell! All the filming is wasted, utterly wasted, because I haven't said the word 'mackerel' once.* There is no way we can hide this mistake with clever voiceover and editing, and an entire night's work is now heading for the cutting-room floor. I am furious with Jeremy but inside I chide myself for being a fool. I knew they were mackerel so why did I doubt myself and trust a man who doesn't even own a fishing rod? I look up at the stars and the Milky Way as we head for shore. My Uncle Matheson appears like Obi-Wan Kenobi with a bright aura around him.

'You can do this, Robson, but first you must believe. Trust your instincts,' he booms majestically across the night sky.

Elusive Giant Grouper

Jeremy tries to make amends by telling me the size of the giant grouper I am going to catch this morning. He says, arms outstretched, 'They grow up to two thousand pounds.' *Wow*, I think, totally forgetting the fact that he's not a marine biologist. Grouper do grow to that size, but not here off the coast of Spain.

But off we go into the void, me as trusting as a child. It's like *Living in Oblivion* with Steve Buscemi.

We are fishing using glass-bottomed boxes that you put in the water and which act like large goggles. Groupers are stout ambush predators with vast mouths: their jaw pressure is around 800 pounds per square inch; a man's clenched fist is only 35–40. Their powerful mouths and gills can suck their prey in from a distance, a bit like Simon Cowell. The species are also hermaphrodites: born female, they can turn into males if there aren't enough cocks in the shoal, so to speak. (And we thought such versatility between the sexes was a modern phenomenon, when fish have in fact been gender-bending for millions of years – and a bit more realistically than RuPaul.)

We submerge the box in the water and wait ... and wait and wait. There's bugger-all down there! And after not hours but *three days* what do we catch? Diddlysquat. It has been a complete waste of time and I have come to the conclusion there's nothing in the sea. It's empty. And do you want to know my theory? It's those damned Spanish fishermen, who, by the way, we pay millions and millions of pounds every year to fish off the coast of Africa whilst our own British fishermen struggle to survive. And then they come and illegally plunder British waters as well. Not to mention the bureaucratic idiots who started the practice of discarding, whereby tonnes upon tonnes of fish are thrown back every year because of the stupid EU quota system. And these muppets get paid like footballers and only work on Wednesdays so as not to spoil both weekends. Don't get me started! But you can do your bit by supporting Hugh Fearnley-Whittingstall's incredible 'Fish Fight' campaign to bring an end to the madness and terrible waste.

Back on the boat, my patience has been tested to the max by the 'sardine' and grouper debacles. I talk to Jeremy about how the show is going and he tells me he thinks it's going swimmingly. I say, 'But we didn't catch anything today.' He replies, 'Robson, it's called fishing, not catching.' I want to strangle him.

Seeing as we have caught bugger-all so far, save the catfish, Hamish suggests we push on to the Canary Islands to see what we can find there. Everyone is winging it and it's not a comfortable feeling. Behind the scenes, Hamish is foaming at the mouth like a rabid dog. He has seen the rushes of Spain – uncut footage that will later be edited into the final programme – and says we have no more than five minutes of a show. This really is our last-chance saloon.

'Go and catch a marlin, Robson,' he says on the phone to me.

'Easier said than done,' I say. 'Haven't you read Hemingway's *The Old Man and the Sea*?'

'Make it happen. I believe in you.'

Uncle Obi-Wan Matheson echoes the sentiment in my head: 'Believe.'

But today, much like the rest of the trip, there is plenty of behind-the-scenes drama that the TV audience doesn't get to see: it transpires that our marlin fisherman in Tenerife, the one we are so heavily relying on to save the show, has had a skinful the night before and crashed his boat! So our first task is to find another contributor. Mercifully the production team manages to track down a Scottish guy called John with a big boat. Crisis averted.

I shake hands with our Scottish fisherman, who is tanned like leather. He has brought his wife and another old seadog along and boy do they all love to drink. It's like a bleeding episode of *Eldorado*.

'How's it looking today?' I ask.

'Looks great. Great weather – nice and hot,' he says.

'Fantastic. So what brought you to Tenerife?'

'The sunshine.'

'Not the fishing?'

'Nope, the sunshine.'

It quickly becomes apparent that this guy isn't remotely interested in fishing; he's just an old sailor who likes going round the islands topping up his tan.

'When did you last catch something?'

'Haven't caught anything in, er, three years.'

Oh. My. God.[1]

We end up fannying around with Scottish John for two days and – surprise, surprise – we catch nothing. I'm in mental decline.

After a day of not even catching a sea cucumber, the biggest insult to an empty-handed fisherman is to make him taste another man's fish, but the team is running out of ideas. I look at the camera and say, 'It's called escolar – because it looks like it's wearing reading glasses like an academic or "scholar". It's also called butterfish.'

The escolar is a bottom feeder and scavenger that hoovers up the dead, decomposing things that lie on the ocean floor – a bit like a vulture does on land. Part of the snake mackerel family, it is highly toxic and has to be prepared in a certain way to make it safe for humans to ingest. It's so dangerous that eating this fish

1. After the first series we always remembered to ask contributors if they had ever actually caught a fish and how long ago that was. It was a steep learning curve.

is banned in some countries – but not here. The islanders absolutely adore it; in fact, they can't get enough of it. Apparently it has a lovely buttery taste – if you get it right . . .

Joni Cejas, a restaurant-owner and chef, is going to show me how to prepare this dangerous fish. He is a silver-haired Spanish Del Boy who has his fingers in lots of pies, and now fish. A large escolar is waiting for me on a butcher's slab in the kitchen. The leathery prehistoric creature has large, frightening eyes, razor-sharp teeth and an obsidian tongue. I only have to take one look at it to know I don't want to eat it. It's as if my response has been evolutionarily hardwired to my brain because an ancestor way, way back in time, some 60,000 years ago, once ate one of these fish and puked himself inside out and everyone in the Green tribe was really worried and said, 'Was it the oysters, Brian?' 'No, the escolar [puking sound effects].' And they all said, 'Gosh, well, we won't eat that again' – and that knowledge was planted in my DNA in an attempt to protect me to this very day. However, today I am going to ignore all of that good sense and eat it for the sake of entertainment on Channel 5.

Enter Joni waving two large knives at me. He shows me how to remove the toxins and cuts the meat away from the spine because this is the most hazardous part of the fish. Although any part of the skin could also send me to hospital with blue lights flashing – it's like playing a game of deep-sea Russian roulette. I wring the oily poison out of a piece of the filleted fish as if it's Russell Brand's bed sheet, and we pour loads of salt on the fillet, just as you do when you spill red wine on the carpet; in the case of this fish, the salt draws toxins out rather than wine.[2]

2. Except I've since learnt that sparkling water or white wine are much better for carpet stains, as well as being very refreshing drinks.

Joni fries the escolar without oil or seasoning for a few minutes and lunch is served. We move through to the dining area to
taste our handiwork. It's like being a guest of Blofeld. I put the
poison to my lips; like a fussy child attempting to eat broccoli, I
open wide and nibble a small piece. It's like motor oil – but not
Castrol Edge, more Mick's Garage's own brand. I turn to camera
and my face starts to lie like a cheap Spanish watch.

'Mmm,' I start to say.

I chew some more and have an epiphany: 'Trust your instincts,
Robson,' I hear Uncle Matheson say.

'That's horrible! That is shocking. I'm sorry, I can't eat that.
What *is* that? The islanders love it? Are you mad? Mmmm, the
lovely buttery taste . . . It tastes like shit. Oh dear me, I think you
have left some of the toxins in it, Joni.'

But the chef decides that the reason I'm not enjoying it is
because I've put too much salt on, and, oh joy of joys, he gives me
another piece. It tastes a bit better but that's like saying Hitler was
a bit better than Stalin. In that moment, I realise the only way this
show has a chance of working is by me being brutally honest at
all times.

Rock Fishing

The next day I am rock fishing with my old mate the poisonous-
fish chef, Joni, and his brother. Using a twenty-one-foot bamboo
pole, we're hoping to catch some delicious parrotfish, which will
make a nice change from the 'I can't believe it's not butterfish'
that tastes nothing like bloody butter – not even close.

I am unravelling fast today as I had little sleep during the
night, convinced that I was slipping into a toxic coma brought on
by my sampling of the frightening oleaginous scavenger. I

clamber over volcanic rock to get into position for our first take and then stand precariously on a craggy lump of ignimbrite and attempt to explain the topography of the islands on camera.

'The Canaries sit on top of a huge underwater mountain range, causing plankton and lots of fish to well up from the depths below. Argh!'

A large crab jumps out at me from a rock pool, waving its claws angrily. I shriek like a girl and hop across to another rock. Out of nowhere a dog brushes past my leg unexpectedly, which nearly sends me over the edge. The director shouts for me to get into position – bloody easy for him to say from down there on the ground, which is *flat*. It's really dangerous on the rocks, especially as I am currently neither physically steady nor mentally sound.

I used go fishing to unwind and relax but now it's having the exact opposite effect and all I want is to hide in my wardrobe and hug my shoes. As I dangle my hook into the water below, my bottom is like a rabbit's nose on a spring day: twitchy. I've never had this symptom before; my nerves must be shot. Back at the hotel, however, I discover this twitchiness is due to something else entirely: parasites, to be precise (the word comes from the Ancient Greek for 'professional dinner guests'). That poisonous atramentous bottom feeder, the escolar, has infected me with red threadworms that are now feasting on *my* bottom and, well, I'm not happy about it. I should have trusted my instincts: I knew eating it was a very bad idea.

I rejoin Joni and his brother on a local beach to eat the parrotfish we caught earlier. It is nectar – just the most amazing-tasting fish. I share a glass of wine with them but I can't stay long – my bottom's on the move again. I head back to the hotel and take action. Standing in front of the bathroom mirror I address my behind: 'I am not food for worms, yet.' I down a litre of milky nematode-napalm.

'Hasta la vista, critters!'

Azores Marlin

The Azores aren't in the schedule. They are Hamish's last-ditch attempt to save the show, as we have maybe enough footage for about half an episode at this point. We have two days to get some usable footage or we are officially sunk. On the first day there, the heavens open up and it pisses it down. We can all tell it's not worth heading out to sea but the skipper, Ian Carter, suggests we give it a go. I suppose we have nothing to lose.

We power out of the habour into a two-metre swell. All the other boats are coming back, and fast, but we unflinchingly go against the tide. I remain cheery on camera but off it I am staring into the abyss of my own career. It is in fact the barrel of a gun with a knot in the end. That said, dwelling on my private turmoil is mildly better than staring into my breakfast, which is what Ian Lilley and Anna Hassan are both doing. This is the start of their extreme-hurling-fest that would endure for the next two days.

After what seems an eternity, Skipper Ian finally abandons the trip and we head for home. Not only are the conditions dangerous but also the likelihood of us catching even a sprat in this weather is remote. However, the relief of heading back to land is tinged with searing anxiety: we now have less than twenty-four hours to catch a blue marlin or something – anything – or the episode will have been an expensive cock-up and the series will be panned.

There is a saying in acting circles that actors are paid for waiting around and the acting's free. This is entirely different. I feel more like one of the British soldiers waiting for his imminent demise in *Zulu*. The night is a long one and I can't sleep. I toss and turn as if still on Ian's boat on the rough seas. Tomorrow is our last chance, our only chance. We *have* to catch a fish.

The next morning I tear the curtains open. The sun is shining and the sky is blue.

Hope springs eternal in the human breast;
Man never Is, but always To be blest:
The soul, uneasy and confin'd from home,
Rests and expatiates in a life to come.[3]

We head out in Ian's boat for the very last time, on the very last day of the schedule, and, well, you know the rest of the story already. Thanks to Steve Hall's superhuman sense of smell, we are given a *deus ex machina* ending and we catch a magnificent blue marlin. Steve saves the day, and my career, and the episode is a success. You couldn't script it.

As we return to Faial Island, our marlin flag flying aloft, Ian says, 'We don't go out to catch marlin because it's easy, we do it because it's hard. And when it's hard to do something and you get it, you get so much more satisfaction out of it. You have to put in the time and you have to try.'

It's a beautiful maxim, and one I'll take with me on my unfolding adventure.

3. Alexander Pope, *An Essay on Man*.

Chapter Two

COSTA RICA

Frogs, Monkeys and Fish that Eat Fruit

June 2008

After the success of catching my beautiful marlin in the Azores, the producers now want me to recapture the magic by reeling in a sailfish, the fastest ocean predator on the planet. Sure, no sweat! I mean, seriously, where do we go after that? Waterskiing behind a Russian sub? Actually, that would have made one hell of a Bond sequence, but yet again I was overlooked for the job. I mean, what's Daniel Craig got that I haven't – apart from Rachel Weisz?

As I board the plane to Costa Rica I'm feeling calm about the journey ahead. The marlin's given me a massive boost of confidence and I've been dipping into my Stanislavski books to help me up my presenting game. The 'Stanislavski system' helps actors draw emotional truth into their performance. I'm feeling sure that Hamish is going to be very happy with the improvement on camera.

After a two-hour drive from the city of Liberia, we arrive at Playa Flamingo, the largest marina in Costa Rica. It's the rainy season so it's hot and sticky, which would be nice if I were with my wife, but I'm not; I'm with my crew of hairy Brits, who are sweating so profusely they look like human fountains. There will be no romantic beach scenes on this shoot but with the rivers swollen with water, there will be plenty of fish in the sea.

After a quick wash and brush-up at the hotel, we climb aboard Captain Jesse Baletti's boat to go in pursuit of a sailfish. The magnitude of the task ahead of me is starting to sink in and a wave of nausea hits me before we've even left port.

When I started the show I'd been a fisherman for thirty-five years, but the fish I was after were four-pound trout, not ocean predators that can get up to speeds of 70 m.p.h. and weigh as much as 500 pounds. I'm a ten-and-a-half-stone neurotic actor about to go and do something brave – the coward within is screaming. I feel like I'm in the wrong bloody play.

Before I film a piece to camera with Jesse Baletti, I go to the WC to have a firm word with myself.

OK, breathe.

I can't. My pulse is racing.

Here you are again, caught up in this madness, about to play with a monster of the deep, a veritable cheetah of the sea, and you're not prepared at all. Forget Stanislavski, you're screwed.

But what about the marlin I caught?

Luck, a simple case of luck.

'Believe,' says Uncle Obi-Wan. It's starting to get crowded in my head.

I walk purposely up the stairs to interview veteran fisherman Jesse. The American's been catching fish since he was five years old, and all his family are fishermen (the list is like the families in the Bible: it goes on a bit). Anyway, the point is it's in his DNA.

'If we're lucky enough to find a sailfish, the fight could be one or two hours,' he says. I smile and my stomach knots a bit tighter.

'And what type of tackle will we be using, Jesse?'

'What really excites me is catching big fish on light tackle,' he says.

I inspect the rods. If this is light tackle, I wouldn't like to see what he uses on a heavy day. This is so different from trout fishing it's unreal. I mean, usually I would spend my day putting a tiny fly onto a tiny hook and trying to cast as elegantly as I can. But Jesse spends his day baiting one-foot squid lures and preparing for a two-hour wrestle with no referee and no bell-ringing in between rounds. It's like comparing Creedence Clearwater Revival with AC/DC.

First Mate Steve Starbuck (genuinely his name) prepares the lines for trawling. On the lure he puts ballyhoo.

'The ballyhoo are good bait fish,' he explains, 'as they're thin and move well in the water to attract the big fish.'

He puts the lines out from two rods at the side, one in the middle and one on the top deck for Jesse. As the boat slices through the waves I suddenly become aware we are surrounded by dolphins.

'Look!' I point, 'There's about fifty!'

They are on both sides of the boat, and in fact there are

hundreds – possibly thousands. Jesse tells me it's a super-pod of Costa Rican spinner dolphins feeding on a shoal of sardines. Known for their gymnastic displays, the dolphins are leaping out of the water as if for joy. It's an awesome sight, and, for fishermen, often a good omen. The dolphins by the boat look as if they are jumping steeples in a National Hunt race. It's exhilarating to watch. As a boy I once asked Uncle Matheson, 'Why do salmon leap?' and he answered, 'If you could, wouldn't you?'

Jesse says that dolphins like to put on a show, but there's a more serious side. Under the water it's a feeding frenzy: there are dolphins, marlin, tuna, sharks and sailfish all wanting fresh sardines for lunch, washed down with a decent splash of claret. It's a ferocious battle and an orgy of food, a bit like a Mr Wu's all-you-can-eat buffet. On the surface of the water the cormorants and gannets scoop up the scraps. Gannets are not the brightest of birds and they gorge on food, trying to satiate their gargantuan appetites, until they literally can't take off. From the boat I watch them lying on the water, bellies sticking up in the air, like fat tourists on the beach in Magaluf. This is when they are most vulnerable to attacks from sharks, which, after gorging on fish, have a sudden urge for chicken. We've all been there.

'Robson!'

A reel at the side of the boat starts whizzing. Oh, my God, this is it: I'm about to join the fray. I reel like billy-o and am impressed with my strength and resolve. I keep my lines as tight as possible and I am winning. I am winning! The fish comes into sight; it's a tuna – a beautiful yellowfin tuna. Both crews (TV and boat) look disappointed, but I am wild with excitement. I leap into the air like a dolphin. I am heeding the truth within, just as Stanislavski said. I heave the fish closer to the boat. It's about twenty pounds – my biggest marine fish, save the marlin, but this time I'm landing it.

Steve Starbuck is unimpressed: 'It's a bit small.'

'Small? It's one of the biggest bloody fish I've ever caught!'

We heave her onto the boat. Her Latin name is *Thunnus albacares, albacares* meaning 'white meat'. This powerful torpedo-shaped creature is capable of bursts of speeds over 40 m.p.h. I think, as with many creatures we harvest, that we take tuna for granted because it comes in tins and has become a staple food in our diet. But I believe we should revere and honour this truly magnificent creature. Sadly, like her cousin the bluefin, she is increasingly becoming overfished due to the 'purse-seining' methods of many commercial vessels. They use sophisticated technology to locate entire shoals and scoop them up in one net that can hold as much as 2,000 tonnes of fish. Unfortunately they tend to scoop up turtles and dolphins, too, which is why, where possible, you should always opt for dolphin-friendly or line-caught tuna.

But today we aren't going desecrate this beautiful tuna with cheap oil, brine or vegetable broth, which they use to preserve tinned tuna in the States; we're going to sushi it! It's an amazing feeling eating tuna a couple of minutes after dispatching the fish. It gives your taste buds a unique flavour that can only be described as clean. And you don't describe fish as clean-tasting very often, do you? The tuna is healthy, fresh and bloody good for you, and today I'm eating it at the finest restaurant in the Pacific: Jesse's boat. In Costa Rica they have a saying, 'La Pura Vida', which strictly means 'pure life' but translates loosely as 'It doesn't get any better than this' – and now I know what they mean ...

Room 25, Santa Cruz

The hotel doesn't look that bad from the outside, but the ordinary exterior hides the horror that lies within. I mean, I've heard of hotels with cockroaches, I've even complained about mosquitoes in a hotel, but I've never come across a hotel that has a problem with crabs. Not one or two but thousands of the buggers.

At the beginning of the rainy season the tajalines, or land crabs, come up from their underground homes in droves and travel to the coast to lay their eggs. And they don't let *anything* get in their way – not even six-storey hotels. I try to sweep them out of my room but they are everywhere: in my bed, my bathroom, my drawers (honest!) and my shower. I banish most to the verandah and try to get some kip but all I can hear is them scratching with their tiny little claws at the door: 'Let me in. Let me in.' An army of Cathys at the French windows: 'It's me ... I've come home. I'm so cold, let me in at your window ...'

I put a pillow over my head to muffle Kate Bush and that's when I come cheek to cheek with cold exoskeleton. I scream and the night turns murderous as I embark upon a killing spree. I stove the crabs' heads in with my trusty priest – not a local Catholic Father, but the wooden tool I use for knocking fish on the head. And now crustacea, too. Die!!!

I return to bed, *fruits de mer* splattered across the room, put my empty wash bag over 'me night fishing tackle' and try to get some shut-eye. In the morning I close the door on room 25 and leg it from the scene of the crime. It's a room I won't forget in a hurry.

*

Director Ross Harper asks me to do a PTC about my crab hell. As I explain why there are so many of them, I pick one up for a more visual effect. Yes, it's definitely more visual: the blighter nips my little finger, and as I pull my hand away its arm comes off. Oops. There's an inhalation of breath from the crew and a squeal from me as I realise its nipper is still pinching my finger. The cameraman pulls the detached arm off. I tell viewers it will grow back, and indeed it will. I mention nothing of the crab pâté in room 25.

Upala

As you can imagine, after the night I'd experienced, I am feeling pretty rotten. Plus there was no hot water either, so morale is low. We get in the minibus around 4 a.m. and travel several hours by road to meet a man called Alex Arias, the president of El Club Nacional de Pesca de Costa Rica. The club is a big deal and I need to impress the main man. However, I am not impressed by what Alex proposes I do. He wants me to float down the hot, muddy, crocodile-infested Río Pizote – without a boat. And, what's more, while being swept down the river in only my shorts and a life-jacket, I have to fish for the toothy first cousin of the piranha, the machaca. This is madness. I need to speak to my agent – except I haven't got one.

I turn accusingly to the director and ask why he hasn't let me in on this secret before now. Ross says, 'Because otherwise you'd never have agreed to it.' Fair enough. He's right – but angry emails are going to be written later.

The thought of having a limb removed by a reptile, or my nadgers munched off by a machaca, doesn't half focus the mind. Alex, a dark and handsome smooth-talking bar steward, smiles and says, 'Don't worry, Robson, it'll be fine – but if you see a sign saying "Welcome to Nicaragua", then you've gone too far.'

'Great,' I say, grinning, beginning to draft my incandescent email to Hamish.

'But seriously,' says Alex, 'if you get to the border you need to turn around and swim upstream very fast – the guards are bored so they might "shoot you up". Understand? Apart from that, this method of fishing is perfectly safe.'

I look down at the river from the bridge. It's in full flood and swimming upstream would be impossible. A river like this in the UK would be declared unfishable – and besides, it's swimming-pool temperature, so I imagine the fish are half-cooked already. Alex says, 'Shall we jump off the bridge, Robson?'

'No, Alex, let's not. Let's leave that to Daniel Craig.'

We are using spinning rods with little lures to attract the machaca, which takes me back to when I was a lad messing about on the River Coquet in Northumberland with Matheson. When I was about twelve or thirteen, we would spin for trout using Mepps that spun through the water like shiny two-pence pieces. A fly-fishing purist like my uncle wasn't really keen on spinning but it was a guaranteed way of catching a fish or several – either that or using worms – and then you were definitely going to go home with something to cook for supper. Fish tend to swallow worms so using lures reduces the risk of damaging the fish, as the hook will usually catch the side of the mouth. This is the best method for catching and releasing a fish, whether you need to do so because of quota, size or because it's a female carrying eggs.

Alex and I put on our life jackets and wade into crocodile alley with our rods. The water soon sweeps us away. Surprisingly the machaca, considering they are members of the violent-crime piranha family who specialise in 'waste management', are vegetarian, save the occasional insect. They love to gorge on the wild figs of the *Ficus tonduzii*, known locally as the Chilamate tree, which grows along the riverbanks, its branches overhanging the water. As well as figs, the fish also eat various flowers, palm fruits and wild plums. I've never heard of a fish like it. Rumour has it they also love a cup of lemon and ginger tea after a hard day at yoga and are rather partial to tie-dyed T-shirts.

We cast our lines out as we travel downstream, trotting a piece of bait along the riverbed. It's similar to the 'drop minnow' method I use to catch trout on the Coquet, which is, as we say up north, 'deadly', basically because the bait is carried by the fast water into the mouths of the trout waiting in ambush. Thankfully, back home, we do it from the relative comfort of the riverbank, not in the drink.

Alex gets a bite but struggles to reel it in because we're in such deep water. It's a machaca but it quickly flies off the hook. We retreat to the bank and watch as fruit drops off a tree into the water and a hungry machaca snaps it up. Bam! It takes it and is gone. I'm not only really keen to win one of these fighting fish for dinner but I'm also hell-bent on joining Alex's club.

We walk up the riverbank and find a spot to wade in and see if we have better luck fishing on our feet. It's late morning and as I stare at the water I have a flashback to the tajalines crab massacre in room 25. I imagine the chambermaid's scream. My rod is yanked forward: I've got a bite. I set the rod up and let it run. Then, very slowly, I reel in the fish, which is fighting like a featherweight champion. I get it to the bank and pick it up. It's tiny, no more than a pound, but I turn to camera and proudly say, 'Look: my first ever cuchaka.'

'Machaca,' interjects Alex.

'Fuck! Machaca.'

'Machaca,' he repeats.

'Machaca,' I say, reddening with embarrassment. I pop the fish back in the water and he swims off. According to club rules any fish under a pound has to be put back in the river. The club is like the British fishing bodies, there to safeguard the health of the river and the fish, as well as to promote the sport. Alex also hooks one and it's a good size, so we're keeping it for our dinner. I carefully hold the vicious fish while delivering a piece to camera.

'Look at that: beautiful Costa Rican machaca – and what's great is, I can't believe how many fish are here. What it tells us all is that this is a very, very healthy river. This fella is for dinner. Well done, matey,' I say to Alex. 'Whoa!'

Suddenly the fish makes a bid for freedom, plops into the river and is gone. I am mortified.

'I've just lost your fish – oh, fuck! Oh, shit, I've just lost the fish!'

Alex looks at me like I'm a right member – but definitely not of his exclusive fishing club. I apologise profusely.

'It's OK, buddy,' he says.

'I'd be knocking me out if I were you.'

'Next time!' he laughs. 'You're paying for lunch anyway!'

'Because I've lost the fucking fish!'

Off camera it was even worse. I also managed to stand on Alex's best and most cherished rod just after I lost the 'cuchaka'. So stunned was I at dropping the fish that I stumbled backwards like a startled wildebeest and laid waste to his rod as if it were no more than a twig. I'll never forget the look on his face or my own toe-curling anguish. However, in spite of the mishaps, Alex still made me an honorary member of his prestigious fishing club. Dunno when I'll use it, mind!

Maleku Tribe

The next day we take a five-hour drive north, deep into rainforest. We are heading for the village of Impala to meet one of the last indigenous tribes of the region, the Maleku. The Maleku people still speak their own language and are fiercely protective of their traditions. They've been living here for over 1,200 years, so if anyone knows about jungle river fishing it's them. I greet Ulysses and two of his fellow Maleku tribesmen, 600 of whom still live on the reserve.

'Capi, capi,' they say, tapping me on the shoulder twice. I return their welcome: 'Capi, capi.'

Ulysses tells me I won't be fishing today as they are taking me on an armadillo hunt.

'OK,' I say, looking at Ross.

He shrugs and we decide to go with the flow. Well, the extreme part of it fits in with the show, at least! As we hack our way through the rainforest I am reminded of Tony Last in Evelyn Waugh's *A Handful of Dust*, who disappears in a South American rainforest and is held captive by a man who forces him to read the entire works of Charles Dickens. I wonder what would be the modern equivalent of such literary torture? Perhaps the complete works of Jilly Cooper, Jeffrey Archer or even Katie Price.

My heart misses a beat when Ulysses' machete swings dangerously close to my knee as we slowly but surely pick our way through the thick undergrowth. The rainforest is the Maleku tribe's supermarket, building supplier and pharmacy. After an hour we stop for a breather near an unremarkable-looking bush. The Maleku medicine man, a dead ringer for Frank Zappa, cuts a leaf off and motions that he wants me to try it. I look around at the director and assistant. They're both nodding, saying, 'Try it, Robson.' *Why don't they bloody try it?* I think to myself.

I put the leaf in my mouth and chew. It's vile and bitter. I spit it out. Suddenly I can't feel my tongue or throat – my whole mouth is numb! I try to speak but I sound like I've had a smack in the mouth, a root canal and then another smack in the mouth. I start choking to bring my throat back to life. Frank Zappa tells me the sensation will subside and I'll be back to normal in half an hour. Great. Meantime I'm thuppothed to prethent a thhow. He goes on to tell me the tribe uses the leaf for numbing the mouth in order to extract teeth. In fact, many of the pills and potions we have in the West are synthesised from these natural rainforest plants. It's fascinating. I chew gum manically to get some kind of feeling back, and slowly it starts to return. I realise I wouldn't last five minutes on my own in the rainforest.

After three or four hours of trudging through the unbearably humid rainforest, the Maleku locate an armadillo burrow and start digging the creature out. It takes a very long time and I come to the conclusion that they must *really* like armadillo. One of the tribesmen disappears down the hole, three others holding him by the ankles; he fumbles about and then shouts something back. He is hauled up, victorious – clutching an armadillo. I tell them they really should invest in a Jack Russell.

Instructed by the tribesmen, I knock the strange-looking creature on the head and return to camp with our supper. It's boiled up by the village ladies and served with soggy bananas. The

Maleku believe eating armadillo is good if you have asthma and it is apparently also a rich source of iron. I wonder if it helps panic attacks. My new friends all watch me take a mouthful.

'It tastes like pork,' I say.

They lean in closer wanting to know my verdict. I tell them, 'I prefer fish.' They laugh.

Man, I am looking forward to a good night's sleep. I'm dead on my feet but what an amazing day it's been. I am shown my hut in the camp . . . and I immediately wish I could be back in room 25 *with* the crabs. It's a bleeding mud hut with a crappy wooden door that doesn't fit, and to top it off I'm sharing it with Ross Harper and George Hughes, the assistant producer.

As we settle down to sleep I imagine I'm in my bed at home in Surrey with Vanya. My son Taylor's tucked up in his room, safe and sound, and I have clean sheets and Siberian goose-down pillows and . . . suddenly my dream is interrupted by a loud rumble. Half asleep, I come to and find both of the guys are now snoring heavily and I am stuck in between them, and the armadillo and bananas are having a very negative effect on the camp. I wake them up.

'Ross, George, you both have to go. I can't sleep with you. *You* snore like a bush pig and *you* have a bottom like Bhopal.'

They willingly rush off to nearby accommodation with running water and proper beds. I resist and I snuggle down as best I can on the hard floor. *I'm not doing a Bear Grylls and skipping off to the nearest five-star*, I think. *I want an authentic experience.*

What is it they say? Be careful what you wish for . . .

Thud! Something hits the roof. Thud! What on earth? I search outside with the flashlight. The hut is under a bloody mango tree. Thud! I look closer. A monkey is throwing the mangos *on purpose*! I go back into the hut. The monkey starts pelting the roof with mangos – it's like throwing-out time on Saturday night in Newcastle. Eventually the monkey gets bored and decides to make loud calls instead. I do breathing exercises to relax my frazzled mind and slowly I start to drift off again … *Zzz!* – a mosquito flies past my ear. *Zzz!* Then a cockerel starts cock-a-bloody-doodle-doing every twenty seconds … and it's only 1 a.m. Dogs are barking, ants and mosquitoes are biting me, birds are tweeting – all that's missing is a bloody brass band. I am in the seventh circle of hell – get me back to room 25! I would rather read *Martin Chuzzlewit* surrounded by tajalines crabs for eternity than stand this for another night. I desperately need sleep.

Sadly, I get none. The next morning my face is creased and blotchy like a wanton hussy's bed. I tell Ross I need to phone my son, Taylor, as it's his eighth birthday. He tells me the only phone in the area is three miles up a mountain. I give him a Mel Gibson snarl and get jogging.

'Tay? It's Dad. Yes, it's really me – come on, it hasn't been that long! Happy birthday, little man. Are you all right? Me? I'm fine. Well, actually I'm not. [Cue tears] Daddy hasn't slept for three days and I look terrible and that's every actor's nightmare and they gave me this leaf to chew which made my mouth go numb and I've been attacked by monkeys, crabs and mosquitoes and … [sniff] I killed an armadillo …'

At this point Taylor hands the phone to his mother.

'What's wrong?' she asks.

'I'm sorry, I'm a bad father. Tell him I love him.'

This was meant to be all about my little boy and his birthday but the conversation became all about me, my utter exhaustion and obsession with my career. I drag my sorry self back down the hill. I must do better as a dad.

I pull myself together and embark on a five-kilometre hike with the Maleku through the jungle to catch the elusive machaca. After losing Alex's fish in such a humiliating fashion, I am determined I'm going to hook one of these veggie fish and keep it, maybe even frame it. On the way, tribesman Oscar shows me a poisonous frog that can kill you stone dead, bullet ants (among the largest on the planet) that will put you in A&E for a few days, and a beautiful chameleon that thankfully is benign. I look at this amazing creature and say to camera, 'Out of all the colours in its repertoire, vibrant yellows and greens – he chooses a dull shade of brown.'

The Costa Rican soundman, Alberto, pipes up: 'Stop! I can't hear anything.'

This is unsurprising as he has insisted on taking a forty-foot cable attached to the camera everywhere we have ventured, land or sea. Most other soundmen are usually connected by wireless because of the dangerous type of terrain but not Alberto, he's old-school. Earlier on today, after getting caught in the under-growth, he fell down a steep slope taking the cameraman, Tim, with him. We stop filming to assess the extent of the problem.

'Is any of it useful or shall we film that piece again?' asks Ross.

The sound guy replies, 'Well, sometimes I hear and sometimes I don't.'

Ross: 'So did you hear any of what Robson just said?'

Sound: 'Sometimes I hear and sometimes I don't.'

Ross: 'Has this happened on any other occasion whilst we've been filming?'

Sound: 'Sometimes.'

Ross (now losing it): 'So are you telling me that sometimes you couldn't hear Robson on the boat, or with the tribe or river fishing?'

Sound: 'Sometimes I hear.'

Robson: 'Are you kidding me? Why didn't you tell anyone?'

Sound: 'You are a bad man, Robson, shouting at me! The people will hear you sometimes.'

And thus the soundman became known as 'Sometimes'. We later found out that much of the sound was poor quality but we manage to muddle through.

We trundle on through the forest. Morale is rock-bottom until, through the trees, we see the sparkling Río Venado. We hurry through to the water's edge. It's nice to get out into the open air; the forest is hot and oppressive whereas the water is clear, cool and about ten feet across. For the first time since arriving, I feel back in my comfort zone; being on the riverbank somehow restores my equilibrium.

We are using methods the tribe have relied on for 1,200 years and today our bait is the machaca's favourite food, figs. I sniff the fruit.

'Smells very nice. Can we eat it?' I ask.

Tribesman Oscar nods. 'It's nice.'

I take a bite. The fig is hard and tastes terrible, all sour and musty like grandma's tights. I spit it out. Oscar and the other lads chuckle.

I take my line with a hook baited with the horrible fruit and throw it into the middle of the river, using the minnow-drop method that Alex and I had previously tried. I suppose this could be called a fruit-drop – and anyone attempting it in the northeast would be called a reet bloody fruit-drop.

'I'm in! I'm in! Please let that be a fish! Yes. Yes! YES!'

After a decent fight I reel in a machaca and I get the name right on camera – back of the net! The fish, known as *Hiki Maleku* by the tribe, has an impressive set of razor-sharp teeth like its Amazon relative, the piranha. Its scales are silvery and tinged with green, probably from eating its five a day, unlike its crazy carnivore cousin. *Perhaps that's why one species of piranha is red-bellied, from all the blood*, I muse. I land a second fish and am thrilled. Oscar and his mate have had an unsuccessful day but are pleased that my two modest fish have made me hysterically happy. They laugh at my crazy behaviour.

'La Pura Vida!' I shout.

In spite of the arduous five-kilometre trek back to the village, I am still buoyant, and I am beginning to feel fitter and more sure-footed. Back at camp, we smoke the fish and serve it with – you've guessed it – bananas. The bananas are rank but the fish is lovely and tastes a bit like grouper, with big meaty flakes and a light texture. The machaca is such a healthy, powerful fish, mainly because it is constantly swimming against a strong current. It's no wonder the Maleku tribe are such healthy people, both physically and mentally. They enjoy a natural stress-free life and a good diet: the Omega-3-rich fish, coupled with mineral-rich bananas and a good two-hour yomp to find your food, is a winning combination. Not to mention their iron-rich armadillo – it really does tick all the boxes.

Sailfish

My journey in Costa Rica is almost over but I am returning to the Pacific to have one last outing with Jesse Baletti and Steve

Starbuck, in search of the fastest ocean predator on the planet. We meet at Playa Flamingo and head out on Jesse's boat. Hopefully this time we will manage to hook a legendary sailfish.

The midday sun beats down, making the waves shine. We've been at sea for nearly five hours now and nothing has been attracted to the lures, but all the signs are positive: the birds are scattered over the water, the dolphins are feeding, and, with the gentle sea breeze, the temperature is perfect. This is my last chance to catch this majestic billfish but I am realistic.

Suddenly the line explodes off the outrigger. *Perhaps it's another tuna*, I think. I harness up and take the rod from Steve. I've been taught all the basics of what to do but in reality, when you see the bend in the rod, all you can do is hang on for dear life. Whatever is on the end of the line is packing thirty pounds of tension on the reel. This is power – the clutch is fully on and the line is still zinging out as the fish takes off at full speed. It strips over 250 metres of line. Jesus Christ! As I play the fish, my muscles burn and I remind myself that it wasn't long ago men were fishing such creatures with hand lines. The chance of this being my ultimate prize is still remote, though. This ocean is teeming with all manner of fish. It really could be any number of species on the end of the line.

As I slowly lift and deliberately wind, the fish torpedoes out of water about 100 metres from the boat. Whoosh! It *is* a sailfish. I can't believe it! The sail is just visible and it jumps two or three times before diving back under the water, where the battle continues.

Jesse shouts over from the helm: 'All right, keep your line tight, keep it tight. It's about a hundred-and-twenty-, hundred-and-thirty-pound fish.'

I am trying to keep my cool.

'What kind of line have we got on here?'

'Ahh, you got a forty on there,' says Steve in his Carolina drawl.

'This is not salmon fishing,' I say, straining. 'He is just holding and I can't do anything. Ha, right, come on ... oooh, yes, he's starting to run again. Whoa! Gotta run, run, run, keep reeling, Robson, keep reeling. Ah, man, he's coming up, keep the line tight, keep winding – this is when it's dangerous.'

I decide to take it nice and easy with this fish, it's a once-in-a-lifetime catch and I don't want to blow it. He is near the boat, about ten feet away, and I can see his sail a metre from the surface.

Suddenly the long, slender creature flies across the crest of a wave, his navy and purple sail at full mast, iridescent like taffeta in the sunshine. The fish is dark blue on top with a bistre and silvery underside, and he has a spear like a marlin. But his sail – his sail is sublime.

After fifty minutes of playing the fish, Steve pulls the line to the side of the boat. He bills the fish and hauls the tired creature onto the side of the boat. He unhooks its mouth and unfurls its now-pitch-black sail. I hold the fish with Steve and touch the silky sail and slippery skin. Its Ancient Greek name is *Istiophorus platypterus*, which means 'to carry a sail'. The incredibly complex hydrodynamic design makes this billfish capable of extraordinary bursts of speed, the fastest in the ocean.

Steve tags the fish in order to help marine biologists understand more about these incredible creatures. He returns it to the salty waters holding it by the bill allowing oxygen back in the gills, and when it is strong enough he lets go.

What a baptism of fire. How on earth am I going to top that?

I fly back to the UK, safe in the knowledge that in Costa Rica we have made a great show.

Post-Production Meeting One Month Later.
Hamish looks me straight in the eye.

'Robson, you look good, the episode's fine, but the voiceover's shite. It sounds like your balls are up your ass. Give it some passion, some grunt.'

I am astonished. How dare he? Hamish looks at the editor.

'Well, what do you think?'

'Truthfully? It's quite boring.'

'Boring? It's fucking soporific!' adds Hamish.

I storm out of the editing studio, squeaking a few insults back at him and racking my brain for the definition of soporific. I google it and loathe Hamish even more. But you know what, he was right. The voiceover *is* terrible. I had felt I had improved so much in Costa Rica and was beginning to grasp what I was meant to be doing, but in the end I dropped the ball before the final touchdown.

Chapter Three

CANADA AND
BRITISH COLUMBIA

'The Curse of the Ocean Pearl'

November 2008, Series 2

Who'd have thought it? The four episodes of Series 1 prove to be a hit for Channel 5 and a second series is commissioned. And this time we've got eight episodes to play with.

I pack my suitcase, mentally preparing to leave my wife and son again. People who travel a lot on business, especially soldiers, will know this feeling – the wrench of leaving your nest and familiar surroundings, to face the unknown. As I lay out my three holdalls, the sense of adventure is palpable.

I spy Taylor out of the corner of my eye. Packing is a ritual I usually do on my own but this time Taylor wants to be with me. The first holdall is for thermals, fleeces and puffa jackets. The second for all types of footwear, from Arctic boots to trainers. The third is for my smalls, socks, shirts, jeans and pictures of my family – something I always take with me.

'Tay, tell me something about Canada,' I say.

'Um, there are lots of black bears and polar bears and grizzly bears,' he says, growling.

I always ask him to find out some interesting and unusual facts about the places I'm about to visit; each one I use in the show is worth a quid. It's a nice little earner for him.

'Very good. And did you know Canada is from the Native American word *kanata*, which means "village" or "settlement"? No? Well, now you do.'

He rolls his eyes at me and leaps onto the bed like a salmon.

I say my goodbyes and hug Vanya. The long absences are not easy for her. Then I turn to Taylor, who has been holding it together well.

'It's all right, Tay. I'm coming back. I will think about you every second of every day, and even though I'm away I will never ever leave you. I will kiss your picture goodnight every night until I return. Will you do the same for me?'

'Yes,' he says.

'Good lad.'

It physically hurts to get in the car and I wave and wave until I can't see them anymore. Five minutes later I phone Vanya.

'Is he OK?'

She tells me that, as soon as I turned the corner, he went to watch *SpongeBob SquarePants*. Kids these days – so shallow.

Jet lag is like being in a really crap musical you don't want to be in: you're singing the songs and dancing the dances but your mind and heart are elsewhere. It's as if you're watching yourself from the wings, wondering how you will ever reconnect with that dancing, singing twat on stage. My nightmare musical would be *Salad Days* – I bloody hated that one. After ten hours in the air, my body and mind are truly smashed, but I gaze glassy-eyed out of the window at the mountains, vast lakes, emerald-green forests of British Columbia, and they take my breath away.

Black Gold

It's 4.48 a.m. in Vancouver and my head is bouncing off the walls. In the UK it's nearly lunchtime. I witter to my diary cam about how I'm losing the plot and I really am. Unable to get back to sleep, I'm dressed, fed and ready to go by 6 a.m.

The iconic Fraser River flows through the city of Vancouver and just a few miles upstream is the largest freshwater fish in North America, the mystical sturgeon, which can grow up to five metres. To try and help me catch this prehistoric giant is Randy Beck – yep, Randy – and, seeing as there's only him and me on the water today, let's hope he doesn't live up to his name. Men can get kinda lonely fishing sometimes.

It's a cold, grey day. We jump out of the minivan at our meeting point on the Fraser River. Randy wanders over to greet us and shakes my hand firmly. He looks like Tintin's mate Captain Haddock but without the hat. I jump aboard his fishing boat and we head upriver. It really is bleak and wintry out here but the mountains in the distance lend a stark beauty to the misty monochrome scene.

We're casting from the boat today because if I hook one of these fish from the bank I'd probably end up waterskiing in its wake. Think of sturgeon fishing as a tug of war with a small car.

They grow so large because they gorge on the millions of salmon whose life cycle ends here, and in order to catch this extreme fish we are going to need some extreme tackle. Randy drops anchor unexpectedly. Clank! My heart skips a beat before going into overdrive. My nerves fray even more when Randy introduces me to what he calls a 'mangina'. I've worn one before but never heard it called that. It is basically a harness that wraps around your waist with a little codpiece at the front to accommodate the butt of the rod (it's all getting a bit Julian Clary). I tell Randy it reminds me of the heavy-metal band Saxon's lead guitarist, who wore one of these to spin his guitar mid-song. It seemed an apt story, given Randy sounds exactly like a roadie at soundcheck, but sadly the pop trivia is lost on him. I quickly move the conversation on.

'OK, Randy, let's just pretend I know nothing about sturgeon fishing.' *Er, you do know nothing about sturgeon fishing, Robson*, pipes up my internal monologue. 'Shut up!'

'What?'

'Not you, Randy. Jason, the director, was coughing.'

'No, I wasn't,' says Jason Holmes from a second boat across the way.

'So what tips would you give in order to catch a sturgeon?'

'Three things that are essential for this type of angling are courage, power and strength,' he says.

I'll get my coat.

I am lying through my teeth, telling Randy I've spent five days a week at the gym for six months preparing for this moment, when, all of a sudden, I get a nose-full of a putrid stench. If that smell is coming from Randy's bottom he needs to see a doctor *immediately*. It's like someone's just opened a coffin next to a sewage plant. I discover the culprit is Randy's bucket of 'green death' stink bait. It's shocking, a full-on dirty bomb attack on the senses. Sturgeon love putrefied salmon, it's like fishy crack and they know it's bad-quality gear, but they're addicted to it. I place the bait on the hook and am gagging. I cast out fifty yards of line and drop the lure into a natural feeding channel behind the boat. All we can do now is wait. *Please bite*, I think, *I've travelled nearly 5,000 miles and feel like I'm on a bad acid trip.*

We're using ninety-pound breaking-strain line with thirty-pound tension on the reel, as some of these creatures can weigh over 500 pounds. The odds really aren't stacked in my favour. Randy tells me that, because the price of caviar is so high, one decent fish can be worth up to $100,000 and it's not uncommon for boats to be held at gunpoint and asked to hand over their catch or else they'll be sleeping with the fishes. The thought that I could be murdered for a fish takes time to sink in. *I need to try these damn fish eggs*, I think.

Suddenly, something begins to stir in the depths and the rod gives a small but significant twitch.

'There we go!' shouts Randy.

The rod is resting in a cradle on the side of the boat; I wait for Randy's command: 'Hit it! Hit it! Hit it!' I swing the rod skywards to hook the fish – 'Reel, reel, reel!' – and I wind with all my might, but nothing's on. We've missed it. My heart is pounding in my chest.

'Bloody hell, Randy, I nearly had a heart attack when you shouted: "Hit it!"'

We don't have to wait long before we are in again.

'Now, now, now! Reel reel reel!' yells Randy.

'Yeah! I am!' I shout.

The bend in the rod is near breaking point; I feel as if I have hooked a mini submarine. The bend increases and the rod almost folds back onto itself. I wind and pull up but every time I wind in two yards, he takes me out two yards.

Finally, after what seems an eternity, the fish reveals itself close to the side of the boat and it is the most extraordinary sight to behold. It's about five feet long and forty pounds in weight. We heave her on board. I try to hold her up for the camera but she's such a strapping and awkward lass that I struggle, so Randy takes the tail and I hold her head. She is an astonishing creature whose family has survived two ice ages. She certainly looks prehistoric with the white, diamond-shaped scutes patterned down her sides, like the armoured skin of a crocodile rather than fishy scales. The Native Americans used these scutes as cutting tools, arrowheads and piercing instruments. The sturgeon was also prized for its oil content, and just a hundred years ago these beautiful fish would even be stacked at the sides of rivers or lakes, to use as firewood. ('Throw another fish on the fire, there's a good lass.' 'Throw your own bloody fish on the fire, you chauvinist pig!' Whack! Getting smacked around the chops with one of these fish could be fatal.) It was also common to see steamboats sailing along the Mississippi powered by sturgeon oil, until legislation led to the cessation of overfishing. Now they are under attack because of their eggs, which are known as 'black gold'. This particular fish is worth around £20,000, but because sturgeon are endangered, and thankfully protected in Canada, we are going to put her back.

So, I am no longer a sturgeon virgin and I'm very happy. These fish love Randy's stink bait and soon we have another strike. This one feels like the Daddy and it's moving away from me at an alarming speed. I struggle, winding and lifting, winding and lifting. Suddenly he whips round to the left – I spin with him. Now to the right – 'Where's he taking me?' I am propelled forward – he's diving down. The downward load is putting a massive strain on my back and I am not as young as I think I am. I am beginning to wish I really *had* trained for six months because I am fighting a perpendicular battle and my back is not strong enough for the struggle. There are shooting pains flying down my legs and into my boots but there's no way I'm losing what could be the biggest fish of my life. The world record is an astonishing 994 pounds, and this feels very close. I throw my hat on the floor. I am sweating profusely, the inside of my lime-green anorak smells like Randy's bucket of green death. I wrestle and struggle some more. Randy is getting a wee bit enthusiastic and decides to increase the tension on the reel to try to slow the fish down. I plead with him not to, as we are nearing the breaking tension of the leader line, but he turns the tension wheel clockwise and shouts, 'Come on, Robson. COME ON!'

'I think you need to take some tension off, Randy. He's gonna fucking take me over. Seriously, guys, get a fucking hold of me!' I yell as I lose my footing.

'I've got you,' says Randy, putting his arm around my waist, laughing wheezily like Muttley from *Wacky Races*.

I am in the hurt locker.

'Look at that – he's away. This has to be the biggest fish I've ever had on my line.'

'He's coming, buddy. Get him, get him,' Randy points.

'Come on then, son!'

I wind and lift the rod up with all my might. Snap! I fall backwards onto the deck – the sturgeon has broken off.

'Ohh, fuck!'

I swear incessantly for about three minutes. There are no other words for the feeling of loss, frustration and despair. It was 200–300-pound sturgeon – it had to be as it's just broken off a 90-pound trace.

Ever the professional, I turn to camera and say, 'But the thing is, the fish win sometimes and it's going take a better fisherman than me to bring that fish out the water. Oh, bollocks!' In reality I'm thinking, *It's all flipping Randy's fault. He put too much bloody tension on the line. I knew it and I did nothing about it. I know, Uncle Kenobi, I know I should have trusted my instincts, but it's a bit bloody hard to when I'm the novice and haven't caught one before.*

Director Jason tries to dampen the blow by offering me Champagne and caviar for dinner that evening. Pound for pound, caviar is the most expensive food in the world and it's strange to think that I'm about to put something in my mouth that is from the bottom end of a fish – but then I do like eggs from the bottom end of a chicken so why not?

'Sturgeons' eggs might be black gold, but are they worth it?' I say to camera.

I taste a small amount on a blini. The answer is, quite simply, 'no'. To my mind, caviar is a bit like some WAGs I could mention: zero calories, little taste and a total waste of money. I wash the salty eggs down with the Champagne and pour another glass. Now that stuff is worth every penny.

Kayaking, baby!

We are heading for Gabriola Island and it's blowing a hooley. I do my Kate Winslet impression at the front of the ferry but I am really not looking forward to going canoeing in this weather. I tried kayaking last year in South Africa and Costa Rica – it's always a bloody disaster and the footage is never used. Kayaking and me go together like the press and Hugh Grant, democracy and China, Scargill and Thatcher. But at least it was warm in South Africa; today it's gonna be as frosty as a miner's wife on washing day.

I meet Kim Crosby, a camp kayaking evangelist who will have to perform a miracle to convert me today. Unfortunately it appears he wants to perform something else. He peers into my canoe, his face dangerously close to my crotch. I point and bite my nails at the camera. I'm going to have to keep a weathered eye on this old sea otter. We paddle out into the Straits of Georgia, where there are sea lions, killer whales and . . . sharks. It is effing freezing and I really don't want to fall in. 'Chin-up, chest out, Robson, and stroke, stroke – no, Kim, not me, the water!'

We are heading for a reef where lingcod live – not a relative of Pacific cod but in fact a long, slender greenling. The lingcod are fierce predators with massive mouths and sharp teeth, and they can grow up to eighty pounds. Kim says the biggest fish can take the kayak with them, dragging you for hundreds of metres. I say to him, 'Stay close.' Worryingly he replies, 'Don't worry, I'm with you, baby.' I have been on some dates in my time, but this one is unique.

We arrive at the spot near some rocks where Kim suggests we throw out a line but this isn't easy and the strong wind keeps blowing us off the reef. He gets me by the paddle, trying to steady me in the waves. It's an impossible task and we are both blown and tossed further off course. I hold on tightly to his kayak, our canoes gently rubbing against each other in the bumpy waters.

I ask Kim that if by some a miracle I should catch a lingcod today and get it to the boat, how the hell do I dispatch it?

'We just grab into the gills, pull it in here, punch the shit out of the fish and down it goes.'

Right. That sounds lovely. I have a feeling that Kim might be sniffing glue or that he's two lingcods short of a picnic – and right at this moment a picnic or any kind of food seems very doubtful indeed. In two hours I have only managed ten minutes of fishing. The wind is taking the canoe in one direction and the current is taking the lure in another, meaning it's not sinking to the bottom but rather is floating on the bloody surface, which is no bloody good for attracting lingcod.

'This is fucking stupid! Ocean kayaking is meant to be breathtaking, but I think this is piss-taking,' I snap.

'But you are looking marvellous,' says Kim, trying to appeal to my vanity. Well, my vanity fucked off long ago and is currently by an open fire, sipping single-malt and puffing on a Monte Cristo cigar, and I want to join it.

We of course catch sod-all. My bottom is numb, I can't feel my toes and I've really had enough. In my eyes, Kim's credibility is at its nadir, unlike our lures. Unabashed, Kim says, 'I dropped some prawn traps earlier today. How about some lovely prawns for lunch?'

'Prawns. Perfect. Whatever. Get me out of this kayak!'

We head out on Kim's boat to pull up his prawn traps set 100 metres down. Right now I'm so hungry my stomach feels like my throat's been cut. I start to haul up a trap. It's hard work but finally it reaches the surface and ... 'Fucking hell, Kim, it's empty!'

There is not a single prawn. I feel like a right one, but Kim is a prize langoustine.

'It's OK. There are two more traps,' he says irritably.

I say, 'It's a bad omen; it's a barren wasteland out there.'

I strangle him on camera when the second one is empty as well. There is one more pot and as I yank the rope up, lunch hovers into view – a couple of handfuls of what in the northeast we call 'shrimp', of which you need to eat about fifty in order to consider it an appetiser. I wave one in the air.

'A prawn. I'm so happy.'

Kim puts his face in the camera and says, 'Extreme fishing, baby.'

No, it's not – and don't call me 'baby', punk.

Port Alberni

'I'm really looking forward to today because I've never been in a fishing competition before but I think my chances are good. There has been a question mark over my fishing ability during this show but I think a lot of questions are going to be answered today.'

I deliver the PTC by an open fire, soft-lit like a 1980s porn film.

'Today this is my type of fishing, exactly like fly-fishing on the Coquet, the Tweed or the Spey, surrounded by peace, quiet and tranquillity...'

Cut to loud rock music and us roaring up the Stamp River, battering into grade-five rapids in a shallow aluminium speed-boat, its engine terrifying anything within a five-mile radius. There's obviously no time for poncey scenery today.

I am here to challenge the self-proclaimed Angling King of

British Columbia, the Jedi Knight of steelhead fishing, Roly Hider, which is a totally made-up name and a really crap anagram. We decide it's the most fish that counts, not the biggest, and the loser has to swim naked in the Stamp lagoon. Roly sits cross-legged on his boat, shades down, cool as fuck, so confident in his ability, so smug and unflappable. I do hope he got bullied at school. If I lose, the water will instantly freeze my tackle off. I *have* to win or I'll become a castrato forever and be forced to duet with Aled Jones on our album, *The Very Best of Songs of Praise*. (What ever happened to that show? Mum used to love Harry 'Seagoon' Secombe singing. I always found it a bit surreal and he wasn't even very good. Don't say a word: three number ones. I was always great; it was Jerome who was tone-deaf. I carried him for years, you know. Just kidding. Love you really, Jerome.)

It's a good start: I have a fish on before Crap Anagram. I lose it but quickly coax another. It puts up a good fight and I have to concentrate hard to reel the fish to the boat, but I manage it and land my first ever steelhead. Steelheads are also known as sea-run rainbow trout or salmon trout, and the only difference between them and the plain old rainbow trout is where they spend their lives feeding and maturing. Stream-resident rainbow trout live their life entirely in freshwater, perhaps with short periods of time spent in estuaries or near-shore marine waters. Steelheads, however, leave freshwater as juveniles and migrate long distances in the ocean, where they grow to maturity before migrating back to their original streams. As they travel to the ocean as little'uns their scales turn a steel blue, hence their name.

I admire my steelhead. What a stunner! She is about five

pounds and with the most vibrant magenta hue along her side that morphs into a stunning bronze gilt around the rest of her form. After a quick 'donk' on the head it's time to get back to work. I am in the lead against the world's cockiest Canadian and I'm planning on it staying that way. Time ticks by and it's one-all, but Roly soon hooks another. It's a fabulous fish but as he reels it towards the boat it suddenly turns and is off. Oh no, he lost it! So sad. Never mind.

Three hours and fifty minutes later, it's two-all with ten minutes to go. I hook a fish and lose it. Damn. With only several minutes left on the clock, Roly shouts: 'Fish on.' He lands the steelhead during injury time and I am gutted. 'I am not going in the drink,' I mutter. 'Oh, yes, I believe you are,' he says, perking up.

Everyone is goading me from the boat. The water is a balmy seven degrees – that's only two degrees warmer than the water that killed the passengers of the flippin' *Titanic*. I'm going to die and he only beat me by one fish. But I am a man of my word. *Stiff upper lip, Robson. For Queen and Country and the Commonwealth, including Canada, which we still rule – suckers!*

I walk in *au buff*.

'I do this every day in Newcastle – not a problem!'

I dive in and burst out of the surface for air.

'Fuck! Jesus! Jesus! Oh, my God!'

My testicles retract, I sing a perfect B-flat – I have never reached that note before, or since. I run out of the water using a dead salmon to protect my modesty, which is more like a mole peeping though a set of curtains by this time.

You might think that's the worst thing that could happen, but you'd be wrong.

The Curse of the *Ocean Pearl*

From the look of the eerie trawler and its rabble crew, my instincts tell me not to board, but as usual I don't fully tune in.

'Robson, I've been looking forward to this,' shouts Captain Bob Frumani, his voice raspy from years of hard living. It's exactly what a killer would say, just before he carves you up. Bob is an unforgettable man, a man on whose face are etched the frightening things he has played witness to. His eyes are haunted – he has seen too much. His crew stand behind him like wraithy heavies from a ship long gone, except instead of wearing swashbuckling kit they are wrapped in black hoodies, which only add to the menace. Nature has played nicely with me so far but I am now about to witness her at her most despicable. I board the *Ocean Pearl* from a small fishing boat and the cameraman, Mike Carling, the director, Jason, and the sound guy, Stuart Bruce, follow me up the metal ladder. The associate producer isn't coming. Why? 'I've got loads of work to do here.' I later discover he suffers from terrible seasickness. He made the right call that day.

We've had sight of the weather forecast and it's looking untidy, to say the least. Sleet and snow are predicted, so it will be not only stormy but also freezing. We are heading out to a notorious stretch of the Pacific off the Brooks Peninsula. Explorer Captain Cook called it the 'Cape of Storms' and Bob does nothing to soften his punch: 'This is serious high seas ... It's like going to another planet. This is extreme fishing. I'm serious.'

As we head out I'm having serious doubts about this. I mean, come on, guys – it's only a bloody TV show. Isn't this too much of a gamble with all our lives? I am pacified by the director, who is between a rock and a hard place – he has to make a show or the production company could lose a lot of money. He updates me with the weather report. The storm will be heading north so we'll miss the worst of it, thank God, but we're still going to get mixed up in a gale.

I take Bob to one side to voice my concerns in private. I don't want his burly crew to know I'm scared. We go up to the wheelhouse from where he captains the trawler. As I start to relate my fears we enter the beginnings of a two-metre swell. The vessel starts to heave up and down and rolls powerfully from side to side. Bob tells me this is nothing compared with what's to come. He's really not helping.

Bob: 'When you come out here you gotta be ready to focus because it's high-end. If someone really doesn't want to come fishing with me, I don't take them. I never phone my crew guys, I never phone 'em and say "Will you come with me?" No way. They gotta wanna be here and it's the same as when you're captain: you have gotta wanna be here, so you're absolutely at your best.'

My internal monologue cranks up. *But I don't want to be here! I don't want to go fishing! I am not at my best and no one will let me get off this fucking boat! I wish you'd understand that!* I stay silent and swallow my frustrations.

Bob: 'I've been in some very serious storms where I really thought that this wheelhouse was gonna get knocked off the boat ... and you know, what I'm saying is, I've been scared before.'

'OK,' I whisper. *Robson, you pillock, listen to me – if he's been scared, you're fucked. I mean, look at the man! He's gnarly, nails, hard as fuck. He's like out of another time, where sailors wrecked four or five ships a career and that was normal.*

Bob: 'You know when you're four hundred, five hundred miles off shore and it's blowing so hard you can't even hear it ... you think that it's peaking ... it's just screaming, it's just woo, woo, woo, woo, woo, woo, wowowooo ... and you think it's peaking and then it just comes: wahhhhhhhhhh ...'

I swallow.

Bob: 'And the whole boat's just shaking and you literally think your wheelhouse is gonna get knocked off ... That's, erm ...' – he turns and looks me straight in the eye – '... when you do really see God, believe me.'

I do, I see all sorts of horrible storms in those haunted grey eyes – it's like looking into one of those snow globes all shaken up, but there's a ship in there being gobbled by the waves.

'Thanks for the chat, Bob. It's really helped.'

For fuck's sake, I'm going to die. I'm seriously going to die. I feel light-headed, my teeth feel too big for my mouth, I'm delirious and I need to breathe, but the boat is all over the place and I'm on board for thirty-six hours.

As we slowly head northwest towards the Cape of Storms, the waves are already four metres high and rising, just as the temperature is plummeting. Well, at least, according to the weather report, we're going to miss the worst of it. But somehow, as time slowly ticks on, it really doesn't feel that way. The swell continues to rise and rise and the wind speed increases. Bob admits this is gale force now.

'But don't worry, Robson, this trawler is built for a hurricane.'

I do not want to test it out, I think to myself.

A conservative description of the ocean would be 'lumpy'; the reality is that its peaks and troughs are about twenty feet high. It's like driving over the tummy-lurching Northumberland Hills at breakneck speed whilst, at the same time, being thrown violently around by some prison animal who wants you to be his bitch.

'I thought we were missing the storm, Jason,' I spit.

He shakes his head: 'We're going straight into it. The weather pattern changed at the last minute.'

I am so unimpressed. To Jason, it's terrific news – this is his *Deadliest Catch* moment – but for Mike, Stuart and me it's terrifying. Especially as those guys are carrying such heavy equipment and don't have an extra pair of hands to hold on. The wind screams. I am frothing with ire.

'How dare you put us in this situation?!'

Boom! Boom! Waves hit the side of the boat and spray the deck. I am glad I'm wearing a survival suit: it'll give me three minutes of important thinking time should I fall in. That's enough time to mentally say goodbye to everyone I know and love. The crew have located their marker buoys so I need to help them get what they've come for. The sablefish are located two miles down in waters chilled by the Arctic winds. The reason why these guys risk life and limb week after week is that black cod, as it's known in high-end Asian restaurants, brings top dollar. On a good day, the *Ocean Pearl* can land £100,000 worth of sablefish. It's black gold to these men, and as we all know riches can corrupt the mind ... and indeed it has done, because these guys are fucking mental to do this job. But not only are they addicted to the booze, the women and the lifestyle the money brings, they are also addicted to the thrill and adventure. As these men prove, the life of a sailor hasn't changed much over the last 500 years.

Deckhand Seamus is showing me the ropes. We need to bring up the pots that the crew baited and set a mile off the ocean floor a couple of weeks ago. A machine starts winching them up. We need to turn into the weather to get the catch on board, and as we do so a wave smacks me in the face like an angry wench. Her hand is bitter cold. As I recover I ask Seamus at what age he started doing this.

'Fourteen!' he shouts.

'Fourteen?' *Why on earth does he do this? There must be easier ways to make a living,* I think.

'Fucking and fishing: that's what Dad taught me.'

Wow.

Actually, Seamus and the rest of the lads are men of a certain ilk: strong, dependent on one another, courageous, fearless, and, in a strange way, really caring. Like soldiers or miners, brothers in arms in the face of adversity – in this case, Mother Nature. Their bond is essential because if there's no trust they literally could die. The number of times Seamus pushes me upright or catches me before I fall is amazing, as if he has a sixth sense for my safety. The guys work their arses off, heaving and lifting the catch onto the boat, all the while being tossed around like toys. I suddenly understand what having your sea legs means – it's not only being able to withstand the physical urge to vomit but also to move with the boat as it lurches left, right and centre.

I am put in charge of the gutting the fish. Seamus picks up a very large knife, takes a sable and bumps it on the head, then decapitates, disembowels and throws the flesh down the chute. He continues with the next fish: three bold moves with the knife and on to the next. The blow to the head of the first fish was just for TV; in reality the sablefish are decapitated before they can blink, if they could. I take the knife and wield it dangerously as I try to remain upright. I steady myself and chop the deep-sea creature's head off, gut it and throw the carcass down the chute. The smell of rancid guts is pungent and inescapable. I continue with the next. Head off, guts out, down the chute. It's a brutal, hellish scene of certain death, with potential death all around us.

Head off, insides out, down the chute. Another and another. Seamus watches over me but I can take no more. I run to the side of the boat but quickly realise I can't vomit over the edge as it will blow back in my face. I puke on deck, all over my boots, a lurid yellow goop. But, unlike with a tummy bug or after an excess of piña coladas, I get no relief; I just feel even worse. As the men heave another load onto the deck, so do I. Our work rate is in sync: every ten minutes another haul, another hurl.

It's dark now and a bit like being tossed about by a cat that's popped your eyes out and eventually will eat you whole, just not yet – there's more pawing, chasing and batting mid-air to be done – and all I want to do is die. Bob guides us through a rising swell to more marker buoys. He is a worried man tonight, not because of the weather but because he needs to balance the books. The last two locations haven't been yielding.

I have been on board for twelve hours now, working, falling and puking. I'm dog-tired. With the light gone I have no sight of the horizon and no perspective of which way is up. But although I am weakened, the anger inside me is growing and seething. As we pull up by another marker buoy, I help the lads land another pot. A wave hits me clean in the face. I can't breathe as I inhale the icy seawater. It's up my nose, in my lungs and stinging my eyes. As I try to recover another wave comes. POW! I am punched backwards and in that moment I think I'm going over into the swirling black nightmare. As everything breaks down into slow motion I yell inside: 'I don't want anyone else to be Taylor's dad. I'm his dad! I want to be there for him, no one else.'

Seamus picks me up. What I need now is a good slap but no one gives it to me so I am going to pass one on to someone else. I summon all my strength, stumble across the deck and swing for Jason: 'Bastard!' He's stood by all this time watching me puke and fall and he's the one who got us into this bleeding mess in the first place. I boom: 'Turn the fucking boat around!' The Arctic winds scream around our heads as another wave smashes port side. We fall. In the film version this is the point where I get Jason by the collar, pin him down on the butcher's block, chop his head off and gut him and throw him down the chute. As if reading my mind, Jason scrambles away.

The soundman has fetched Bob from the wheelhouse – *fuck, who's driving?* I stay on the floor. I don't want to fall anymore. Bob shouts down at me over the winds, which sound like a million banshees.

'We can't turn, Robson! The boat'll flip and then it's night-night.'

He offers me a hand up. I accept but am immediately bent double for another projectile puking fit.

Another wave smashes the side. At this point I decide to give in and accept that this is how it's going to end. I've never been a religious man but in this moment I am having more words with the Almighty than ever before. I think, nowadays, in the age of science and reason, many see religion as anachronistic and irrelevant to them, but all I can say to those without faith, including myself, is perhaps we've never been in a position where we've really needed it? Out on the high seas or on the battleground or

at a refugee camp, cold reason and science are just not enough.
For the first time I pray that I will be reunited with my family. I
pray with all my heart and soul and I vow never to complain
about being an actor again, as I don't know the meaning of hard-
ship. All the while I'm having my spiritual epiphany, the crew of
the *Ocean Pearl* graft away, landing pot after pot without a break,
undeterred by the vicious storm.

Seamus takes me and the TV crew below deck. He confirms it's
a force-10 storm, which is two off a hurricane (12) on the
Beaufort wind force scale. The waves are over twenty feet high
and the wind is reaching speeds of 65 m.p.h. He offers us some
fried black cod, but we all shake our heads in unison and snaffle
another couple of seasickness pills, which are bloody useless. He
shows us to our digs. There are four bunks to a closet. I share
with Mike and two fishermen and, like a nightmarish version of
The Waltons, we say goodnight. The other three guys snore as if
they all have serious medical issues. I diagnose sleep apnea and a
very bad case of bulimia for myself, as I need to get up every ten
minutes to puke.

Finally the wind drops a few knots and Bob is able, very slowly,
to make a turn for home. Bob and the crew are happy to stay out
fishing, but my pleading every five minutes with Jason has obviously paid off. It went something like this: I'm lying in the closet
on the bottom bunk, I shut my eyes, oh God going to be sick, I
run to the toilet, dry retch, dry retch, flush, wash my mouth out
and knock on Jason's closet door: 'Please, Jason, I can't take anymore! For the love of God!' I go back to bed and repeat the
process. It was worth the begging, though, because *we are heading home*. I get a burst of energy and rush up to the wheelhouse
to see if it's really true. Bob, being the hero he truly is, has taken

pity on me after thirty-six hours of hell and guides us back to safer waters. The crew are apparently pissed off – they're losing money and it's our fault. I apologise.

Bob offers me a glass of red wine and a fillet of black cod, which the crew eat for breakfast, lunch and tea.

'I couldn't, Bob, I'm sick to my toenails.'

He insists I drink with him. As I sip the claret I feel as if I've taken a quantum leap back to the seventeenth century.

'Thank you for the experience. I will never forget it, Bob.'

His face cracks into smile. We finish our drinks and shake hands.

After dropping us off, the crew head back out to endure another five punishing weeks at sea. I honestly don't know how they do it, especially in light of what I found out several days later. Just weeks before we arrived, Bob had lost an entire boat, out of his fleet of a dozen trawlers, in a force-9 gale. Sadly, eight of the crew members were also lost at sea. It's a sobering thought and one that should make us all value our fishermen all the more. So when you're next eating black cod, give a nod to Bob and his crew – and whatever happens don't you dare waste a morsel!

As soon as we reach the shore I ring Vanya. She has been trying to get me for days. She was worried and knew something was wrong. Taylor knew, too.

'I can't wait to be home with you,' I say.

Nothing on the face of God's earth is as important as my family. I've been humbled by the experience on the trawler and have discovered a new-found respect for Mother Nature, not only in her beauty but in all her might.

Chapter Four

ALASKA

'Thanksgiving'

November 2008, Series 2

Everything is alabaster, including the sky, frozen by the White Witch's own hoary hand. It's bitter, harsh, perishing, arctic, glacial, numbing, polar, penetrating, raw, COLD! But unlike in the *Narnia* books, I haven't just fallen through the wardrobe to get here; instead I have endured another commercial plane journey, over 2,000 miles this time. It's more mundane than magical – well, the flying bit is definitely magic, but the loos and the tea not so much. I mean, that's the paradox of the human spirit, isn't it? We can make a tube of metal fly through the sky with all our clobber on board but we can't improve the food or the plumbing! Well done, the Wright Brothers; buck up, Gate Gourmet.

A clinically obese passenger across the aisle from me asks, 'You been to Alaska before?' I shake my head.

'It's staggering,' he says. 'Over a hundred thousand glaciers and most places you can only get to by plane. I hope you got your warm clothes and boots or you'll be getting chilblains.'

He then goes on to tell me about the terrible problems he has with his feet. I look concerned but inside I'm thinking, *Yeah, you can't keep them out of the bloody pie shop, mate.* (Will I go to hell now?)

I walk like a zombie to a waiting transit van to begin a six-hour butt-clenchingly awful journey due south from the city of Anchorage to a place called Homer. We are driving in a blizzard in the dark, which makes *Ice Road Truckers* seem positively tame.

My *Extreme* team comprises Jonathan, the AP whose job it is to make sure all the filming runs smoothly, director Jamie Goold, Mike Carling on camera, soundman Patrick Boland and location fixer Hector MacKenzie. They have all been in Alaska for two weeks doing a recce, but it would seem in that time Jonathan still hasn't gained confidence behind the wheel. The conditions are treacherous and the van is slipping all over the place. We are all on edge. Jonathan is a luvvie like me and really shouldn't be the designated driver. I vote for Hector, who emigrated to Alaska with his wife twenty years ago. He's an old-school rough, tough, no-nonsense Scot, and, I'm betting, a superior ice-driver.

Jonathan is craning over the wheel. He can't see the road, the windscreen is frosting over and . . . what's that? He hits the brakes and we go into a spectacular skid, turning round and round until we end up parked on the wrong side of the road. We have all had enough. I strongly suggest Hector drives. Jonathan is only too happy to hand over the task but starts having a tizzy because he feels the journey is just too dangerous; he doesn't want to be on board anymore. I know the feeling. He starts hyperventilating. In a bid to calm him down, Jamie suggests we change the tyres to studded ones to make it a bit safer. Unhelpfully I tell him to 'man up', hypocrite that I am: 'As my Uncle Matheson says, no place is worth going if it's easy to get to.'

Finally, after a change of driver, tyres and underpants, we arrive at our first Alaskan angling destination – Homer on the Kenai Peninsula. The Kenai, which is as big as the UK, Italy, France and Spain put together but only has a population the size of Newcastle, is a Mecca for salmon fishermen from all over the world. The fish are healthy and plentiful in this unspoiled paradise and only the very lucky, like me, have the chance to cast a line here.

It's really beginning to sink in that I am going to places most professional and amateur anglers can only dream about, and no one more so than my Uncle Matheson. For decades he has dreamt of dipping his fly rod in the Kenai River and exploring the unspoiled Alaskan wilderness. And what's more he's a trained taxidermist so he would doubly love it here, because at every turn, from the airport to the hotel, from the shopping mall to people's homes, there's always a stuffed creature, or usually several, on display. It's a fishing and taxidermy utopia. *I'll bring Matheson here one day*, I think, *but right now what I need is a stiff drink.*

Home from Homer

My first impression of Homer is, well, that I can't see a bloody thing, save a small wooden cabin otherwise known as the The Salty Dawg Saloon Bar. I enter; the smell of stale hops hits me. This is a place where men are men and moose are frightened.

Dollar bills are pinned to the walls and hanging from the ceiling, with all manner of messages written in marker pen: 'Shelly loves Buck.' 'Noah will pistol-whip Buck if he touches Shelly.' An old salty dawg sings Country and Western songs in the corner, strumming his guitar and puffing on a harmonica – except that they're more 'Cold and Northern' songs about being chilled to the bone and coming back from fishing and getting the dry-land blues. I feel slightly melancholy.

Keith Kalke introduces himself. He's an all-American hunter with a camo baseball cap, an impressive moustache and eyes that could pierce steel. Unlike the former governor of Alaska, Sarah Palin, Keith started hunting and fishing with his father aged just five. (In 2011, it was discovered that Sarah wasn't quite the outdoorsy girl she'd claimed to be.) Keith orders a beer and I order a white wine. No one including Keith bats an eyelid at this, which is disappointing as part of me (the mad part) wants a bit of a ruckus. There is none. Apparently, there are one or two Alaskan fishermen who enjoy a glass of Pinot Grigio as much as I do. Well, it goes very well with king salmon and there's certainly no shortage of *Oncorhynchus tshawytscha* (from the Ancient Greek meaning 'hook nose') up here. We'll be searching for the king in the morning, and Keith is very confident we'll catch.

I raise a toast: 'To good king salmon fishing!'

'Slammin' salmon!' says Keith, and we will be.

At this time of year, millions of Pacific salmon of all species, including the king (or chinook), pink, chum, sockeye (or red) and coho (also known as silvers), are making their epic journey back to their freshwater homes after years of feeding in the ocean. And what's more amazing is that they are returning to breed and then die. This life cycle is known as semelparity – from the Latin *semel*, 'once', and *pario*, 'to beget' – although no one knows why Pacific salmon (*Oncorhynchus*) expire after breeding while Atlantic salmon (*Salmo*) survive. It's one of life's eternal mysteries, but without their sacrifice the ecosystem in Alaska would struggle to thrive. These fish not only support human life in this winter wonderland but also the lives of birds, otters, bears – and the forests themselves. The salmon bring with them vital nutrients from the ocean, such as nitrogen, sulphur and phosphorus, which, via the wild animals that love to feast on them, fertilise the trees and plant life. Almost every organism around the river basin of Alaska has salmon in its DNA.

After a breakfast of tinned hot dogs, waffles and cream at our Travelodge-type hotel, I meet up with Keith and his son, Ross. We are going out on his boat, the *Ocean Hunter*, in pursuit of piscatorial royalty, and I'm excited. We drop anchor near Yukon Island in Kachemak Bay, part of the vast estuary where the Yukon River meets the mighty Pacific. Keith begins to explain the method of fishing we'll be using.

'We're running a twenty-five-pound test line with a flasher. This is gonna be like a school bait fish. All it's going to do is attract and get their attention and they'll come up and look at this and they'll see the bait dragging behind it,' he says in his rugged way.

'You give them a little tease and then they bite,' I say, nodding.

We're also putting on a downrigger, a weight to keep the bait at a depth of fifty feet.

Almost immediately Keith shouts, 'Fish on!'

'You are kidding me!'

The line is away. I take the rod. The odds are stacked in my favour because unlike the fly reels I use, which are basic storage facilities for the fly line with little or no tension at all, these reels provide up to fifteen to twenty pounds of tension along with a line that has a twenty-five-pound breaking strain. Nevertheless, if you don't keep yourself focused and the line tight, you will most likely lose your prize. I land the fish.

'King on deck!' says Keith.

In over thirty years of casting a line for salmon and trout, this is Keith's fastest bite ever.

'That took us, what, a minute?' says Keith.

Thirty seconds, more like. I try in vain to deliver a PTC that will enlighten, educate and inspire the viewer but what they get is, 'Hey . . . Woo, man, that's a FISH! You're the man, Keith! You're the lad!' I present my catch to the lens saying, 'This is the number-one salmon of them all. You've got your sockeye, your pink and your chum salmon but this is why we came to Alaska. Every salmon fisherman's dream is the king salmon.' I then drop the fish. I bloody drop it. Keith and his son share a look of incredulity. Their silence speaks volumes.

Some time later, I manage to mend bridges when we start talking of our shared passion for fishing. Ross says, 'Once you get addicted, you're done.' And he's right: it is an addiction, but what a healthy one – and you don't need to spend months in the Priory to get over it, which is a key point to underline to loved ones when explaining long absences and substantial financial investment in the sport. 'Yes, I know it's expensive, darling, but if I gave up fishing and took up crack . . . In the long term, fishing would be cheaper.' Google the cost of the Priory. You could come to Alaska five times over and still have cash to spare for bone fishing in the Bahamas!

*

Was that first king a fluke? Not on your nelly: within five minutes I have my three kings – a salmon hat-trick off the coast of Homer. Extreme location, extreme temperature and wonderful company – when catching salmon, it doesn't get any better than this.

Later that evening, although it's hard to tell whether it's day or night because it's dark most of the time, I cut the fish into steaks, cover them in lemon and butter and fry them on a shovel over an open fire on the beach. It's Newcastle's answer to *The Galloping Gourmet*.

There's a Moose Loose

The next day Jamie, the director, thinks it would be funny to film a PTC of me trying to attract a moose with loud calls. I think it's a stupid idea. I mean, is he trying to finish my acting career off? The only thing I'll be good for after this show is Maynard's Wine Gums – 'There's a moose loose aboot this hoose.' That's worse than Rob Brydon's Toilet Duck low. Of course I end up doing it.

Cue my moose mating calls. I stand in the middle of the woods and attempt to find one of the elusive 150,000 moose that live here. My male moose sounds like a cow and my female call to attract a male (bloody hell) sounds like I've popped my own testes with a plastic spoon. Awwwwwwwahoooooohhoooaaaaa! I wail into the icy tree-lined void for half an hour but to no avail. Unlike my lady fans, they don't come running, clutching their bangers and a Robson & Jerome CD, free with *Take a Break* magazine. Never mind – apparently nine out of ten men who try moose prefer women. I'm assured by Jamie that it's TV gold. I love Jamie but he is also a buffoon.

So where next for this Green fisherman? Fishing for northern pike with a nine-pronged spear through six feet of ice in the middle of bleeding nowhere, of course. After another epic journey in our uncomfortable van we arrive in Wasilla, where former Alaskan governor and prospective Veep (Vice President) Sarah Palin cut her teeth as mayor, and what a mare she is! It's 0600 hours and it's bloody cold with a high of −7°C, according to a very depressed-sounding radio weather forecaster. It must be like *Groundhog Day* at this time of year: 'What's the weather like?' 'Cold.' 'And later?' 'Colder.' *He needs to eat more salmon,* I think to myself – a portion a day will give you 90 per cent of your vitamin D intake (which is important when you're not getting enough sunlight) and it's rich in calcium, phosphorus and Omega-3.

Two people who aren't lacking fish in their wild diet are hunters Howard and Deborah Tieden. They've invited me into their home, which is a bit like a natural history museum. It seems after enjoying a good meal they like to remember it forever by having it stuffed. I imagine Howard looking up at his mounted caribou head and thinking, 'Those were the best goddamn hot dogs I have ever had.' Uncle Matheson would love this house – there's a creature at every turn: a bear, an antelope, a pheasant and a moose ...

'Hey, I found one, Jamie!' I say, pointing.

Maybe the Tiedens have eaten all of the moose and that's why we haven't seen one yet?

In Alaska everyone with a resident's permit is entitled to shoot one moose a year during the season, which runs August through September. Howard's weapon of choice is a bow and arrow, but today we will be using a spear, because thankfully we're going in pursuit of a much smaller but nonetheless incredibly ferocious predator, the northern pike. Howard passes me the fishing spear, which looks more like Ruprecht's trident in *Dirty Rotten Scoundrels* or a really rubbish garden rake. Howard assures me it's a spear.

'We're going to use this under the ice,' he says.

I'm ready to hit the road but as I head towards the truck Howard shakes his head and opens the doors to a massive double garage, in which is parked a gleaming white plane. It's so small it looks like toy. *Oh, great*, I think. I bloody hate light aircraft.

'Where we're going is two hundred miles into the interior and only accessible by air,' says Howard.

I make Jamie check the map. Howard's right. Out of the 300 million lakes, he had to pick one miles from a bloody road.

My guide insists that the best pike are found in this lake at the bottom of Sleeping Lady Mountain, which is a mountain that – yes, you've got it – looks like a Native American lass flat on her back knocking out the zeds. Howard is an extraordinary bush pilot who fears absolutely nothing as we hurtle along at 200 m.p.h. ten feet above the treetops. His landing is perfect, and, after another change of underwear, we get down to work setting up our camp, drilling and sawing into three feet of ice and then setting a canopy over the hole we've created. It's a spin on the ancient Native American method of ice fishing that has fed families for centuries. In fact, it's pretty much the same save the tent, a better rod and the plane to get here!

We are fishing at a depth of eight feet. After laying sliced potato segments at the bottom of the hole, to reflect the light and show the outline of any predator that swims past, I dangle my simple red and white fish-shaped wooden lure down the hole and stare into the icy water below. The pike (*Esox lucius*) is an ambush predator that lies in wait before selecting its target and WHAM!, it quickly takes down its prey with its deadly jaws and teeth. Its long, slender and compressed shape is perfect for propelling it at high speeds over short distances. What I need is focus, speed and lightning reflexes – three things I lack. I open my eyes wide and raise my spear, primed for attack. I stare and wait and stare and wait. It looks almost instantaneous on camera but in reality it takes bloody ages. A long, black silhouette appears below me and smashes into the lure.

'Hit it, Robson!' Howard shouts, and in one swift movement I launch the spear into the back of its skull. It's over in a second. I have just speared my first-ever northern pike – and a fine specimen it is, too. I pull my spear out of the water and haul up an ugly and fearsome-looking creature with an impressive set of gnashers. I can see why the Latin name translates as 'wolf fish'.

Back in the UK, pike are a catch-and-release quarry, as 99 per cent of anglers believe that the fish are far too bony to eat. But it's the water quality that makes the difference. Out here it's gin-clear, whereas in Britain the lakes are earthy, which undoubtedly affects the flavour. It will be interesting to see how this pike tastes.

This lake used to hold salmon and grayling but once the pike were introduced there was only going to be one outcome: anni-hilation. As a consequence, the pike feed on pike in rampant piscatorial cannibalism.

'OK, let's do something about that and see how many I can land for our dinner before they eat each other,' I say.

Within minutes I spear my second *Esox lucius* and for the next three hours it's non-stop action. After that the only thing to do is take off from the soft, squidgy bottom of the Sleeping Lady and head back to the Tiedens' stuffed-menagerie HQ in Wasilla to poach our pike.

It's a beautiful sunset flight back to Howard's house and I am more relaxed after a good day's fishing. Howard tells me about the time he got stuck for nine days at the Sleeping Lady lake with two other pilots and nine Japanese tourists.

'It was 9/11 and the authorities closed the entire skies. We were told there was no way we could take off so we made a camp and survived on pike until the restrictions were lifted and we could go home.'

After that experience I'm surprised Howard ever wanted to eat pike again!

We land smoothly on the runway next to his house. Howard, the crew and I jump out and together we push the small plane back into the double garage. I am coming round to the idea of small planes. I mean, how cool would it be to have one in your garage? Deborah is waiting to relieve us of the pike, which she pops in the oven with butter and lemon slices. We enjoy a beer around the kitchen table before sitting down to sample Mrs Tieden's pike supper. It's absolutely exquisite. I tell them many people in the UK don't eat pike because it's supposed to be bony; Howard says it is, but only on one side, and that the flesh is easy to pull off the bone. I have to say the taste is up there with my top fish suppers. It might even have just knocked haddock off the top spot.

The Kenai

It's been a lifelong dream to come to the Kenai, a large peninsula jutting from the southern coast of Alaska, but the question is, will it live up to my expectations? The icy water is crystal-clear, tinged with an iridescent mineral green that adds a Pre-Raphaelite romanticism to the setting. Snow-dusted pine trees line the water's edge, shaken only by the occasion fish eagle jumping into flight to skim the water and take its prey. A brown bear casually tosses a half-eaten salmon aside and wanders into the forest as we arrive. It is everything I had hoped for and more, and I haven't even got out of the van!

In 1985 a ninety-seven-pound salmon was landed out of the river and it still stands as the biggest salmon ever caught any-where in the world. But today I'm after rainbow trout, with the help of the Collette Bros. Carl and Billy are no ordinary brothers, and these are no ordinary rainbow trout – they're some of the best in the world.

Billy says, 'Let's just say they're not on the Weight Watchers programme. They're real big and they're real fat.'

Carl and Billy were, in their own words, born to fish. They also have a penchant for chewing tobacco, and as we row out into the river there is a 'phut-tink' every sixty seconds. At first I think they are unwell as I watch them perpetually hack and gob. Perhaps it's the flu or maybe bronchitis brought on by the cold? However, I soon deduce the reason they both have protruding lower lips is not owing to bundled forceps deliveries, as I had first thought, but to their sizeable pouches of tobacco. As Carl speaks I catch a glimpse of his 'gobbet' just in front of his stained yellow teeth. Within just five minutes of being in their company, I can tell that my time on the Kenai is going to be memorable.

It's as cold and quiet as a cathedral out on the river and there couldn't be a more spiritual setting for a fly-fisherman. The snow-covered mountains create one of the most dramatic backdrops I have ever seen. Otters feed greedily on the shore of the glacier-fed river and a large bald eagle watches over me from a leafless tree. Phut-tink! Carl spits another gobbet into the water. I watch it disperse like congealed blood.

As I prepare for my first cast on the Kenai, I am tingling with excitement. I am using an egg fly as my lure. Salmon eggs are the reason why these rainbow trout and steelheads, like the ones I caught with Crap Anagram in Canada, are so fat. Most are stream residents and it's difficult to tell the anadromous[4] fish apart. When the female salmon lays thousands of eggs in her riverbed redd, or nest, many are simply washed away by the current into feeding channels, where hefty rainbows are ready waiting for them, gobs open. Our plan is to replicate nature by gently floating downstream and through a series of turns, casting the egg under the noses of the rainbows that lie in wait below the surface. The water is so clear that I can see the fish moving about fifteen feet down and I can tell by their darting moves they are hungry.

Fly-fishing has a rhythm to it. I relax into my casts and remember a few tips Uncle Matheson taught me. I gently take the rod back, whisking the line over my shoulder until it's nearly straight; I pause and then, bringing my arm gently forward, watch the loops of the line unfurl and straighten on the water about twenty metres in front of my rod. I am happy with my cast. I feel a nibble and set the rod by quickly bringing the tip up from the water to

---

4. Meaning they spend most of their life in the sea but return to freshwater to breed.

the sky. This action hooks the lip of the fish and, as we say on the show, 'I am in.' I can see the trout: it's about seven pounds in weight but is fighting like a twenty-pound salmon! She runs, taking twenty-five metres of line with her. These rainbow trout are true Olympians of the river – think Jessica Ennis (well, any excuse!). Her run is continuous, powerful and downwards. That's the difference between rainbows and brown trout: rainbows fight deep, whereas browns flap on the surface.

There is no way this fish is going to come in quickly. I just need to keep her away from the fast-moving current, the boat and the hungry eagles lurking in the treetops, ready to launch at an unsuspecting angler's quarry. I let her run again and she takes the line upriver like a champion. Then, very slowly, I begin the retrieve and reel her towards me, keeping the line tight. She runs again but after about fifteen minutes the angling stalemate is over. She is spent, and I am able to gently guide the fish into the landing net and celebrate her beauty with the world. Her scales are pinks, greens and yellow hues, all the colours of the rainbow.

A hundred years ago prospectors came looking for gold in the Kenai but today I struck something else that is far more precious – and, more importantly, edible: *Oncorhynchus mykiss*. I give her one, mwah, and, holding her under the water for a slow release, allow the oxygen to gently circulate in her gills. I let go and she darts away. Closed-season rules dictate we must release our trout today – these rules protect the species and allow them to thrive and prosper.

Nanwalek

The last part of my journey in Alaska is to travel further south along the Kenai Peninsula to the incredibly remote village of

Nanwalek, home to the Sugpiaq tribe who will be taking me fishing for an Alaskan legend, the silver salmon. Although it's not far, the only way to get to Nanwalek is by plane – another very small plane. I turn up at Terminal 1 – it's a shed. What's more worrying is that the pilots are children, who toss a coin to determine which of the spotty adolescents will take us. The thirteen-year-old loses the toss to the eleven-year-old.

'Isn't it past your bedtime?' I ask, begging the director not to make me board.

He reminds me that boats can only occasionally make the crossing, and it's impossible to reach by road.

So my eleven-year-old pilot turns out to be Alaska's answer to the Red Baron (I was going to say Douglas Bader but then had images of an eleven-year-old being known as 'Stumpy' and it all got a bit messy in my head). It's a twenty-minute flight through freezing fog and a white sky. It's a bleak landscape and I get a good view of it as the ground comes up to meet us fast, but the child lands the plane perfectly.

'Well done,' I say, tapping him on the shoulder. God, not only do I feel inadequate as an adventurer, but I feel bloody old!

Over the years, the Sugpiaq tribe have seen Russian and then American rulers, after Alaska was sold to the US by Russia in 1867 for $7.2 million, which is under 2 cents an acre! Just think what you pay for a 400-square-foot flat in London nowadays – it was a steal. The tribe now govern themselves and village chief Wally Kvashnikoff is at the airport (another shed) to greet me.

Although Wally's name sounds like a heavy-assault weapon, he is a modest man of few words with kind eyes. He is also an excellent hunter and fisherman. Owing to the remote location, everything has to be brought in and out by plane, so the villagers are almost completely self-sufficient. In fact, 95 per cent of Wally and his family's diet comes from the land, the sea and the rivers, so angling isn't a sport for him – it's survival.

Today Wally and I are going in pursuit of the silver salmon (or coho), which we'll eat at a village feast tonight. It's 27 November and Thanksgiving here in the remote American state of Alaska. Everyone is looking forward to the party, so Wally and I cannot return empty-handed. At this time of year, as the silvers arrive home from the Pacific to the quiet backwaters where they were raised as parrs, they quickly turn from silver to red and green, showing that they are sexually mature. It really is extraordinary to think that the final act of these beautiful salmon before they die will be uninhibited lovemaking with their partners ... so at least they'll pass away with a smile on their faces! I comfort myself with this thought but I can't help feeling choked by the sheer magnitude of this species' journey, followed by such a tragic yet passionate end. It's their beautiful and poignant sacrifice that touches my luvvie soul. That said, I still want to catch one for our supper – especially seeing as it's going to die anyway. They can't all be for the bears.

The snow flutters down as we cast our lines. I am freezing to the bone and need to stamp my feet and clap my hands every few minutes to keep my circulation going. Wally quietly casts, seemingly unaffected by the cold. After two hours of non-stop casting the fishing, like the conversation, is going nowhere.

'Are there fish in here?' I ask Wally.

'Yes, we just have to find them,' he replies.

Honestly, if my family lived and relied on my fishing prowess to provide food, sadly they would starve and eventually leave me, standing alone with my rod like an impotent angler. But November is a difficult time to catch a fish in this part of the world; these guys are weakened, waiting to die, and therefore not really in the mood for feeding.

Time after time salmon between ten and twenty pounds swim into view, but even when I cast right in front of their noses they're not interested. As salmon are technically unable to feed once they hit freshwater, because their stomachs can't digest food, I need to provide an irritant to the fish. The males become incredibly territorial and very possessive over their area and their partner, so any intruder, no matter how small, would wish they'd never ventured anywhere near the horny salmon. I cast a spoon lure, which has worked for me before on the River Coquet, and – yes, you guessed it – absolutely nothing. Time after time the fish just don't want to know.

I deliver my final PTC informing the viewers that on tonight's menu is fish surprise . . . the surprise being that there is no fish. It's a sad angling end to a beautiful backdrop but just as I'm reeling my line to the bank to perform my last cast of the day, WHAM! I get a take! My spoon is no more than ten feet from the bank but astonishingly a female silver has decided to attack my lure. Everyone is astounded and no one more than me. Even though this girl's travelled thousands of miles, has spawned and is on hunger strike, about to die, she fights like a woman possessed.

She runs, and just when I think I have her she leaps five feet out of the water and runs again, taking another thirty metres of line with her. All I can do is keep the line tight. One of us has to tire and this time it's not going to be me. Wally and his large family are expecting food on the table and they are relying on me to get it there. I reel her in and get her to the snow-covered bank. She is a fifteen-pound silver, a dark burgundy colour, similar to a sockeye salmon. I pick her up to inspect her and she is covered in snow like icing sugar. Her tail is worn from creating her redd (nest) on the gravel riverbed, in which she will have laid her eggs. This tail is so powerful that it has not only migrated 4,000 miles but then also dug a hole while fighting the current – and all on an empty stomach.

'Happy Thanksgiving, Wally. Last cast! Get in!' I say.

I am so chuffed not to be going back empty-handed and also proud that I have landed a silver on the famous Kenai. Wally says he never doubted me for a second . . . Millions would, Wally, millions would.

Wally's wife prepares all the ingredients for our Thanksgiving feast, including locally grown vegetables as well as herbs and spices. She uses every part of the fish save the entrails. The fish head is used to create a delicious soup. All I'm thinking is that I hope it tastes as good as it smells, because the aroma is unbearably beautiful. We all agree fish tastes wonderful when you have caught it yourself – though these people have probably never tasted the supermarket stuff.

That said, many of the tribe do not eat as healthily as Wally and his family. Unfortunately the Sugpiaq suffered terribly in 1989, along with their fellow Alaskans, when the oil tanker *Exxon Valdez* spilled over 10 million gallons of crude oil. The spill, at that time the largest in US history, affected 1,100 miles of Alaskan coastline and killed or poisoned almost all the fish. As a result the tribe was sent an abundance of processed food by

American charities and well-wishers. Concerned about contamination during the years after the spill, native people abandoned about half the wild foods they would normally have eaten. Their bodies were unable to assimilate the imported food and sadly there is now an obesity crisis within the tribe, just as there is across most of the West. Hopefully, with Wally at the helm of the tribe, the Sugpiaq people will return to their healthy lifestyle and the eating patterns of their forefathers.

Down at the village hall, the party is underway. Thanksgiving is the celebration of the first time native people shared their food with British settlers. Four hundred years later they are just as generous. We arrive with our stewed salmon and soup and I sit down and join Wally and his family at the table and tuck in – it's delicious. I try other food on offer, too. With a little Nanwalek ketchup, which is seal blubber boiled down into a waxy paste. It tastes like, well, erm, seal fat. It kind of has the Marmite effect: you love it or hate it, and let me tell you I hate it! I later discovered that it has been known to cause botulism. This strangely didn't concern me. Well, I work with actors with faces full of botox – a deadly strain of the bacteria. A couple of air kisses could be as lethal as a bad portion of seal fat – it's a good reason to avoid kissing Simon Cowell, ladies! Anyway, before you think of freezing your faces in permanent surprise, digest this: botulism is a lethal toxin that blocks nerve function and causes paralysis. I mean, what muppet wants to inject that into their face? All I can say is it's bonkers.

After a bellyful of delicious local food there is only one way to end this Thanksgiving evening, and that's with a song. I get hold of a guitar and perform an old northeastern folk song entitled

'They Don't Write Them Like That Anymore'. I can see one of Wally's teenage daughters thinking, 'Thank the Lord for that.' I hit the final chord.

'Goodnight, Nanwalek, it's good to be back! Happy Thanksgiving, everyone.'

Chapter Five

BOSTON AND CAPE COD

Follow that Fish

November 2008, Series 2

As I walk through Boston Arrivals I spot the director, Jamie Goold, among the throng. Immediately I can see something's wrong. He walks purposely over to me, stony-faced.

'What's happened? [pause] Is it my dad?'

'Yes.'

'Is he dead?'

'No, he's had a heart attack.'

It's a surreal and emotional introduction to Boston.

I phone the Freeman Hospital in Newcastle. Dad is in intensive care but able to talk.

'Are you OK? Jesus, Dad.'

'I'm all right, son.'

'I'm organising a flight home first thing tomorrow.'

'Don't you dare get on the plane. All the family are here, and we love you and I am fine.'

'But I want to be there.'

'There's nothing you can do. I know you were in *Casualty* but an actor in a hospital is about as useful as a chocolate teapot,' he laughs, short of breath.

I really didn't want to stay. The truth is that I was scared to death and I wanted to be with my family. I had never faced the possibility of life without Dad before and it shook me to the core.

'Dad, did it hurt?' I ask, like one of Job's Comforters, part of me wanting to know how serious it was, the other what it will be like when I go through it later on!

He says, 'I have never felt pain like it.'

This is a man who has worked down the mines all his life and has suffered slipped discs and a crooked back, like his father, a miner before him, all of this resulting in a perpetual stoop when he walks. He's endured severe nerve damage in his fingers (vibration white finger) from working at the coalface but never complains. He's always managed the pain by swimming for miles in the North Sea, irrespective of what time of year it is. Now that's hardcore.

'Imagine you are in a room and the walls are closing in,' he says. 'And they start to squeeze your ribs from right to left and the crushing is not stopping and the pain is getting worse. It takes a lot to drop me to my knees.'

I imagine him bent double in searing agony. I've never seen my father vulnerable before. Growing up, Robson Senior, or Big Rob, as he is known to his mates, was the hardest man in the village. He's only five-foot-nine but stocky with huge shoulders, built like a juggernaut. When people ask me to describe my father, the best word is 'huge'. He is huge both in character and stature, not an ounce of fat on him, and boy, could he handle himself in a fight – of which there were many. Like the time when a young guy knocked all my teeth out and Dad went round to his house, pushed him aside and chinned his father! Or if ever he was woken up by people on the street outside, he would thunder down the stairs, give someone a smack in the mouth and ask questions later. No one dared to interrupt his sleep. If David, Joanna, Dawn or I did, we knew not to be in the same postcode.

My younger brother, David, inherited Dad's build and toughness, but that gene wasn't passed on to me. I always say, 'A runner is better than a fighter and an ego heals faster than a broken jaw.'

'Make a good programme, Robson.'

'I will, and I'll be over to see you in six days.'

The phone clicks off. I exhale deeply, feeling as though there is a tight band around my head. I am poleaxed by anxiety and want to blub like a child.

Tonight we are meant to be going out on a trawler for three days in pursuit of Atlantic bluefin tuna, a fish that can grow to record sizes of over 1,400 pounds. Men risk life and limb to hunt these creatures because one that size could be worth around half a million dollars on the Japanese market. Our timing is perfect: the bluefin are running. But after the news of my father, and indeed the ordeal of the *Ocean Pearl* a few weeks ago, I just can't face it. Mercifully Jamie has asked the trawlermen if we can postpone our trip until the morning, explaining the situation, but my dad being poorly means nothing to them – they have to make a living – so they go without us.

Jamie calls a production meeting with Jonathan, the AP from the Alaska episode, cameraman Mike Carling and the sound-man Patrick Boland, and we decide to go out on the trawler at the back end of the week. We'll just have to pray we haven't missed the bluefin run. We re-jig the schedule as best we can. Luckily Jamie is an expert at thinking on his feet.

After the meeting Mike takes me to one side.

'What you're going through with your dad – I've been there. If you need to talk I know exactly how you're feeling.'

Mike is ex-army and built like a brick shithouse. He's also got a massive heart. We'd bonded on the *Ocean Pearl* trawler, during thirty-six hours of hell, which was a hundred times worse for him with a heavy camera on his shoulder, but, unlike me, Mike never complained once. Over the next few nights I talk about my dad and how to face the inevitable. I regale Mike with stories of my childhood, such as the one and only time Dad took us out fishing in Devon, when I was seven and David was five. David and I were really seasick so the captain suggested he turn the boat around but my father said, 'No way, I've paid five pound. We are staying out 'til we get a fish.' We came back with one mackerel, which Mum cooked and made a right mess of. Dad doesn't get fishing – to him it's inactive and boring. His favourite hobby is drinking; he loves it and could have won many medals had dipsomania been an Olympic discipline. I once witnessed him devour eighteen pints and still manage to walk home – I have never been so proud. He fell over the hedge in the front garden but it was a grand effort all the same.

Cape Cod, Massachusetts

Seeing as we aren't going out on the trawler to catch tuna, we have to find something else to film. So we decide to do a PTC on Cape Cod and the history of the name. In 1602, a chap called Bartholomew Gosnold, an eminent English lawyer, explorer and privateer, went fishing and caught a few cod with a collective weight of 1,000 pounds, as you do. (Sadly we're not going to catch any today as the cod are too small due to overfishing and therefore not extreme enough.) Having rather a lot of sway and also having discovered the area first, he decreed it should henceforth be known as Cape Cod. He also named Martha's Vineyard after his daughter. I wonder if they'll name a place after me one day? Perhaps a cricket field in Northumberland – Robson's Green – or a bridge I once fished off. I can dream.

(I actually wasn't named Robson when I was a baby. Believe it or not for two days my name was Gary Green, but then Dad turned up, took the band off my arm and gave me his own name. Thank God he did. I can't think of many hip Garys off the top of my head. Well, there's Gary Oldman: extremely cool. Gary Lineker: quite cool. Gary Glitter: hmm, death penalty springs to mind. I'm very glad I'm Robson. It's a name that belongs to the mining communities of the northeast and it's common for the eldest son to have a surname as a first name. In fact, in my class at middle school there was me, Robson Green, and my mate Robson Brown. I kid you not.)

Anyway, the history of this part of New England is also pivotal in the founding of modern America. In September 1620 the *Mayflower* set sail from England and that November she landed on the shores of Cape Cod, most probably near Provincetown, aka 'P-Town', nowadays the gay capital and party town of Massachusetts.

Probably not what the highly religious Pilgrim Fathers had in mind, but I've heard Burger Queen is worth a visit. In December 1620 the Plymouth Colony was founded and the rest, as they say, is American history. But there is also another important historical fact associated with the Cape and this one I actually know a lot about. Here's a clue: the famous score is just two notes played on a cello, over and over again. Dur-nur, dur-nur, dur-nur-dur-nur ... faster and faster ... That's right, it was the setting for *Jaws*. Over the summer of 1974, when Steven Spielberg was just twenty-seven, they filmed all around here and Martha's Vineyard. Usually movies were shot in a studio, but the young maverick Spielberg wanted to prove himself and took the gamble to shoot in the ocean. There were many near-drownings and the film was fraught with setbacks, not least when the $250,000 mechanical shark was finally ready for his close-up and turned out to be cross-eyed and a bit, well, rubbish-looking. He also sank to the bottom of Nantucket Sound and all his electricals had to be overhauled. Not to mention that Jaws was worse than me in the high-maintenance stakes: every night he had to be hosed down and freshly painted. Spielberg knew he was facing a flop so he went back to the draw-ing board. He later said, 'I had no choice but to figure out how to tell the story without the shark. So I just went back to Alfred Hitchcock: "What would Hitchcock do in a situation like this?"' He realised 'it's what we don't see that is truly frightening', and thus made a classic by featuring the shark as little as possible.

Great whites are in fact rare off Cape Cod but there are plenty of other sharks, such as the vicious mako, which is what I'm off to catch this morning. Known round these parts as 'the taxman', mako can take 70 per cent or even 90 per cent chunks out of your quarry when fishing, which is known as being taxed.

A giant wels catfish that, I have to say, bears no resemblance whatsoever to a cat

'OK Robson, be interesting, insightful and entertaining.' And . . . action!

Let's just say this carp is no stranger to the dessert trolley (or isn't on the Weight Watchers diet!)

A super-pod of dolphins. A rare and extraordinar sight that just makes your heart sing

Show-off! If I could leap like that I could be my own stunt double

The sailfish. The marine equivalent of a Ferrari!

'Sometimes I hear, and sometimes I don't!'

Dinner is served, Costa Rican style

A survivor of the terrible massacre in Room 25

The setting for the iconic 1970s movie *Jaws*. I don't think my tackle is big enough . . .

A bluefin tuna that really put the *Extreme* into Extreme Fishing

Two crayfish and a prawn

Has anyone seen my drum kit?

Even in the Amazon jungle there's always a pap lurking in the undergrowth. Thankfully I'm not topless

How on earth are we going to top this? I came in search of the ultimate angling experience, and I think I've found it!

Check out the mahi-mahi (and the Mangina!)

It's the only way t
travel, especially i
I'm at the control

The last picture ever
taken of the bloody
cockerel that kept me
awake in Costa Rica

An actor with a
harpoon, what could
possibly go wrong

Mine's bigger than yours, Tarzan

If I run the caiman gets me, if I swim the piranha get me, it's a Catch-23 (which is like a Catch-22 but worse!)

Cuba. A 1950s paradise, and one of my favourite places on the planet

A rose between two thorns. Or should I say barracudas?

What more does an angler need? Well, a bathroom would be nice!

And then a storm removed our humble abode from the earth

As I walk down to the aptly named Green Harbour (hopefully not named after a forebear who lost his life to a shark), the only question is: are we going to need a bigger boat? I meet Tom de Persia and his son, Jeff, who run several sports fishing charters off the Cape. Today we're heading two hours east into the Atlantic to go in search of this ultimate predator. It's beautiful out at sea, the sun is rising, the dolphins are swimming, but bloody hell, Tom is driving the boat like an utter madman. It's obvious he hasn't skippered in a while by the way he is battering the boat at speed into the waves. Jeff is more of an able seaman and is losing patience with his father's incompetence. As we are all thrown around the boat, Jeff shouts, 'What the hell are you doing, Dad?' Let's just say they seem to have a somewhat strained relationship. I think Tom is just desperate to be on camera.

The mako shark is the fastest shark in the ocean and the third-fastest creature on the planet. They are capable of jumping twenty feet out of the water and are responsible for taking many a chunk out of fishermen who land them on their boats. We will not be landing our mako, as shark fishing is part of a catch-and-release programme, which means any taxmen we catch will be electronically tagged so that marine biologists can study feeding, breeding and extreme fiscal pillaging, and other habits of this fearsome creature.

To attract these predators we have got to get the smell of blood in their nostrils, so out goes the chum crate full of ground-up smelly fish. We drag the crate behind the boat, to encourage sharks to head straight for us – it's definitely counter-intuitive. I am looking for dorsal fins in the water, trying to act casual. When the sharks do get near the boat we are going to try to hook one using balloons.

'Are we throwing the mako a party?' I ask.

Jeff explains that the balloon acts as a bobber, so when the shark bites the balloons pop. Because of the waves and the swell it's sometimes difficult to see where the bait has dropped; in this instance we're using bonito, which is a medium-sized mackerel-type fish. The bright-coloured balloon is an extreme version of a fish float, and if we accidentally fall asleep (which is quite possible when out fishing) the loud bang will hopefully wake us up. Well, that's the theory.

Jeff has been fishing since he was born. In fact, when he came out of the womb, the first thing his parents gave him was a rod – well, almost the first thing. They probably gave him a kiss and then a good glug of milk and *then* the rod. Jeff is fascinated by sharks and saw *Jaws* before he went on his first shark-fishing trip with his dad. He has seen the film twenty-six times at the cinema. I myself saw *Jaws* six times at the Newcastle Odeon (now a car park) with my best mate Keith Jobson; we watched *Star Wars* sixteen times.

As I wait for a bite, I jabber at the crew and camera. The sun gleams on the water and I check every bump and ripple for signs of movement. I really don't want to spot a grey dorsal fin cutting through the waves like a scalpel, but then again I really do. What is it about humans and the need to scare the shit out of ourselves? Spielberg is right, it's the things we can't see that scare us the most, so I suppose shark fishing is a way of facing your fears, literally. It's also borne out of pure curiosity to see and know more about what lurks beneath. To my mind it's bloody bonkers, but I am contractually obliged!

I imagine I'm in the barrel scene of the movie. The shark is circling Quint's boat. Quint loads a harpoon and attaches it to a plastic barrel. He shoots Jaws. The predator is now very pissed off and takes the barrel on a very fast journey. He disappears and so does the barrel. Where's the shark gone? John Williams's cello music is playing in my head: dur-nur, dur-nur, dur-nur. Every glimmer looks like movement and my eyes are in overdrive. I'm seeing shapes everywhere. I stare at the balloon waiting for it to pop. I wait. But a watched balloon never bursts.

Two hours later and we've got bugger-all, I am still in one piece and I'm bored. I'm also absolutely freezing my nuts off out here. Quint never looked cold but then, compared to Orkney Islander Robert Shaw, who played the grizzly fisherman, I am a soft Southerner. He was probably warmed up by rum, as he wasn't shy of a drink. Shaw was an incredibly talented man and actually wrote the USS *Indianapolis* monologue scene in which Quint explains his violent hatred of sharks. Watch it again, it's brilliant. He died in 1978 of a heart attack but is on my imaginary list of top five people of all time to go on the lash with, the others being: Oliver Reed, Peter Sellers, Errol Flynn and, weirdly, Michael Bublé.

Suddenly I swear I see something break the surface of the water. Jeff isn't sure. The balloon starts moving towards us very slowly. I don't think we are going to need a bigger boat. It's about the pace of a Chihuahua paddling under the surface. We pull up the line – 'It's a shark!' Just the wrong bloody kind. It's a small spiny dogfish. I grab him by the tail and hold him up to camera. He's got two small dorsal fins and really rough skin, and reminds me of an ex-girlfriend.

As we pop him back, Tom suggests we perhaps try to catch a bluefin tuna instead. Jamie says no, because we are now going to do that on a trawler at the end of the week and our catch is likely to be much bigger than it would be here. We all agree to stick with the shark fishing. But right at the time of the discussion, Jamie's phone starts beeping. It's a text from the captain of the trawler 100 miles out at sea. It simply says 'They've gone', meaning the tuna.

'Thank fuck we didn't go out with them. It would have been a complete waste of time,' I say.

I have never been so happy in my whole life to miss three days on a blinking trawler without the prospect of catching a single fish. And it's all down to my dad.

Jamie looks at his phone for a while.

'OK, let's catch a bluefin,' he says.

Thank God for that. I'm always happier catching a fish we can actually eat, rather than one that wants to eat me. We head further out into the Atlantic, now in pursuit of *Thunnus thynnus*, which can grow to the size of a small car and put up one hell of a fight. The birds are feeding, which means only one thing: big fish are gorging on bait fish.

We set out our lines, baited with plastic jelly skip bait that replicates sardines or mackerel in the water, and begin to trawl. Jeff can see bluefin tuna leaping 100 yards away. We head towards them. The suspense is killing me but after half an hour there are still no bites. Surely I'm not going to miss out again. All of a sudden, one of the reels starts to scream. I take the rod, with the help of Jeff, and plug it into my special 'mangina'. The pull on the line is incredible. It feels like a massive bluefin tuna but that could be wishful thinking. The muscles in my back are stretched to their limit but still the fish keeps running.

'This is a big fish! Such a strong, powerful, ocean-going Ferrari!'

I slowly wind in but the fish takes out more and more line.

'You hear that? That is the sound of power. He's turning me round, he's turning me round. Oh, stop, please! This is some beast, I'm telling you now we're in for some shock if we get this on board,' I yell out to anyone who's listening.

After twenty minutes he seems to tire and I can wind him in again . . . As the fish gets nearer, the pull gets stronger. I am in real trouble; my back is knackered and I'm in serious pain.

'Oh, it's going under the boat!' I shout.

Shooting pains are making me feel sick but I can't lose this fish. I ask Jeff if I am doing something wrong or standing incorrectly.

'No, this is what they do to you,' he says, as I heave the rod up and reel with all my might. 'You're gonna want to stay right in this corner and swing him out. There you go, get a crank.'

'I can't!'

'There you go, you're doing good,' says Jeff. 'We got colour!'

I look at the side of the boat. It's a monster. How on earth are we going to get it on board? I am dizzy with pain.

'Ready, 3, 2, 1 . . .'

Jeff and Tom heave the tuna on board and I go mental, like a schoolboy with ADHD, shouting, 'That's why we came here! Look at that fish! Oh, yes, man, get in! Whoah! This is why we came to Boston, this is why we came to Cape Cod. We did it, Jeff, you're the man. Tom de Persia's the man. What have we got, a hundred and twenty, hundred and fifty-pound?!'

Jeff confirms it's a 150-pound bluefin. It's astonishing. I suddenly experience a release of tension; all the anxieties I have been storing up about my father are exorcised in that moment. This bluefin symbolises that everything is going to be OK. I sit on deck holding the fish in my arms, completely overwhelmed. I can't stop looking at every inch in admiration. The Latin name *Thunnus* means 'to dart away quickly', which is spot-on because this shinning metallic and silvery creature is made of pure muscle and is one of the fastest animals on the planet. Its design is incredible: the dorsal fin fits into a slot and comes up like a small jib when needed and then goes down again into a groove to make it streamlined, like a jet. It is beautiful, quite beautiful, but its striking eyes seem doleful and part of me is sad to have taken this creature from its home in the ocean. It's a paradox of emotions: I'm overwhelmed at the hunt but it's tinged with melancholy at the fish's sacrifice. However, nothing will go to waste and that is how we show respect for the creatures whose lives we take, by not wasting a morsel and, like the Native Americans, giving thanks in our hearts. This fish will now become a part of me, and much bigger parts of my hungry crew.

Bluefin tuna is around $40 per pound, so ours is worth over $6,000. We take a slab of the vibrant pink meat to a sushi restaurant near the harbour, where Kong the chef prepares it. He explains that the best part of the tuna for sashimi is the o-toro cut, which is the fattiest part of the belly, up near the head. It's a very pale pink meat that melts on the tongue. Other cuts are the akami, pure red meat from the back of the fish (my favourite), and chu-toro, marbled pink belly meat that is rich and buttery in taste. We eat with Tom, Jeff and the rest of crew. The sushi is delicious, among the best I have ever tasted; just like the tuna I tried off the coast of Costa Rica, it tastes clean.

Back at the hotel I have a shower and phone Dad. He is feeling better and tells me he is going to be fine. He's hoping to get 'released' tomorrow. I tell him he inadvertently saved me from another trawler journey from hell.

'Saved you from a bit of hard work, eh?' he chuckles.

I lie on the bed reflecting on how different our lives have been. Compared to his life down the pit, it is amazing how lucky I've been and I know he is very proud of me. Dad started out as a putter (pushing the coal carts), then a face worker, and worked his way up to deputy leader of a team – a role that demanded the respect of the lads underground, which he had in abundance. Whatever he asked, they delivered. However, his favourite job was looking after the pit ponies. Dad adored horses, just like his brother, Matheson. It was their shared passion.

As I lie there I swear I hear a whinny followed by a long neigh. I sit up on the bed. My mind is playing tricks. I must be exhausted. I lie back down. No, there it is again. I sit up and listen intently. Now more like a short groan, the kind of sound I make when I put my socks on in the morning. Another whinny accompanies the groan – someone's in pain. I suddenly twig: it's the elderly couple in the next room going 'at it', pensioner-style. Oh, my God! Whatever they're doing sounds sore. I head downstairs for a pint of American lager, trying to rid my head of the sepia imagery. I take a sip of my Sam Adams. I am lobster fishing tomorrow. I smile as Peter Cook and Dudley Moore's Jayne Mansfield/lobster sketch pops into my head. Now, that would be sore.

Lobster Fishing

Lobster boats go out in all weathers to get their catch, and thinking about how cold it is at the moment I opt to wear a survival suit, a special type of waterproof dry suit that will protect me from hypothermia should I end up in the drink. Unfortunately I am roasting like the proverbial trussed up like this, and when I meet Jim Ryan, he is dressed in only a pullover and waterproof dungarees, *not* a full-on survival suit. Now, unlike women, men freak out when they aren't dressed the same and at this party I have turned up wearing the wrong kit – it's embarrassing and Jim takes the piss immediately. I warm to him instantly. He is a jovial soul with a laugh like The Joker from *Batman*. For eight hours he doesn't stop laughing.

Jim and his first mate Matt harvest and bait up to 400 lobster pots a day. The forecast is for rough seas but we head out anyway. These are normal conditions for lobstermen and there is no turning back. After the curse of the *Ocean Pearl* in Canada, I laugh in the face of a mere choppy sea.

We bring up the first pot, which has two lobsters in it. Anything that has a body measuring between three and five inches is a keeper, anything smaller or larger must go back. It's only a three-man boat but there is still a pecking order. One of them catches the pots; the second job is to remove the lobsters, size them and put elastic bands around the claws to prevent the amputation of fishermen's fingers or other lobsters' pincers when they get a bit feisty, and the third job is to re-bait the pots before putting them back out to sea. Rather like Peter Mandelson or Camilla Parker Bowles, I am the third man. You'd have thought an extra pair of hands would have been helpful to a two-man crew, but in reality I am a bloody hindrance. Re-baiting is the job you give to the genetically challenged bloke – it's pretty straightforward: you fill the traps with cod skins, which are honking, and throw them back out to sea – but I *still* can't master it and am slowing the whole process down. The closed season is limited to only three months a year (January–April), which means these guys need to catch as many lobsters as possible five days a week. I fear I am beginning to have a negative effect on their bank balances.

'Jim, I'm covered in fish guts, you can't go home to your girl-friend smelling like this ... or maybe she likes the aroma of rotting herring ... cod skin and rotting herring, guaranteed a girlfriend or your money back,' I say, still baiting the pots.

Jim beams at me and cackles like The Joker. These guys absolutely reek of fish and now so do I; cod skin is in every pore. They fish all day, go to bed and then fish all the next day. I don't think they've seen a bar of soap for months. It's like when Napoleon sent the apocryphal message to Josephine: 'Home in three days. Don't wash!' So typically French. Whether it's true or not is unimportant; let's just say we all know why the French invented perfume.

Matt gets me to start bringing up the pots, and nineteen later I'm exhausted – it's tough work. Jim says: 'It's not for everyone.' He works ten hours a day, doing 400 pots five times a week, and why? Because he absolutely loves it. For some, like Peter Cook, it would be possibly 'the worst job they've ever had'.

Jim gives me a *Homarus gammarus* anatomy lesson. Each lob-ster has a crusher claw and a pincer claw, and can be left- or right-handed depending upon which side the crusher claw is on.

'The female tails are fatter and the crusher claw is smaller,' he says. He turns one over: 'See that he's got two pricks? They're hard.' He picks up a female: 'See her, she got soft ones, kind of like real life, right?'

I tell him it's a family show.

To explain more fully, lobsters have feathery appendages called swimmerets under their tail, which help them swim and also helps the female carry her eggs. The first pair of swimmerets closest to the head are soft on a female and hard on the male. These are what Jim was referring to as 'pricks'. Lobsters nest in rocky areas where they can hide, but they also burrow like rabbits in the sand and live in depths of up to 400 metres or shallower waters. Their main diet is a daily platter of *fruits de mer*: crab, mussels, clams, starfish (not the chocolate ones), marine worms, small fish and shrimp. Another bit of trivia is that the creature's anus is at tip of its tail, so bear that in mind next time you order lobster arsehole salad.

Back on dry land we cook the lobsters for a feast on the beach. The correct way to kill a lobster isn't by tossing it in a pot of boiling water, but in fact by placing it in a pan of cold water and gently heating it up. The warm water sends the lobsters to sleep before the water begins to boil, and it is a much more humane method of killing these creatures. The major pigment in lobster shell is called astaxanthin, which in live lobsters is bound to proteins that change colour, to green, greenish brown or blue. As we cook the lobster the bond between the proteins and the astaxanthin is broken down to release it to its free state and true colour: red. So now you know why their shells turn scarlet!

We settle down and eat our bounty. Jim and Matt cover theirs in loads of butter ('Butter makes everything better,' Jim smiles.) I have mine steamed with a hint of lemon, just like I do at J. Sheekey's in London. I'm such a ponce. They slurp the butter like gravy, dipping their bread in it. The lobster tastes remarkable, not that they'd know it as they may as well have had Krispy Kreme doughnuts with theirs. I suppose eating lobster gets boring after a while. I'm glad there's such a good perk to a very tough job.

Wild Bass Chase

Cape Cod isn't all about heading out into the wild Atlantic; some great fish lurk in the creeks and rivers that feed the Cape. However, winter's on the way and finding fish that haven't migrated south yet is going to be a real challenge. I meet Mike Rice, who will be showing me where to catch striped bass. The thing I love about the striper is that it's covered in black and white stripes just like my beloved football team, Newcastle. To catch a Geordie of the ocean is my destiny.

I shake hands with Mike, a good-looking, charismatic, lean guy who reminds me of Jon Bon Jovi. At this time of year, the local fishermen here have to cooperate on an almost military level to maximise their chances of catching, so we join Mike's fishing buddies, Brian, Pete and Scotty, to discuss strategy.

'So, what's the plan, Mike?' I ask.

Mike's all over it: 'What we'll do is split up. Pete's going to one area, Scotty's going to another, we're going to go to a small creek. They're all pretty close, within twenty minutes of each other, so if one spot starts to get active we can jump in the truck and be there pretty quick.'

These fishermen tell us the striped bass are in their thousands in this area and it's just a matter of finding them. I'm excited – the chase is on! Mike and I head for Scorton Creek, which is flat and marshy but conditions are perfect for catching bass on the fly. The light is constant and not too bright, and I'm starting to feel pretty confident.

After three or so hours of relentless casting I am tired and very bored. 'I don't think there's anything here,' I say to Mike. 'But you know it's not just about catching fish, is it?'

'No. It's about being out here,' he replies.

'And the companionship,' I add.

'Some of my best days on the water have been when I haven't caught a thing,' he says nonchalantly. Alarm bells ring in my head. I remind him I've travelled 4,000 miles.

'I've got a wife and kids, Mike. A personal reputation. There's a career at stake here,' I say.

Mike knows I'm not going to be dicked around on some kind of wild bass chase. He is under pressure so he checks to see how the others are doing. Brian's caught and released a fourteen-inch shad. If shad are feeding, the bass could be, too. Time to head to Brian's spot to see if we have better luck there. We arrive at Sandwich Harbour and the first thing I see is a seal. This is not a good sign as they like to eat all the fish, but the other lads caught here earlier so we decide to stay in spite of the competition.

We cast our lines out again and again in the hope that maybe, just maybe, we'll bang into some striped bass. Twenty minutes later it looks as if Mike's hooked something. The seal is interested, too.

'That seal's just gone for Mike's fish,' I say to camera. 'It's just gone for Mike's fish! Oh, he's right here, he's right in front of me. Look at him. Lovely to look at, but at the moment that seal's a right bastard.'

Jamie wants me to deliver more lines about the seal to camera while the pinniped (from the Latin *pinna*, 'fin', and *ped*, 'foot') is still in shot. I continue: 'People may look at the image of a seal and think, "What a wonderful, inspiring sight" – but to an angler they are a menace as they scare off all the fish and, surprise, surprise, today our fate is sealed. There's no bloody fish here!'

In the middle of the take a car pulls up in between me and the camera on the road behind. A guy jumps out.

'Hey, guys, you makin' a movie?' he asks in a distinctive Brooklyn drawl. 'The name's Mike, from Mike's Automobile Collectibles. How yoo dooin'? What's the movie called?'

'Well, Mike, thanks for destroying our take. It's called *Extreme Fishing with Robson Green*,' I say, grinning at Jamie, who is looking distinctly pissed off.

'That's awesome. Who's Robson?'

'Take a wild guess, Mike.'

'You're Robson? That's awesome! Here, I got some caps for you all with my logo on it! Google me. I buy and sell old cars . . . I'm *on* the Internet. I've had four hundred thousand hits!'

'I think you're *on* drugs, Mike . . . Could you please get out of my shot?'

'Have a keyring and my card. You guys are awesome . . . Robson, we definitely got something going here,' he says, shaking my hand.

'Yes, Mike, it's called mild irritation,' I say, putting on one of his hats.

He gives us a wave, jumps in the car and drives off. Basically he wanted me to plug his company on the programme – and actually, you know what, you have to applaud the guy's chutzpah. Mike is going all the way! However, had my dad been here he would definitely have chinned him! I chuckle at the scene in my head of Big Rob throwing Mike across the bonnet of his own car. I look round at fisherman Mike and imagine doing the same to him. I'm beginning to get tired of being Yanked around.

After another fruitless hour we are heading back to Scorton

Creek, again. Morale is low and everyone is frustrated. In the truck, I try to lighten the mood by regaling Mike with tales from my glittering music career.

'The act was called Robson and Jerome. We knew we had to stop when a woman brought her two guinea pigs, Robson and Jerome, on a show called *Animal Hospital*. Rolf Harris says, "What's wrong?" She says, "It's Robson, he's not right." And then, in front of millions, Robson wobbles about on his back, fitting. Rolf says, "There's only one thing to do about this poor little fella." The vet gets a large needle out and live on TV they put him down. Robson died! My mum rang up, "Have you seen you're on the other side? You're a guinea pig." "*Was* a guinea pig, Mum." And in that moment I realised that's exactly what I had been – Simon Cowell's bloody guinea pig. Thankfully I've moved on (considerably richer) and he's now practising vivisection on One Direction.'

Mike is completely uninterested in my stories and I miss Jim the Joker. He was my type of guy – laughed at anything.

It's three o'clock when we arrive back at the creek. The tide is in and everyone thinks this is now *the* place to hook a striped bass. I'm determined to be the first to get one. But as the light starts to fade, none of us has caught a single fish. I've been thrashing the water for six hours, my hand is blistered and it looks like the bass have buggered off.

'Where's the bass, Mike?' I yell.

Mike and his mates conclude that we have missed them and they will already have travelled south. Defeated, we head back to the hotel. On the way we pass a psychic's 'salon'. Jamie and I look at one another. It's time for drastic measures. We are now willing to try *anything*.

The Clairvoyant

The next morning I find out that Dad is being released from hospital. He's got to have a stent fitted and possibly undergo a bypass but at the moment, owing to flu-like symptoms and a kidney infection, he's not well enough for surgery but he is well enough to go home. I can't wait to see him. Perhaps the lady I am seeing next will tell me exactly when that will be.

We walk into the psychic salon and meet Tammy the psychic. I shake hands with the buxom blonde, who is a cross between Doris Day and Kirstie Alley at the height of her drink and junk-food problem. She looks into my eyes, still holding my hand, and no word of a lie says, 'How's your father?' I gasp. Now, on reflection of her subsequent bonkers behaviour, I've taken this to possibly be less a comment about Dad's heart attack and more a how's-yer-father, nudge-nudge, wink-wink, fancy-a-bit scenario. Either way, this whole psychic thing is playing tricks on my mind. We sit down at a table and Tammy reads my palms, her tarot cards and my mind. She looks into my eyes seductively.

'Robson, I honestly believe, on this journey, you are in a location where you are destined to be, but you're not in the right spot. There is a spot and you will find what you are searching for. You're going to become a winner – you always have been, and you always will be. You're a lover, not a fighter. You will succeed in what you're looking for.'

I only hear the words 'winner' and 'lover'.

Robson: 'Tammy, can I ask you a question?'

Tammy: 'Sure, sugar.'

Robson: 'Will you be my agent? No one has ever said those things to me. And if not my agent, will you marry me?'

Quick as a flash she gives me her ring.

Tammy: 'Yes, here's a ring. Just put it on me.'

I suddenly realise I'm in unchartered and dangerous waters here. She wants my number ... so I give her Jonathan's. Thinking it's mine, she clutches it to her enormous bosoms. What on earth have I done? *You haven't bloody thought it through again, that's what,* cranks up my inner monologue. *You have just asked a lonely woman of a certain age to marry you and she doesn't see it as a joke; she thinks you are her white knight finally come to free her from the shackles of perpetual loneliness and suffering, like Prometheus bound to the mountain every day, an eagle pecking at her liver. And then you ride into town and offer her a glimpse of hope to break the bonds and stop the pain. You bloody fool, you've really gone and done it now.*

Tammy ends her reading by saying: 'You are not catching fish because the fish have moved. You need to follow the fish.'

Jamie: 'That's brilliant – she's a genius.'

'*I* could have told you that!'

But Jamie is already out the door shouting, 'Follow the fish!'

Back at the hotel it's all hands on deck as we plot where the fish have gone and how we're going to locate them. Mike and his gang think they have moved to Manhattan, and that's exactly where Jamie wants to go. I'm not so sure it's a good idea but he wants to shoot the unfolding story of us trying to track down these elusive stripers. Jamie calls Hamish in Glasgow, who thinks it's a brilliant idea, so it's settled: we're going to New York.

'Are we going to fly there?' I ask.

Jamie: 'No. We are going by van.'

Robson: 'What? But it's miles!'

Jamie: 'No, it's less than an inch on the map.'

Robson: 'Jamie, this is America!'

I am reminded that there is no money left in the budget because of me. I shut up.

Jonathan's phone rings. He answers. It's Tammy-the-psychic trying to get hold of me! I signal that I am not here, shaking my head vigorously. He tells her I'm unavailable. She calls back a few more times but by late afternoon the calls have stopped, and we think she has got the message that I don't really want to marry her.

Later that evening we wander down to the hotel bar to get a few drinks and something to eat. Standing in the lobby is Tammy. Before she sees me, I turn and leg it up the stairs, leaving Jonathan to deal with her, again. She tells him she really needs to talk to me. Jonathan tells her I'm not here. She says that's not true because she's been waiting out in her car and she knows I haven't left the building. She's been staking me out! Jonathan finally persuades her to go and we hit the bar. It has slightly freaked me out but then I think, if she'd been any good at clairvoyance, she should always have been ahead of me. Now that would be scary.

The next day we embark on a nine-hour road trip to New York in a van. I'm dreading it but it actually turns out to be one of the nicest journeys I have had. We really bond as a team, stopping to eat burgers and nachos and all kinds of other really bad junk food, and singing songs. We are all squished in – well, they are. I am at the front, of course. It's the *Extreme* boy band on tour.

The next morning, our new striped bass expert finds us in the restaurant of the hotel having breakfast.

'They're here,' says Tooch in a sharp Bronx accent.

He looks like a character out of *The Sopranos*. We head over with him to Sandy Hook Bay and meet his friend Brian. It's very early but these guys are wide awake and bang up for action. As we head out across the sparkling water on a small speedboat, the hazy silhouette of New York's skyline unfolds in front of us like a giant poster ... Wow. It's awesome to be here, especially as Brian tells me we are definitely going to catch striped bass today. Brian receives a text from another local fisherman: the bite is on and we're heading at full-throttle to the spot. We have found the fishing G-Spot, as foretold by the Boston stalker, and I'm excited about going in for a tackle against the Alan Shearer of the ocean.

The birds are feeding and the bass are here in their thousands. Unlike trying to catch the bass on the fly, as I did with Mike (even though they were here all the bleeding time), today we're not taking any chances. We are sinking lines and using toby lures to try to tempt the fish. Brian says that if we want to eat tonight this is the most practical method – there's no time for purist sentiment on this boat, I want me a striped bass! If dynamite were another option I'd have gone for that as well.

Ten minutes later Tooch has a striper on the end of his line. The camera crew and I are ecstatic. Brian and Tooch are taken aback by our reaction. Tooch's fish has to go back, as the legal size is twenty-eight inches, but it's a stunner, a piscatorial zebra.

At last I get a bass on the end of my line as well. It fights like a rainbow trout, as it's strong, fast and likes to run. It's crucial I keep my line tight and don't put too much drag on it or the fish will come off. After a couple of runs, including one under the boat, the fish tires and I reel him in. He shoots! He scores! He lands a bass! Sadly it's too small to keep so I have to release it, but what a stunner. It's like a skipjack tuna but stretched. Under the water they appear dark green but in the light you can see the black and white curved stripes. I pop it back. I don't mind; I'm one very happy fisherman.

With the Empire State Building in the background, it's a fantastic end to a fantastic trip. Don't go to New York for the shopping – go for the fishing.

A week later, back in the UK, Dad is as right as rain. I visit him at his huge eight-berth caravan near Bamborough Castle, where he lives with his girlfriend of seven years, Yvonne. He loves the outdoors and would have had us all growing up in a caravan if he'd had his way.

'Are you taking it easy, Dad?'

'Yes, Robo. I'm drinking less, which is a bloody shame but I did have a swift pint at the Black Bull last night with Plum. First time out since the attack, mind. Plum says to me: "Big Rob, your lad's never off the TV." I said: "I know, we call it interference."'

Chapter Six

THE PHILIPPINES

Robson Crusoe

February 2009, Series 2

Hamish Barbour and I are enjoying a good lunch at the Two Fat Ladies in Glasgow, talking about the possibilities of Series 2. We gulp more wine and come up with a few ideas, Hamish as excitable as ever. I regard him across the table – he looks like a Swan Vestas match, with his tight red hair and pale lean body from all those triathlons he does at the weekends. The comparison suits his personality, too. He ignites all the programme ideas by slowly getting the wet logs (the TV suits) to light up about something, anything. It's an unenviable task and he almost burns himself out trying to get them to finally spark. I suppose Hamish is a creative firestarter; if he had crazier hair and Keith from The Prodigy had an eating disorder, they could be twins.

'What about *Robson Crusoe*?' says Hamish, combusting, 'You

are cast away for twenty-four hours and have to survive on your own, using all the skills you've learnt to feed yourself from the ocean?'

'Fantastic! But maybe I should do it for seventy-two hours because I have learnt a lot, Hamish. I think I really would be fine for that amount of time. A bit loopy, granted, but fine. I've been watching a lot of Ray Mears, which should come in handy.'

'Great. Great. Twenty-four hours will be fine, Robson. I'll get Helen Nightingale [the series producer] to set it up. [To the waiter] Can we have the bill, please?'

The NeverEnding Journey

The *Extreme* team and I are travelling 7,000 miles to the 7,107-island archipelago of the Philippines, on the western edge of the Pacific Ocean. It's a three-day journey and Jamie Goold wants to film the first few minutes of the show on my diary cam. He says I'm not to shave because I need to film the intensity of the journey and its effect on me. Well, thanks, Jamie. It's the first time I've thought 'Fuck me, I'm middle-aged' and it's depressing. I'm entering the autumn of my years but today it looks like bleak midwinter. Jamie, Craig Herd (a Kiwi cameraman), and Peter Prada, the soundman who from this point on becomes part of the *Extreme Fishing* furniture, are with me on this odyssey. We travel via three different planes, each getting progressively smaller, until the smallest finally takes us to Manila. It's a terrifying flight and I'm glad it's over.

As we drive through the capital in a brightly painted minibus I realise that we couldn't be any more conspicuous. The city is a chaotic mixture of traffic, noise and humidity. Thousands of tuk-tuks, all beeping, zoom down the streets, there are minibuses crammed full of people, high-rise flats line either side of the road, and there is a hot, damp smell of fuel, drains and people. Every time we stop in traffic, the locals stare at us. It's a place where you need to look like you know where you are going, because if you don't, urban predators will smell your fear. This is a Third World country with Third World problems, including great poverty, corruption and violent crime, and because of that we have a team of security guys to look after us and they are tooled up to the max. I later find out that the kidnapping of Westerners for ransom is fairly common.

As we approach the edge of the city, Jamie reveals that he wants to film the rest of the journey with me travelling in a tuk-tuk behind the van. So while the rest of the crew are sitting in relative luxury, I am forced to endure a three-hour noisy and very bumpy journey to the coast southeast of Manila. It's like taking a motorised chair from Newcastle to Liverpool. When we finally arrive, my bottom is numb and I'm feeling cranky but it's straight onto a boat for another three hours, heading to our final destination: the teardrop island of Siargao in Surigao del Norte province in the Philippines Sea.

It's an open-topped boat and we've barely left port when it starts to pee it down. We are not prepared – no one is. Even though we are filming a TV show, the fixer has overlooked the fact that we would have all of our camera equipment with us. In order to save the thousands of pounds' worth of recording equipment, we are forced to surrender our waterproofs and get soaked through. It's like a hairy wet T-shirt competition on board. I feel sick. Apparently it rains a lot here. *Maybe staying on a desert island for twenty-four hours is not such a good idea,* I think. *Rubbish, it'll be fine, you big Jessie,* replies the other voice within.

*

Siargao is a tropical paradise, white sand and a clear blue sea, as well as dense mangrove forest and wetlands that help protect costal areas from erosion and storm surge. We are staying at one of the Philippines' best-kept secrets, the Pansukian Tropical Resort. This place is so amazing and opulent that even the president stays here. I'm staying in his room, aptly named the Presidential Suite, where there's enough space to swing a cat, a dog and a bleeding horse, and all the crew's 'quarters' are the same: absolutely massive. It's been well worth the ball-breaking effort to get here. I clean my teeth and look in the mirror. I am dishevelled and look so much like my dad, who has thankfully now made a full recovery and is back up to flying speed. *Why do we have to perish and decay?* I wonder. Still, at least with age some other things have improved, like my monobrow now being consigned to the past. I didn't even know I had one until I started dating Vanya. Pretty much after our first date she attacked me with tweezers. I used to look like Frida Khalo and didn't even know it.

Before Tweezers   *After Tweezers*

With that thought in mind, I crawl into bed and black out.

*

I wake up at 6 a.m. and walk outside onto the verandah. The ocean is twenty metres from my door, iron flat and turquoise, with only beach between us. Men, women and kids are fishing in bancas, traditional dugout canoes with crude bamboo outriggers to keep them stable. They are all using basic hand line methods, about a dozen of them floating in the shallows pulling up fish. It's wonderful to see, but these families are not fishing as a hobby – it's a way of life and they need to put food on the table. Jobs are hard to come by in the area and people live off the land as well as the ocean, growing rice and breeding animals. To most people here, every day is about survival.

Junior

I meet Junior Gonzalez, one of the finest fishermen on the island, I'm told. There are loads of fish here and they are varied but, as I discover, they are very small. The locals either eat them or sell them at the market. Junior has no technology to help him catch fish, no GPS, no sounder, no mobile phone, no two-way radio and not even a compass. He does what families have done for generations in Siargao: he relies on his knowledge of the stars, landmarks, tides, the weather and the moon. He also uses bird life to guide the boat, knowing certain species never fly far from the shore, and high birds or feeding birds mean fish. Low-flying birds, skimming the waves, tend to be just passing through, using the air from the waves to save energy on their journey.

Junior has fished like this since he was a little boy. He appears to be around sixty years of age but could be younger; he has a face that is well lived-in. We head out on Junior's banca, which looks more like a tourist river boat that he's hurriedly converted into a fishing vessel by putting a couple of pipes on it to hold rods and the odd plank to rest your feet against. Junior's six-teen-year-old son, Grieshan, is in another banca and to be honest I've got ship envy. His is way better.

Junior starts the engines. It sounds like a cross-channel ferry – the fish will hear us coming from about twenty-two miles away – and I stick my fingers in my ears. We get a gentle speed up but the boat is all over the place, rocking and lurching. Thankfully it doesn't matter too much today as we're staying 500 metres from the shore, but tomorrow we'll be travelling to the Philippine Trench. I hope he's got a bigger boat. At a maximum known depth of 6.54 miles, the trench is the third-deepest body of water in the world, the deepest being the Mariana Trench, near Guam, which is 6.86 miles deep. It's mind-blowing stuff, like considering the size of the universe and what it all means when you're really, really tired. It's so much to ponder that it makes me feel queasy. But then again, that's probably just Junior's crappy boat.

We try to fish from the diesel-glugging beast but to no avail. I look over the way – young Grieshan is hauling them in. I suggest, very strongly, that we change boats, and my request is granted. As we head back to shore, Junior tells me a story of the time he went out with Grieshan, aged four, to catch a swordfish. Swordfish are nocturnal deepwater fish so are caught at night when they come up to feed on squid. He was forty miles out over the Philippine Trench in an oversized canoe with a toddler and no GPS, radio or phone, in the middle of the night, when the mother of all storms hits. Storms in this area tend to come very fast and out of nowhere. Junior and Grieshan are tossed about in their banca until it's eventually smashed to smithereens and sinks. Never letting go of his son's hand for one second, he flings Grieshan on his back and, clinging to a piece of wood, begins to slowly swim and float to shore. Since that day they have been inseparable. It's an amazing tale that completely blows *Life of Pi* out of the water.

I switch boats.

'This one's much better, Junior!' I say.

He smiles. It's quieter, too, which is what we need to catch coral reef species and pelagic fish that live near the surface of the ocean, not the bottom. We're hoping for wahoo or maya maya (red snapper) to come our way. The red snapper is a beautiful red fish, which strangely makes it an excellent predator, because in the underwater spectrum of light, red isn't seen, so the fish is almost invisible.

Nine hours later, I finally get a bite. It's a dog tooth tuna and it's not coming in easily. It's fighting the current and the speed of the boat, and even though it's small it's still quite strong. It's a hard fish to land and I don't want to get my fingers anywhere near its ferocious canines. A member of the *Scombridae* family – not a mad Highland clan but a subclassification of fish that includes bonitos, mackerels and tuna – the dog tooth tuna, in spite of its name, has more in common with its bonito cousins than with pure tunas. It's fast in the water but it's the impact and bite that kills the prey. *One down*, I think to myself

My next fish comes five minutes later. It's a good fighting fish and we have a decent tussle. I reel it in but am unfamiliar with the species. Junior calls it an 'oyung-oyung'. It's definitely my first one of those. I manage to land it. It's a strong, compact fish with a powerful jaw lined with triangular razor teeth and a blue-green skin. Junior tells me that in English it's called a bluefish. Bluefish are found all around the world in coastal areas favouring continental shelves, surf beaches or rocky headland. (I've got a continental shelf problem: everything's on the way down.)

My mood has soared and we all head en masse to the market to see what we can get for this brace of fish. I tell Junior about my desert island experience in two days' time and he says, 'Robson you are a natural, you could survive on any one of these islands.' Then he gives me double thumbs-up. I am optimistic. *I am actually really good*, I think.

At the small open-air market I get 200 pesos, about three quid, for our catch. I give the cash to the children of the locals who have gathered around to watch us film and everyone's happy. The people here are incredibly charming and friendly in spite of their abject poverty. It's paradise here but surviving in paradise is far from easy. I'm sure I'll be OK for a day and night, however.

Port Pilar Harbour

Today we're heading out to the mighty Philippine Trench forty miles from the shore, and our target is dorado. I have the idea that we will only eat what we catch for breakfast, lunch and dinner. We have cooking facilities on board our fishing boat and I intend to show off my culinary skills like a Northern Rick Stein. The four deckhands, wearing classic lampshade hats, ask me if they can bring some food on just in case. I say, 'No way. We'll catch loads of fish. I caught two in five minutes yesterday.'

'Yeah, after nine hours.'

'Shut up, Craig. Right, everyone turn out their pockets for contraband. If this show's going to be a success we have to play by the rules. I don't have anything on me. Does anyone else?'

They shake their heads.

'Are you sure?'

They nod.

'Good.'

We set out to the trench. I am experiencing a great high today. The sun is shining; life is good. Deep down, I wonder if I am experiencing one of my manic episodes but I don't think so. I breathe in the air. *I am a fishing god*, I tell myself, and I am buzzing with energy and chat. As we are trawling, Junior explains he is looking for bird life, floating debris, which makes false reefs, or any other natural indicators that put us in the right place for a magnificent dorado. We are fishing as nature intended and I can't wait for our first strike.

Junior says, 'One year I went fishing every day of the year to work out the best days.'

'Three hundred and sixty-five days? Wow. And what did you discover?'

'The fourth day before a new moon is the best.'

'Is that today?'

'No,' he laughs.

I suss out the tiny kitchen area, which is basic and no more than two feet wide. As I leave a deckhand enters and places something quickly in a cupboard. I open the door and find a tin of corned beef inside. I look at him.

'Oh, ye of little faith. I'm very disappointed. That's really bad.'

He looks at me sheepishly. The four of them go into a huddle talking in Filipino, probably calling me a name used by British carp fishermen.

*

Six hours later I am feeling like a prize James Blunt, as we have got nothing. The sea is getting lumpy and the sun is due to set in seven hours' time, which seems a long way away but we need to get back to shore in that time.

Jamie says firmly, 'We have to catch a fish and we'll stay here all night if necessary.'

We are starving, I'm feeling faint and I am getting some filthy looks from the crew. I sidle up to the one with the corned beef – I can't remember his name so let's call him David.

'Psst, David. How much for the tin of beef?'

'What?'

'How much?'

We are very subtle; it's like scoring shabú – methamphetamine pills – the drug of choice in South East Asia. I give him a large amount of pesos and wander casually down to the toilet to gorge my contraband. After seven hours of nothing to eat it doesn't touch the sides. As I wander out, Craig catches me.

'You bastard. You fucking sneaky bastard.'

I start to giggle nervously. Craig is furious.

'Jamie! Peter! Robson's just snaffled a whole tin of corned beef.'

I walk upstairs. Peter looks grey with hunger and Jamie regards me like a bitterly disappointed teacher. But I feel much better. I have a new lease of life.

Another seven hours later the effects of the corned beef have worn off and we still haven't had even a sniff of a fish. If I thought I looked bad when I arrived, I now look like I'm decomposing. I hear a rustle and see Craig open a bag of crisps.

'Where d'you get those?'

'Wouldn't you like to know?'

He shares them with everyone apart from me in retaliation for the bully beef. Craig produces another bag of crisps, again none for me. He eyeballs me, munching mouthful after mouthful. I ignore him and talk to Junior.

'Well, the fishing's been great but the catching's been appalling.'

Junior says, 'In all my years of fishing, this has been one of my worst days.'

I believe him. I am a jinx and a corn beef criminal. Suddenly, two terns appear above us out of nowhere. Junior points; they are flying high – they have seen something. We see it too: it's drift-wood, no more than eight feet long and six inches in diameter. Junior turns the boat around; we trawl the lines past it, and bang! I'm into a mahi-mahi. Also known as a dorado or dolphinfish, this creature's brain size in proportion to its body is large. Some say this is one of the most intelligent species of fish as it can follow simple instructions, but I say, 'Did they invent the internal combustion engine? Was Pythagoras a dorado? Let's put it in perspective.' They're about as bright as a Sunderland Supporter after a heavy weekend on the piss.

As I wind in the dorado, he comes to the surface and leaps. He's magnificent, his vibrant green, gold and blue skin glisten-ing in the setting sun. Dorados fight hard and they fight aerially. He jumps again like a Lycra-clad acrobat doing somersaults. Morale has soared, the crew is going to eat and it's going to be delicious.

I shout, 'I have caught us supper. You all doubted me but I did it!'

The aerial fight cranks up a notch; I must bring this fish in. I give it one last leap and he jumps off the hook and is gone. The crew is catatonic with shock and I am in the seventh circle of hell, but Jamie is going mental, shouting, 'That was fucking brilliant!

One of the best sequences I have ever filmed. The under-fish triumphed – adversity works so well on telly.'

We all want to deck him.

'Fuck the programme! We want something to eat.'

I am so pissed off with myself. The deckhands won't look at me, especially the one who sold me the corned beef. He's visibly stiffened with internal rage. To make matters worse, Jamie declares he wants us to fish into the night and catch a swordfish. We beg him to let us go home but the footage has given him a second wind. He gives me a piece of bread.

'Thank you, master,' I snivel.

But Junior has a cunning plan. We are going to drop a line for swordfish very deep, and with six miles below us we're never going to touch the bottom. We bait the rod, which is huge and a bit like a marlin rod. The swordfish is a billfish and is known as one of the 'big five', along with blue marlin, black marlin, striped marlin and sailfish. This striking, dark grey fish has huge black eyes, which help it to see in the deep water over half a mile below the surface, where it resides in the daytime. Its bill is massive in proportion to its body, which it uses like a sword to cut down its prey. It is thus known as the gladiator of the sea, from its name *Xiphias gladius* (from the Latin *gladius*, meaning 'sword').

To help us catch, Junior lets the boat drift using the wind. In order to slow a conventional boat down, skippers use something called a drogue – an underwater parachute that impedes forward motion. Junior doesn't have a drogue because he can't afford one, so ingeniously he uses palm leaves, tied in such a way that they have the same effect. He says nature always solves the problem of a lack of technology. The second part of Junior's plan is to use two kerosene lamps to try to attract squid. We use a lure like a plastic shrimp with upturned barbs on the end. I drop it ten metres and slowly pull it up towards me. I do this about a hundred times before I finally catch a cephalopod (Ancient Greek for 'head-feet', as these creatures have no body). The squid I pull up is seven inches in length and basically a meal for one. By this time I am so tired and hungry I am starting to hallucinate. Junior suggests we use my one and only squid as bait.

I say, 'But I don't want to use it as bait, I want to eat it.'

He says, 'We will catch many with that one.'

I do as I am told and I slowly pull up the hand line.

'Oh, my God, I have got another one!' I cry.

'It's the same bloody one!' everyone replies in unison.

All in all, I catch two. Fishing for swordfish has been a complete disaster. It's the wrong conditions and by 3 a.m. we've all had enough. We've been twenty-two hours without a proper meal and Craig is beginning to gnaw the edge of the boat, like a pony on its stable door. He's started to kick the side of the boat as well; he is not a happy pony. He is even unhappier when, after finally reaching land, he hops out of the boat and promptly breaks his ankle. Cameramen with broken ankles are not good news, but luckily, unlike ponies, he can be mended and not shot.

The doctor back at the hotel bandages it up and tells Craig not to walk on it. We could have saved him a job and the production company a call-out fee. The fixer, Enrico, steps in: 'It's OK, guys. I know how to operate a camera.'

Thank God for that – we can sleep easy now.

'Ooh, looks sore. You OK, mate?' I say sympathetically to Craig.

'Yeah, it's just bloody annoying.'

'Get some rest. [pause] Oh, and Craig, by the way, your broken ankle – it's all about karma. That was for the second bag of crisps. The first bag of crisps was fine. We were even. Level playing field. But not sharing the second, you Kiwi bum pirate? The universe knows, Craig. The universe knows.'

And the universe does indeed know because, back in my room, as I deliver my final piece to camera about how exhausted I am, a bug starts flying around my head, dive-bombing me like a kamikaze pilot. Argh! It's a beetle the size of a blackbird.

'Go away!'

I get a wet hand towel and start to flick at the air, incandescent with fury. Neeeoooooowwww! It goes into flat spin like a World War II bomber at my head, pulling out just before crashing into my ear. I fight back for another ten minutes, waving what I later realised was basically a white flag around my head, before passing out fully clothed and face down on my bed. God knows what it did to me that night. I don't want to think about it.

I'm feeling like shit the next day but if I'm slightly off colour it's nothing to the pain poor old Craig is in. However, he carries on like a true champion cameraman. We're going out by boat to a small island called Kasulian with a guy called Charlito. This area has been declared fishing-free, to encourage fish stocks to recover, and the initiative is going so well we've been given special clearance to fish here – just enough for our supper.

I'm on a banca again and this time we're using hermit crabs as bait. The crabs live in beautiful shells that are shaped like the ice-cream part of a Mr Whippy. Cruelly we have to tease them out and then use them as live bait on our hand lines, but this is what the locals do and I'm not here to judge, I'm here to learn.

'Charlito, I've seen some hermit crabs in my time but these are enormous.'

I look into the turquoise waters at the reef below where I can see there is an abundance of coral reef fish but none is more than three inches in size. We throw out the hand lines while Craig films everything from a special chair. If you watch the sequence you'll see everything is shot from chest height!

Looking into the sea below, it's like a tropical aquarium. We can't be eating these, surely?

'Charlito, they're a bit small, don't you think?'

'Then we need many,' he says.

The hand lining is not going according to plan, mainly because the crabs are four inches bigger than the fish and our bait is actually scaring the fish away! Charlito is becoming restless. Suddenly he produces an enormous spear gun out of nowhere.

'Let's go snorkelling!' he commands.

What is so impressive is that he's made his entire diving kit himself, including his goggles from discarded rubber and plastic for the lenses, and his flippers, which are wooden panels attached to his feet. I decide to be a spectator today. What I'm about to witness is akin to blasting a sparrow with a twelve-bore shotgun. The head of the spear gun is bigger than some of the fish! It doesn't feel right to me but it's completely normal to Charlito, and, more importantly, it works. It's a crude method but it gets results – and the fish he needs to feed his sizeable family.

We eat five of these pretty fish-tank fish each with casaba, a type of muskmelon that is grown on the island and looks like a honeydew but tastes more like a potato. The fish taste nice enough but it truly is like eating Nemo.

*

Back at the hotel, I decide to do some research on why the fish are so small in this area and stocks so depleted. I find my answer swiftly: it's all down to dynamite fishing, a method whereby desperate people can kill whole shoals in one go with a lump of dynamite and an accurate throw. But it's disastrous long-term as whole reefs are disappearing and thus ecosystems are wiped out. And reefs take a very long time to recover. Dynamite fishing is illegal but sadly it's going on all over the Philippines.

This afternoon the production team has arranged for me to meet an ex-dynamite fisherman who is now helping to educate other fishermen about the importance of protecting the reefs. We travel to a very different part of the island from where our hotel is located. It's a poor, dusty village with a collection of sparse shanty huts. We are greeted by Tootya Alvarez, who did six months inside for dynamite fishing, and his judge, Bimbi, who translates for me. As we walk towards a lagoon that Tootya and others destroyed, he tells me, 'I did it because it's very easy to catch fish. We can catch a large amount and it will be big money for us.' And do you know what? If I were in the same position as Tootya I'd probably do it, too. It's a means of escape from poverty.

'How much of the reef has disappeared because of dynamite fishing?' I ask.

'Outside the lagoon, the reefs are not good anymore because they are already annihilated, but inside the corals are starting to grow already,' says Tootya.

Thankfully, with the help of local investment and efforts to conserve the reefs by former dynamite fishermen like Tootya, attempts are now being made to help the damaged reefs to recover. It is now illegal to fish in certain areas, such as the one I went to with Charlito after permissions were granted. This work needs to continue or a bad situation could, further down the line, turn into an environmental and humanitarian crisis, where the local people literally have *no* fish to live on.

Desert Island

Late next morning we leave Siargao. It's castaway time and I will be living on a desert island completely on my own for twenty-four hours. I'm apprehensive but also really looking forward to getting away from this smelly crisp-munching rabble. Craig's ankle is still buggered so we've left him behind and brought our back-up cameraman, fixer Enrico, with us.

We are heading south to the uninhabited island of Tabili. Two hours into the boat trip and I'm beginning to think this is a really stupid idea.

'How far away is it?' I ask.

'About another half an hour,' says Jamie.

'What? You mean I'm two and half hours away from civilisation and, more importantly, help? I thought I'd be just across the way like Lindisfarne to Seahouses and if, for whatever reason, I needed to swim back I could! I'm going to be miles out, in the middle of the Pacific all on my own. What the hell have I signed up to? This isn't funny.'

We arrive at Tabili. It's basically a mound of sand with a few palm trees. I beat my chest in an attempt try to knock down my growing anxiety. *Don't worry*, I tell myself, *you're the Ray Mears of the North. You* are *Ray Mears!*

Are you out of your fucking mind? comes the reply. *That's like saying Dame Judi's bloody Bruce Parry.*

We start shooting some footage of me preparing for the next

twenty-four hours and it quickly becomes apparent that, although Enrico is a lovely guy, he's perhaps not a natural behind the camera. Jamie is getting increasingly agitated but we muddle on as best we can. In the end, Jamie decides that the best solution is to shoot the whole of the island sequence on my diary camera, and with that said everyone buggers off on the boat, heading straight to the hotel bar, where it's trebles all round. I watch the boat become a speck in the distance. I am alone with only my camera and my thoughts. It's a weird feeling but the sun is setting so I need to be practical and make a fire. I gather together firewood that I collected earlier and, using coconut husks as kindling, create a small fire. Well, it's easy when you know how and you have a Bic lighter.

My next task is to make some kind of shelter. Ray Mears made a bivouac on his show so I'm going to do the same, but the light is fading. I um and ah before deciding it might be better to catch some food first. So what's on tonight's menu at the Castaway Café? I could catch a few crabs, or I could cast a line for some small reef fish similar to the ones I caught with Charlito. I walk along the water's edge, half-heartedly looking for crabs. What am I doing here? This is crackers. I think about casting a line out and then I have a much better idea. Hidden among the few supplies I've been allowed to bring is a bottle of white wine and a corkscrew.

I find a coconut and draw a face on it in homage to Tom Hanks in *Castaway*, set up the camera and open the bottle of Chablis. As the last of the light fades, I raise a toast to my new date, Julia (after Julia Roberts, because of her massive mouth). I take a sip of the wine and then drain the contents of the glass. I pour another and another.

'That's better,' I say to Julia. 'It's all a bit more fun now I'm getting pissed.'

As I finish the bottle, and open the Sauvignon Blanc, I start talking nonsense to the coconut and the camera.

'Have you heard of the notion that many dog-owners look like their pets, Julia? Well, they tried an experiment to see how true it was. They took an architect and his dog, an engineer and his dog and an actor and his dog, and under laboratory conditions tested to see how each reacted to a pile of bones in the middle of the room. The engineer's dog goes first and makes a complex cog system with gears, reflecting the behaviour of the owner. The architect's dog constructs a bridge. Next up is the actor's dog. He eats all the bones, fucks the other two dogs and asks for the rest of the day off.'

I roll around laughing but Julia is po-faced.

'You need to lighten up, Jules, have some fun.'

I reel off my CV, and she tells me hers. I feel inadequate but quite horny. I think I'm in with a chance with Jules when suddenly there is a loud clatter of thunder. Boom! As if someone's lifted a grand piano and dropped it. Immediately the heavens open. It's not a light shower but rain of biblical proportions, like someone has a hose over my head and I haven't made a fucking shelter and – shit! The cameras! I manage to get the Z-camera, batteries and the diary cam wrapped up in my waterproof coat. The fire is well and truly out, one torch has died and the other is on life support. I take a swig from the bottle of wine, grab Julia and stumble over to shelter under one of the coconut palms. What the fuck am I doing here?

It pours and it pours and it pours down for over four long and lonely hours and then that's when the REALLY BIG storm hits, and with it there is thunder, sheet lightning and, of course, more rain. The water takes out all the batteries and the Z-camera so all I have is my diary cam. I am soaked to the skin and sozzled and I want to go home – this isn't funny anymore. The only connection I have with the outside world is a satellite phone so I ring Jamie. No reply. I ring again. No reply. I can't get hold of him because he's at the bar with Craig and Peter and they are all off their tits. Bastards. They're lording it up in opulence and I'm sitting here on my own on an island in the middle of the Pacific, under a fucking waterfall, talking shit to a coconut I quite fancy.

I scramble around in the undergrowth, trying to make a last-minute bivouac with palm leaves. The rain has washed away a pile of coconuts under a tree and I can see a polythene bag. I shine my torch on it. It's a plastic carrier bag. *That's odd*, I think. I look inside and my heart stops beating. It's full of money. Oh. My. God. I'm going to be kidnapped by terrorists or drug runners and murdered in a scene out of *Scarface* with a chainsaw. I don't fucking want to be on Treasure Island anymore. I'm in grave danger and I need to get off this fucking island.

I calm down and decide to count the money. It's torrential rain but at least counting gives me something to do. My heart beats rapidly against my chest. There's 68,000 pesos! Jesus Christ, 68,000! It's a big stash. (Which I later discover is only £1,000, but it is still a great deal of money in these parts.) As I put the notes back in the bag I suddenly see lights coming towards me across the water. I shut my eyes and open them; I must be mistaken . . . but I am not. Lights are coming this way and I stop breathing. Very slowly I hide the money back under the pile of coconuts and move back under the tree. This is now not only inconvenient, it's fucking terrifying.

I dial Jamie. There's no reply so I phone the series producer, Helen Nightingale, in Glasgow, and wake her up.

'Hello?' she says sleepily.

'Helen? Get me off this fucking island!'

'Robson, are you OK? Have you spoken to Jamie?'

'I've tried; he's not answering, none of them are. They're all pissing it up.'

She says, 'OK, I'll phone him now. Don't worry, I'll sort it.'

'Send a boat, a fucking pigeon, do whatever. I am going to die!'

I get on the satellite phone again and ring my business partner, Sandra, who has got me out of many scrapes in my life.

'Sandra, whatever you're doing, wherever you are, get me off this fucking island.'

Between them, Sandra and Helen finally manage to get hold of Jamie and the team, now in their beds. The whole team is woken up and ordered to come and get me, immediately.

There isn't an inch of me that isn't wet and I'm starting to get cold. The lights are very close to the island now and I can hear men talking. The rain continues to pour down and they are talking loudly over the sound of the waves as two men drag their boat ashore. I don't move one single muscle and barely dare to breathe. They are just yards away from me and the images of what they are going to do to me flood my brain like a virus-infected computer on its way out. In fact, later on I realise they were actually fishermen coming to shelter from the storm but after discovering that stash of money all I could think of was cold-blooded killers.

Jamie and the team finally arrive around 3 a.m., half asleep. I'm cold, reeking of bevy and exhausted from being terrified.

Jamie thinks the whole thing is hilarious and wants to do some filming but I'm not in the mood.

'Come on, Robson, it'll be great material.'

I tell him where to go. He examines the cameras.

'Are you sure you can't just stay here until the morning, filming on your diary cam?'

'Fuck you!' I roar, throwing the bag of money at him and taking a swing for him. Jamie's six-foot-two, I'm five-foot-nine, and punching high isn't a good way to box. I of course miss. AP Finlay McCray holds me back. Jamie is now furious, too, and also has to be restrained by Finlay. This adventure is now less *Robson Crusoe* and more *Lord of the Flies*. I feel like Piggy, the kid with glasses that they bullied and ultimately killed.

On the boat I change into some dry clothes. I'm so wet my fingers are all wrinkled. I'm not Bear Grylls or Ray Mears, I'm Robson Green. I'll leave those guys to fight the wilds. As we bounce across the gentle waves, I can see there are hundreds of lights out at sea, like street lamps. They twinkle across the water. Each light is a fisherman who, night after night, provides food for his village and family. They are proper fishermen, unlike me.

I have never been so pleased to see a bed in all my life. I luxuriate in it, hugging a soft pillow, and sleep soundly. In the morning, in spite of everything and all the hell I've been put through, I wake up full of warm feelings of love towards my *Extreme* team. After all, they did come and rescue me in the end. Jamie has taken the money I found to the local police and all order has been restored.

Before we head to Manila I decide to pop to the shop to load up with supplies for the long journey ahead, buying fruit, juice, sweets and loads of delicious things for the whole team to gorge on. I walk outside, laden with food, and notice both of the production cars have gone. *That's weird*, I think, looking this way and that. I wait around for a few minutes, imagining they've gone for a quick toilet stop. Ten minutes later no one has returned, and this is when it dawns on me that they have fucked off without me and are on their way to Manila. I am really upset, and what's more I've got no signal on my phone. Fuck! It is twenty minutes before anyone notices I'm not in the car. Each group thinks I've gone with the other but thankfully Peter Prada decides to double-check. He phones Jamie.

'Is Robson with you?'

'No, we thought he was with you,' says Jamie.

Fuck!! Loud screech of brakes.

I'll tell you what, I am devastated. I thought I was part of this great team and they didn't even notice I wasn't there – or maybe they did and left me on purpose? They eventually turn up to get me and I peevishly give all the food I've bought to some random locals. Well, at least they appreciate the gesture and there's no way these bastards are getting a thing from me now. I sulk all the way to Manila. During the trip I turn to Jamie and say, 'I thought we were like a rock band on tour.'

'We are. But sometimes it gets crazy on the road and shit happens.'

He's right, it certainly does.

Chapter Seven

THAILAND

Accentuate the Positive

February 2009, Series 2

It's a twelve-hour flight to Thailand and, knowing that jet psychosis is waiting for me at Arrivals, I decide to follow a close friend's advice and take two sleeping tablets called Stay Knocked. They contain melatonin, the hormone in the brain believed to maintain a regular sleeping pattern – my friend assures me that I will sleep like a baby, awake feeling refreshed and as if I've had a hot shower completely synced to Bangkok time.

I fall asleep all right; I stayed KO'd for the entire flight and am only able to shoot one piece on my diary camera as I'm coming into land. I feel like some deranged squatter has laid waste to the delicate furniture of my mind; the sofa's on fire, the coffee table's broken and he's nicked the telly. When we touch down, Jamie takes one look at me and decides it's best to shoot me in wide because a close-up and the effects of Stay Knocked may scare the children. Bangkok Airport is insane, hectic, nuts, crazy, bonkers, and I'm watching it happen through bevelled glass.

We head out to film in the busy streets, avoiding tuk-tuks, elephants, women whose chest hair goes all the way down to their testicles, spider sellers, scorpion sellers and ladies who have turned ping-pong into a whole new art form. It's all here in this hot, sweaty and vibrant city of sin and serenity. This is the land of contrasts. No sooner am I shown to my room in the hotel than my face hits the pillow and I dream I am swimming with a giant stingray, one of the chief quarries of this particular adventure. It flaps its wings like a rubbery raptor, so graceful in the water. I am feeling relaxed and I touch the creature. It winks at me. I become aware that I'm not swimming alone – there is another man, an Australian. It's Steve Irwin.

'Hello, Steve,' my voice echoes strangely underwater.

He smiles and waves at me. The stingray lifts its tail. Nooo! I sit bolt upright, gasping for air.

Market

Today I am feeling more human but my nightmare has left a residue of acrid fear. Why the hell do I want to hunt a giant freshwater stingray after one harpooned one of the greatest wildlife presenters in the chest? What does the experience add to the show? Oh, yes, I forgot: it's called *Extreme Fishing*. Why on earth didn't I sign up for some gentle fly-fishing?

We hop in a tuk-tuk and go to the Bang Kapi market to meet contributor Eddy Mounce. Originally from Ipswich, he came to Thailand on a fishing trip six years ago and never caught the flight home. He now works as a fishing guide for tourists from all over the world. Here we stock up on bait for our first fishing adventure. My deli counter at Tesco looks nothing like this: everything is fresh, i.e. ALIVE! Fish flap, eels squirm, cockerels cock-a-doodle-doo, crabs scuttle, frogs jump – and one desperately tries to break out of a net bag, attempting to part a hole with its strong green arms. It's brutal; there are about twenty all piled together in the bag. I want to help them but it's how things are done here.

I must admit the market is a full frontal assault on my Western sensibilities, however it also seems more real and truthful. Back home we are shielded from the suffering and visceral, bloody destruction of the animals whose lives we take. Everything is stewed and neatly packaged in ready-meals or cling-wrapped with pretty pictures to mask the violent slaughter and butchery that befalls the creatures. But I am very proud of the animal welfare standards we have in the UK. In my opinion, limiting suffering should be top of the list when harvesting fish or dispatching any animal.

Eddy interrupts my contemplation by shoving a bag of chopped-up mackerel in my arms, which we are going to use as bait. I then have to ask, in my best Thai, for several bags of cow's blood. The woman bends down and reaches under the counter, passing me one gallon at a time. I bung the two transparent bags of burgundy under each arm, pay the woman at the stall and wander off to go fishing with Eddy. This place is as mad as a bag of frogs.

Lake IT

The city of Bangkok and all its madness is a world away from the simple life of many people who inhabit this beautiful country, where once again fishing is a lot more than a hobby – it's a way of life. The humidity smacks you in the face, you are battered by the relentless sun and you're leaking from orifices you didn't think you had.

Sixty miles south we head for a lake known as IT Lake Monsters, and it's a world away from the madness of Bangkok. I'm pleased to be out of the oppressive city and in the countryside, with open plains and tropical vegetation. We arrive at a man-made lake a bit like the ones we have back in the UK, only the weather's nicer and this lake is stocked with some of the most amazing predators from all over the world. Unlike Loch Ness, there are real monsters of the deep lurking under the surface.

Eddy introduces me to Alley Lungtong, the singing fisherman.

'Sawadee-krup, Robson.'

'Sawadee-krup, Alley.'

Alley tells me the lake is stocked with barramundi, tigerfish, alligator gar, redtail catfish and arapaima, and even though some are endangered species, parks like this help protect them, so I can fish with a clear conscience. The arapaima is incredibly rare in the wild. In fact, you have more likelihood of catching an arapaima here than in South America, where it is from originally. I am desperate to catch this great predator today. It hunts by scent so we are hoping it likes the cow's blood. I chuck jam jars of blood across the lake, 'chumming' the water. Much like fishing for shark, the blood will get into the arapaima's nostrils and hopefully bring them towards our bait. I have only chummed for sharks before and never anything else.

It's midday and the heat is overpowering, plus it's 95 per cent humidity, but I don't have time to complain because within thirty seconds I am in. Alley thinks it's a redtail catfish, but whatever it is it's big, and the pull on the line and the heat are wearing me out. Just when I think I can't reel anymore, the redtail catfish comes to the surface. It is about thirty to forty pounds. Its red tail mixes into orange on its underbelly; a stunning creature. We put it back – the policy is catch-and-release here and the lake wouldn't stay stocked for long if it weren't.

I ask Alley what he does while he waits for a bite.

'I like sing-song.'

Perhaps he could be a replacement for Jerome, I wonder to myself, although I'm still hoping to hear back from PSY. Imagine it: Geordie Gangnam Style.

Suddenly I feel a yank on the line.

'We're in.'

Straight away it's off.

'Oh, bugger.'

I teach Alley the correct British fishing phrases. 'Oh, bugger,' he says over and over.

But the wait isn't long before we have another bite. It's an alligator gar! I reel him in and hold him up to the camera. The alligator gar is an extraordinary-looking ray-finned fish that has existed for 100 million years. He's known as an alligator gar because of his crocodilian head and rows of sharp teeth. They can grow up to ten feet in length and are found in the brackish waters of the southern United States, although this fella can survive for up to two hours out of water. No one needs to be in this heat for long so I pop him straight back. This mean-assed predator's got business to attend to in his lake. He's the Godfather fish because he will eat anything and anyone, even turtles and wildfowl.

As we continue to wait for the arapaima to make an appearance, Alley bursts into a rendition of a Thai favourite. I join in: 'I love Thailand, I like Patpong. I like Thailand, I love Patpong,' we croon.

'What's Patpong, Alley?'

I quickly work out it's the Bangkok ladies he loves. Patpong is the 'entertainments' district of the city.

'OK, let's end it there. It's a family show and I'm not Wayne Rooney.'

With no hat on I'm beginning to feel the symptoms of sunstroke. In this kind of heat your blood thickens and takes longer to circulate round the body. I try not to think about a syrupy chum trying to force its way around my veins. I really should take an aspirin but there's no time because I'm 'in' again and whatever's on the end of my line feels very different. As I begin to reel the fish in I can see it's an arapaima (or pirarucu, as the species is known by the Amazonians), one of the largest freshwater fish in the world. I bring in this dinosaur of the deep. Her tail is like an eel's and she has distinctive red speckles on her body. I put her back into the lake, mission accomplished. I shake Alley's hand and thank him for a great day. It's time to head back to the mayhem of Bangkok and not before time. I think my brain's boiled.

After a quick shower and change of clothes at our very kitsch hotel, which looks as if it is made of sequins, and with all the female staff bowing every five seconds, saying 'Sawadee-ka', the crew and I head out to dinner. Assistant Producer Finlay has booked a table at one of Bangkok's top restaurants and I'm looking forward to indulging in some delicious Thai cuisine. But the restaurant's not quite what I expected and the name is truly terrible: it's called 'Cabbages and Condoms'. I reluctantly enter.

The place is packed and there is a long queue for tables. We breeze past the line and a waiter with a johnny on his head (no lie) takes us to our table. He's got it all the way over his eyes and nose, only his mouth is uncovered, and it is inflated at the top. *It must be a femidom*, I find myself thinking. Oh, God – I really don't want to consider this when I'm about to eat. There is a tree made of condoms next to our table, and there are lights, chairs, tables and flower arrangements all made from brightly coloured willy sheaths. Apparently the proprietors are concerned with raising awareness for sexual health and family planning. I'm really not sure if the message is getting through, or whether it's even relevant to the affluent middle-class patrons here, but the food is amazing. I'm not a fan of the doggy bags, though . . .

Mekong Catfish

The next day I'm back with Eddy again. We're heading forty minutes outside of Bangkok to Bungsamran Lake, which in Thai mean 'Luxury Lake'. It's a twenty-acre stock lake containing over fifty species. We're after the Mekong catfish, another enormous freshwater fish, so it should be a good rehearsal for the giant stingray. My heart races and I go weak at the knees when I consider this quarry. Thankfully it's still a few days away.

We put big balls of hard-packed rice husks above a hook and throw them out a good thirty-five yards. It's a bit like casting a tennis ball. The Mekong catfish is sadly facing extinction in its eponymous river, so fishing is tightly controlled. They are threatened partly through overfishing, but partly owing to decreased water levels because of upstream damming in the People's Republic of China.

'There're restrictions now on the Mekong River,' says Eddy, 'so fishing parks like this one offer anybody the chance to hook fish they wouldn't be able to catch elsewhere.'

A 100-kilo catfish was pulled out of this very lake so it's possible I could become a record-holder today – it would be nice to put a different kind of record to my name. In the wild they can grow to between 150 and 200 kilos in just six years. I yank the rod up and we're in. I reel and reel – giant Mekongs love to run. This one takes me up and down the pontoon and round the houses. It has an amazing amount of sustained power. I run up the pontoon again. Where's he taking me now? He tries to go down to the bottom when something in my back tweaks slightly. It feels very sore, like red-hot needles. Pulling him in is a test of stamina. He won't give up but nor will I. Wow! He peers through the surface.

'Look at the girth on the fella.'

He's a good fifty pounds – OK, by no means the biggest, but handsome all the same. Eddy and I pick him up and he looks at us with his big eyes. These Mekong catfish have seriously dangerous spikes on their pectoral fins, which can do some serious damage, so Eddy carefully puts him back into the lake and I head straight to the physiotherapist.

River Kwai

After a quick Thai massage with a happy ending – not a Patpong happy ending, but my back's much better now, thank you – I head west with Eddy and the crew to the Burmese border. We stop off at the iconic Bridge over the River Kwai, which is actually pronounced 'Kway'. Kwai ('kwhy') are in fact buffalo, and many drink from the River Kwai ('Kway'). Two hundred and sixty thousand men laboured on the Death Railway that stretched 258 miles from Bangkok to Rangoon in Burma and was built by

Japan to support its forces during World War II. More than 90,000 Asian labourers and 16,000 Allied prisoners of war died of accidents, starvation and disease during its construction; 6,318 British personnel lost their lives. Others were luckier, including Ronald Searle, the British cartoonist and creator of St Trinian's, who managed to survive the war.

On the bridge a young man in a plaid shirt and jeans is playing the violin. *How lovely*, I think, until I tune into what he's playing and start howling with laughter. I join in: 'Hitler has only got one ball, the other is in the Albert Hall. Himmler had something similar but poor old Goebbels had none at all.'

The busker takes me aside: 'Do you know Hitler has only got one ball?' He puts his finger to his lips. 'Nobody knows – only one ball.' Well, they do now.

Despite the heat I can't resist getting my rod out to try to catch a few perch. Eddy tries all manner of bait, including bananas. I instinctively know we are not going to catch one today, especially with the gathering crowd behind us, so it's time to go. The cows and buffaloes have come to drink, pee and poo in the river.

Indian Carp

In the late afternoon we arrive at Khao Laem Dam, 180 miles west of Bangkok, where I'm meeting Air Lekkham, who's lived on the reservoir all his life. It's like the Lake District with jungle attached to it. This freshwater fishing heaven exists because of the Khao Laem Dam, built in the 1980s to supply water and electricity to the area. It's a world away from the comforts of the city. I spot our hotel – it's a raft with a roof, in the middle of the lake. It's primitive but I'm sure it's as comfortable as the Hilton, and I certainly won't feel fiscally plundered in the morning. Our accommodation is open-plan and we are all sleeping in one room, but it's the only way to get an early start tomorrow.

At 10.30 p.m. we are still sorting out fishing gear for the morning and as we finally settle down for the night the insects come alive and start attacking us. We are covered in them: mayflies like pterodactyls, the high-pitch whine of mosquitoes, moths that are all over me like a busy jumper. I film a piece on my diary camera recording my suffering by moonlight. My therapist said it's good to share, and that's why I got into TV! I am exhausted and I desperately try to settle down to sleep again. I put my headphones on in an attempt to drown out the noise of mosquitoes and Jamie's snoring, which is getting on my man-tits. After what seems an eternity, I finally drift off.

Eddy wakes me up with a start, singing 'In the jungle, the mighty jungle . . .' at the top of his voice. I want to kill him and so does the rest of the crew. I've had only four and a half hours of fitful sleep and this guy has the brass neck to sing. I drag my sorry behind out of bed.

This morning we are fishing for Indian carp (rohu), which isn't native to Thailand but actually originally from India and Pakistan. It's the staple diet for families here, and what they don't eat they sell at the market. However, whatever we catch we are going to eat and I'm excited. No one eats carp back home because it's a bottom feeder and hovers up silt, weed and other gunk, apparently making it taste muddy, so I can't wait to give my verdict on rohu. Carp only feed at certain times, so we wait for sunrise. Eddy asks me to cast out three metres past a float and to the right. I'm so tired I can't hit a barn door but finally I make a good cast. Eddy is impressed but the fish couldn't give a toss; two hours later there is still no sign of life.

'Up at three forty-five, no sleep on a raft, to catch carp. This better be worth it, Eddy,' I say grumpily. 'You've got six rods out there and there hasn't been a bend in one of them.'

I'm hot and tired and I feel like a seven-year-old. Minutes later I moan from the hut.

'When are we going to get one, Eddy?'

'In terms of carp fishing we've been here a very short time,' says Eddy.

He's right, and that's why I don't like carp fishing: it's inactive and boring. The carp fishing posse can 'troll' about me as much as they like on the Internet, I care not. Some people don't like curling or tai chi – I don't like carp fishing.

I take shelter from the burning rays on a 'day bed' in the hut. I just need an opium pipe to deal with this interminable ennui and I'm set for the day. Eddy is the watchman and our six rods are primed. We wait restlessly and another three hours pass before a rod springs into action.

'Keep it pumping, Robson.'

I've got to keep him off the bottom, otherwise he'll be in snags, vegetation or dead trees that hold the fish or catch the line and I'll lose him. I don't lose him and we land the fish. I am very pleased to have caught such a fine-looking rohu and, after a very long morning, I'm really looking forward to devouring it.

We cook the carp five ways: steamed, shallow-fried, deep-fried, grilled and baked. It's a lovely white fish – not in my top three but very nice. We enjoy five courses, including tom yum carp soup. It tastes beautiful and nothing is wasted. Here they even eat the swim bladder that helps the carp float in the water, but this doesn't stay in my mouth long. Rather like prairie oysters, it's an acquired taste.

Buddhist Temple

So the day of reckoning is here: we are going after a giant stingray today and I am wetting myself. We travel to a place called Chachoengsao, fifty miles from Bangkok, and Jamie wants me to visit a beautiful Buddhist temple to bless the day. It's something I've never done on a trip before but I'll take all the positive vibes I can get. Buddhism is an amazing philosophy and one of its key tenets is to accentuate the positive and eliminate the negative.

I deliver a piece to camera: 'Yes, I'm after the world's largest freshwater fish. A fish that can weigh up to one thousand pounds. A fish with a barb so deadly that it can kill in seconds. We're going after a giant stingray!'

One of the crew's phones rings. Oh, for goodness' sake: not in the middle of a take – and in a Buddhist temple, of all places . . . I try not to get uptight. Buddhism is about achieving calmness and training one's willpower to overcome emotional responses and act rationally, so I have a go. But actors are the most unstable creatures on the planet – far worse than francium, the most unstable element in the Periodic Table. Maybe that's why they call it a periodic table . . . *Accentuate the positive, eliminate the negative, Robson.* I breathe in the incense and stare at Buddha. Finlay walks over to me, the phone outstretched.

'Robson, you need to ring Sandra urgently.'

Sandra, my business partner, is my rock. She is Paul Burrell to my Diana. She answers after a single ring.

'Robson. I'm so sorry.'

'Has Dad passed away?' I ask, sensing what has happened.

'Yes, he has. [pause] Joanna, Dawn, David and Yvonne were all with him. He had an aneurysm in his stomach.'

She goes on to tell me Big Rob was with his girlfriend Yvonne watching TV, when all of a sudden he gasped with pain and experienced the fatal burst.

'Did he suffer?'

'No, it was so quick.'

I stagger outside the temple. I'm feeling light-headed and the picture distorts. I desperately search for a corner to break down in but I can't find one. *Keep it together, Robson.* I walk towards a tree, the mobile drops from my hand and I collapse on my knees, sobbing alone in the heat. Two guys are staring at me. Maybe they think it's part of the show. Maybe they are thinking, 'Wow, this guy is really good.' I want to tell them Big Rob's dead but I don't.

Jamie comes and hugs me.

'I'm sorry, Robson, I'm so sorry'. He turns to everyone: 'OK, we are all going home now.'

A Buddhist monk silently makes his way over. He looks at me and holds my hand. His presence is so calming. He strokes my face and looks at me in the eye.

'Was he not well?' he asks.

'No,' I say, still choked.

'He has moved on to a good place, but he is still here with you. He is within you. You look like him. You are him.'

It's an extraordinary moment. I will never forget the way he looked at me.

Later on I realise I have learnt one of the four truths of Buddhism: life is challenging. For everyone. Our physical bodies, our relationships – all of our life circumstances – are fragile and subject to change. We are always accommodating.

I guess grieving is part of accommodating.

Big Rob

I visit my mum first. She's OK, I think because she and Dad parted years ago. She sips her tea and says, 'I was at the Spanish Ballroom in Whitley Bay when I first clapped eyes on your dad. The first thing he said was, "I've been watching you dancing all night. You're the most beautiful woman here." 'Course I knew straight away he was after something and I was right. He said, "Are you here next week, because I'd love to dance with you?" I said, "I'll be here." He said, "Oh, good. Can you lend us ten pence to get the bus home? I'll pay you back." The cheeky so-and-so had spent all his money on drink. Your dad was a wonderful dancer: he glided across the floor – and he paid me back, just as he said.'

I see my two sisters, who live just yards from Mum. They are taking it very badly but my brother David is reserved as ever. As we remember Dad our sadness turns to laughter, especially when we recall his preference for going everywhere bare-chested, including restaurants!

'What about the time in Devon, we were going for dinner and Dad had his top off. The guy at the door said, "You can't come in", and Dad says, "You try and fucking stop me."'

He was as hard as nails. He thought it was completely normal but as kids we knew something was wrong. No one else's dad was half-naked all the time. Come rain, shine or Arctic winter, he never had a shirt on and was always as brown as a berry. I remember him digging the garden on a cold winter's day with only his trousers and boots on. He was a great horticulturist and grew prize-winning vegetables. He also had a beautiful flower garden where he grew roses, carnations and exquisite blue corn-flowers, which he gave to family, friends and local people.

The funeral service is at Whitley Bay Crematorium, with 200 people crammed into a very small space. Dawn and Joanna both say a few words and then it's my turn. David stands by my side as I speak; he is catatonic with grief.

'Dad loved his football and he followed his beloved Newcastle United around the world. I remember a time in Nice when Monaco slaughtered Newcastle. Before the game I took Dad to the Colombe d'Or – a famous restaurant patronised by Matisse and Picasso, who paid their bills with paintings, which are still on the walls today. Dad thought the paintings were shite. "I don't get it. It's not my cup of tea." He ordered the soup; it was gazpacho. He took a sip and in broad Geordie summoned the waiter over. "How! Bonnie lad, this soup has never touched the flame." Antwerp made me smile, too. Dad was very anti-German. At lunch they had all the different flags of Europe on the table. He walks over, seizes the German one and says, "You can take that one off for a bloody start." Next to go is the Italian ensign, which he plonks down on the table. I say, "Dad, you weren't even in the war!" "So what! I still hate those bastard Krauts and I'll never trust the Eyeties." He makes a sudden grab for the Tricolour: "Almost forgot this one," he says. "Bloody collaborators."'

I take a breath and end my speech by plagiarising Jimmy Dean's 'Big Bad John':

Ev'ry mornin' at the mine you could see him arrive
He stood five-foot-nine and weighed two thirty-five
Kinda broad at the shoulder and narrow at the hip
And everybody knew ya didn't give no lip to Big Rob.
That was my Dad.

Stingray

One week later and I'm back at the Bang Pakong River in Chachoengsao Province, ready to catch a giant freshwater stingray. I meet stingray expert Que at his wooden house on stilts at the river's edge. The river is deep, fast-flowing and the colour of British Rail coffee with a hint of long-life milk. I try on the tackle and kit needed to fish for one of these prehistoric giants and Que trusses me up like a Christmas turkey.

We set up the rods on the bank outside his house while Que's mate rows the bait out and drops it in the middle of a brackish river. We use a sardine as live bait. The hook is fastened under the spine of the fish, which is brutal but it's the local Thai method. When a fish is hurt it sends out a distress signal that attracts other fish, and today we're hoping this little sardine appeals to a stingray.

By 11 a.m. the lines are set. There is only a loose tension on them because giant stingrays don't eat immediately and will take the bait somewhere to feed later, so we must wait for the moment they swallow the bait. Come midday there's 100 per cent humidity and the heat is unbearable. I am on the corner of a makeshift bed, trying to rest, and all the team is asleep except for Que, who is our watchman. The jungle behind is alive with the buzz of insects, the squawks of monkeys.

'Fish! Fish! Fish!' yells Que.

We scramble to our feet. I take the rod and it is quickly apparent that the fish is not going to come to us. We are going to have to go to the fish. We set the rod, put it on full tension and jump on a boat to float down the river. I put on the harness and take the rod, keeping it on full tension as I try to pull up. It really hurts my bollocks and my back. This fish is 300–400 pounds or even larger, and it's desperately trying to go to the bottom and bury itself in the mud. I soon realise that, because of the tension on the rod, reel and body, I can't do it alone, so Que takes over. The boat is very unstable and we almost capsize. We need a bigger boat! Considering this cartilaginous fish is a relative of the shark family, this seems appropriate. We jump in a larger model and the fight continues. The rod is bending in Que's hands, almost back on itself. He sits on the rod and it continues to bend over the edge of the boat. I've never seen anything like it.

Giant freshwater stingrays are bottom feeders and hunt for crabs, snails and clams by detecting their electrical impulses through the mud. They have sophisticated electro receptors called ampullae of Lorenzini, named after the seventeenth-century Italian scientist who discovered them, which are also found in other rays, sharks and chimaeras (ghost fish). Giant stingrays are such complex creatures that little is known about them, nor do we know how many still exist, but they are thought to be endangered in Asia and critically endangered here in Thailand. Unfortunately the Bang Pakong River is known to be polluted, with prawns and other fish stocks dwindling, possibly from industrial pollutants upstream. Many other species are endangered here, including the Irrawaddy dolphin, owing not only to pollution but also to overfishing, soil erosion, and getting caught in nets. It's a sad state of affairs, and, with the human population set to rise to 8 billion by 2030, one we need to address before it's too late.

I'm back in the hot seat and inch by inch I'm gaining some ground. It's been fifty minutes; landing this fish is like hauling John Prescott out of the water. Que pulls up the line as I reel in. But even working together the two of us still can't bring it in.

Que's friend takes over – it's become a three-man fight in the searing heat. After an hour and a half the ray nearly takes the boat over and I am screaming in agony – the load is too much. Que helps me. It's piercing agony. The way a stingray moves in the water it's like pulling up a huge plate with water on top: it's the ultimate amount of drag. Suddenly we see the fishing weight appear out of the coffee, and then a wing, flapping like an elephant's ear, breaks the surface. We see her and she truly is like something out of a sci-fi movie. Her wingspan is ten or eleven feet, and her length from head to tail is thirteen or fourteen feet. We guess she's around a quarter of a ton but these rays can grow to over a thousand pounds!

On the edge of her tail is a spike. If it comes near us we are in trouble. The spike can measure up to fifteen inches, is shaped like a bayonet and covered in a sheath of toxic mucus that is capable of piercing bone. A stingray has just killed Steve Irwin, and now Que is telling me to get in the water and hold the fish.

'Are you insane?' I yelp.

All the stingray has to do is quickly flick her tail to the side or over her back like a scorpion, the spike deploys and it's game over. They can kill sharks; they can kill anything. It's like a trigger and it's lightning-quick. I stay back while Que and his friend cover the tail with a blanket, wrapping it round and tying it down tightly. The fish is no longer a threat.

There's no way we can get this creature on the boat so I really do have to go in, according to Jamie, whom I now loathe once more. He was lovely after my father's passing but now he's reverted to his old sadistic ways. I get in the water and wade slowly towards this alien life-form. I am petrified. I hold her with Que and his friend, quickly spout a few facts about this giant to camera, and it's time to let the awesome creature off the hook. We take the metal out of her mouth and she glides gently away back to her home on the bottom of the Bang Pakong.

I wish I could tell my Dad about the experience. I phone Uncle Matheson instead.

Chapter Eight

KENYA

Addiction

September 2009, World Tour, Series 3

As I look out over Kilimanjaro for the first time, I think this programme is actually going to work. It might even be a success. As a team we have started to know what we are doing and it turns out *Extreme Fishing* isn't really a fishing programme at all; it's a travelogue that explores different cultures and places, with the common link of fishing. Fishing is quite literally my passport to the world. (Sir Winston Churchill once said, 'Polo is a passport to the world.' Mine is fishing and I don't need six horses to do it.) I have turned down several acting jobs to do this series but the locations of Manchester, Rochdale and Cowgate in Newcastle didn't really come close to the savannahs and exotic wildlife of Africa, not to mention the record-breaking angling to be had off the east coast. This is the place to catch the big five: blue marlin, black marlin, swordfish, sailfish and striped marlin.

It's the stuff of dreams and it blows *Waterloo Road* firmly out of the water!

As we come into land at Nairobi Airport, it also dawns on me that I am addicted to the show. It's like a fix and when I don't get my hit I feel sad or that something is missing, and that's just the days in between episodes. Time passes slowly when I'm back in the UK – tick, tick, tick – like the hand of a faulty clock stuck on the same minute, unable to budge. But when I'm filming the show I feel so upbeat and occupied in a positive way. If I'm honest I'm a lot healthier because of this gig – fishing has replaced drinking, which is par for the course in this business. I knew I had a drink problem when I found an olive in my urine sample – thank you, Keith Richards.

From Nairobi we take another plane to Watamu National Maritime Park in the Indian Ocean. The light aircraft is falling apart and I spot a gaping hole in the wing mid-flight! It reminds me of the good old days of Dan-Air (aka Dan Dare). We survive the rickety African flight and carry on to our hotel. We are staying at Hemingway's, named after the author, traveller and hunter who spent many years in Kenya. I didn't realise that he'd shot and fished for anything that moved. In 1933, inspired by the legendary hunts of President Theodore Roosevelt, Ernest borrowed money from his wife's uncle and set off on a three-month safari.

I look at the gigantic stuffed fish adorning the walls of the hotel: there's a giant black marlin and a beautiful golden dorado. I'm determined to catch both on this trip. The dorado won't outsmart me this time, as it did in the Philippines. I still carry the sinking feeling of that loss. Totally my fault, but it won't happen again. I've come here to set the record straight.

But first things first: I need a haircut, because right now I look like Richard Clayderman. I ask at reception if they have a salon and they tell me they have an expert stylist who comes in. I make an appointment and continue filming. A few hours later, enter Fatima.

'Come this way,' she says, leading me to a room with bright lights and a mirror. I sit down in front of it. Fatima crosses the room with a pair of electric shears, dragging the lead noisily across the hardwood floor. She plugs the shears in and sets them at grade 3.

'Hang on! Do you have any scissors?' I venture.

'No, I have a comb and shears – it will be fine.'

'But I just want you to tidy it up,' I say, putting my hand up to prevent the shears taking me a step closer to Yul Brynner. 'Just a trim would be great,' I say firmly.

'I am very sad,' she says, sighing.

'What?'

'I just buried my sister. I miss her so much. We put her in the earth at the top of a mountain.'

Inside I am thinking, *OK, that is very sad* – but I still don't want an emotionally vulnerable woman to come anywhere near my head with a pair of electric shears.

'You shouldn't be here, you must be traumatised,' I say, looking at her in the mirror.

'No, I'm fine.'

The tears are streaming down her face as she brings the shears down on my head. She gets to work like a champion sheep-shearer and it's over in a matter of seconds.

I walk outside and find the crew. They take one look at me and their faces fall. I have gone from Clayderman to Charles Bronson within fifteen minutes and now everything we have shot before the 'attack' is unusable because of continuity.

'What the hell happened?' asks Alistair.

'Let's just say she wasn't in the mood for a trim. I think I got off lightly.'

Alistair shakes his head sadly: 'How can you manage to fuck up a haircut, Robson?'

Thankfully I'd brought my trusty Nanogen in my Mary Poppins make-up bag. It's a scalp filler that makes you look like you have twice as much hair. Think David Guest but more subtle. And yes, I carry a make-up bag. Actors and presenters have all manner of tricks to avoid looking shiny, sallow or dog-rough on camera.

If you are an Alpha male, feel free to skip this paragraph but for the gays and ladies here're my top beauty tips: I apply a Clinique green cream, which covers up any redness or sunburn, and it's great if you suffer from rosacea or are a raging alcoholic. Then I apply a primer, which evens the skin tone. Next I lighten under the eyelids and use concealer as necessary. I then apply powder. I add a little eyeliner on the lower lashes because when you are filming in hot, bright countries there is high contrast, so features need to be accentuated. I also use MAC mascara for the top lashes, and on my lips I use Zam-Buk, a green ointment that protects and highlights them. I only wear make-up when I am filming, not every day – honest. And just so you know, even butch men like Matt Dawson, Bruce Parry and Ray Mears all wear make-up on TV.

Anyway, we crack on with filming. It's a hot day but we are all relishing being outside after the shocking weather back home in the UK. However, none of us has applied enough sunscreen so our faces, heads, necks, arms and ears are all scorched by the midday sun. A few hours later we look like *Viz* magazine's 'Brits Abroad'. Peter is singed the worst and that evening I suggest he try my Green Cream to cover his badly burned face.

'I am not putting any of your poofy muck on my face!'

'It's not poofy muck, it's Clinique!'

He suffers like a man; I suffer like an actor.

El Dorado

The next morning I tear the curtains open. I am red-hot with sunburn but the prospect of catching a golden dorado this morning is like lidocaine.

We walk down to the harbour to meet Callum, a strapping Kenyan fisherman and my guide for today. We board his gleaming white sports fishing boat and set off a mile out to sea, to a place known locally as Sailfish Alley. The sun is hot and it's a beautiful day to go fishing. On the way we come across a sperm whale carcass floating on the surface, about forty feet in length. As we get closer the aroma is abhorrent. It is an oily, sweet, rotten stench of death. Callum thinks the whale has either died of natural causes or been hit by a boat, which sadly happens all too often. Every year thousands of whales lose their lives to container ships, like flies on a car windscreen. It's a tragedy that will hopefully one day be preventable through technology. We slowly pass the carcass. It moves strangely in the water, its tail swishing from side to side. At first I think it's gas escaping but then I see a dorsal fin, in fact several of them – 800-pound tiger sharks are taking bites out of the whale like Brie. They are incredible-looking fish, with stripes like the eponymous big cat and just as vicious. I shudder. There are only two types of people who are not scared of sharks: psychopaths and dead people.

After just twenty minutes' motoring across the waves we reach our destination, Sailfish Alley. It's a huge drop-off and natural feeding channel for pelagic, billfish and other species that have a penchant for bait fish. We rig our skip bait, large bonitos, relations of the mackerel family, and trawl the live bait behind the boat. It's not something I'm used to fly-fishing in Northumberland, but it's the way they do it here in Kenya. Almost immediately I get a take. I set the rod and pull the line in tight. It's not a dorado, as the fish doesn't become airborne within twenty seconds, but whatever it is nimbly jumps off the hook. I reel in the bait; half of it is missing. Something has cut through the fish like a serrated knife through butter.

Ten minutes later this happens again: our bait is taken and the predator misses the hook by millimetres. Callum thinks it's a wahoo nicking our bait but on the sixth attempt I catch the culprit. I am convinced it's the same one that's been eating all the pies and now, overfed, has got sloppy and made a fatal mistake. I bring the twenty-pound fish onto the boat. It is a wahoo – the Usain Bolt of the ocean (cue lightning pose). We knock it on the head and keep it for our supper. Wahoo tastes absolutely delicious, as its Hawaiian name suggests. It's a bit like mackerel but with a softer, more delicate flavour.

I don't have to wait long for my next strike and it's gold, as the shining dorado bursts out of the water. I know how tough this pulchritudinous fish is to catch and I'm not going to lose her – she is my greatest prize. She leaps athletically out of the ocean again. If I don't keep her under control she'll turn off the hook and be free. She is so powerful she can exceed 50 m.p.h. in short bursts, and she's smart – I've underestimated the golden maverick once before but this time I play it safe and use all the skills I have learnt to land her.

I've done it! I am ecstatic. A quick bump on the head and we've got a fifteen-pound mahi-mahi (the Hawaiian name for dorado, meaning very strong) for our supper to complement our wahoo – I am a very happy man. As we head back to shore I take in the stunning coastline. Callum points to the starboard side of the boat and as I cross the deck I see a female humpback whale and her calf. We are all rendered speechless. She ejects seawater out of her spout like a geyser while her calf expels a faint mist more like a lawn sprinkler – he'll get there in the end. They swim by the boat for a while, dive down and are gone.

Back at Hemingway's, I eat the wahoo and dorado with the crew and Callum. I look around at the other clientele in the bistro. There are a conspicuous number of rotund German women in their sixties having candlelit dinners with young African men. Around the world, I've seen my fair share of saggy ageing men with fresh-faced nubile girls, which is repugnant, but I didn't know there was sex tourism the other way round. These boys have been groomed by these grey-haired porno-grannies, seduced with cars, money and treats. They say many a good tune is played on an old fiddle, but looking at some of these women, I would definitely take up a new instrument.

Dhow Fishing

I wake up with images of haggard German women on heat and feel sick. At breakfast there are old Italian boilers in on the act and we all decide to get some air. Today we are heading to Malindi, a former port and tourist resort on the east coast. I am dhow fishing with Hassan, Mohammed and Mohammed (Mo for short), three guys who fish together day in, day out and who are like the Kenyan angling equivalent of the Rolling Stones, all with faces that could tell a thousand stories. They are all wearing the traditional dhow dress of plain coloured kilts. We greet one another and I hop aboard their boat.

Dhow boats are Indian in origin and design and have been used in the area for centuries; today we are going out in a vessel Hassan says he has designed and built himself. The craftsmanship is truly outstanding. Coming from a shipbuilding background I appreciate the design and execution. As a lad out of school I was accepted for an apprenticeship as a draughtsman at Swan Hunter, where I worked in hull design and shell expansion, but I quickly realised that, if shipbuilding and I were both to survive, we would have to go our separate ways. I know the industry has been struggling since the 1980s, when I coincidentally worked at Swan Hunter, but I would like to take this opportunity to underline that the decline in shipbuilding in the northeast was down to Margaret Thatcher and not my ineptitude as a draughtsman. Honest!

The men unfurl the sail and we tack across the water. It's amazing how the boat glides through the waves; I feel this is how we are meant to fish. It's so natural and more like the poetry of fly-fishing that I love so much. It is also in complete contrast to the big white petrol-guzzling craft we went out in yesterday. I stare at Hassan, in awe of him for building this boat. As we sail across the sea I turn to him on camera and say, 'This really is an amazing dhow boat, so beautiful and perfect for catching reef fish. I understand you built it yourself?'

'No, I didn't,' he says.

My pupils dilate. WTF? 'Oh? A little bird told me that you had built it.'

'No, a local businessman built and paid for it.'

'Did you have any hand in it at all?'

'No.'

Basically he'd spun me a right old yarn until he realised he was going to be on camera and it might tie him in knots later.

But whatever the genesis of the dhow boat, one thing is irrefutable: Hassan and his friends know how to fish. I've never seen anything like it. They work the lines not only with their hands but also with their feet, playing the fish like puppets on strings. Their feet and hands all bear the scars of their work but over time the skin has hardened and they feel no pain. Each of them pulls up four fish, sometimes two at a time, without ever tangling the lines; it's an incredible feat. They are the masters, with extraordinary coordination and great strength to fight not only the fish but also gusts of wind and lumpy water. They make it look easy but I assure you it is not.

I'm hoping to catch a grouper or red snapper but first I have to don the traditional dhow fishermen dress. Well, it's more of a skirt or sarong that fits from the midriff to the ankles. I feel like David Beckham. In this part of the country it is shameful for men to show their legs, which is unfortunate because I have been told I have lovely legs. Peter Prada needs to cover his; in fact, I don't think they have ever seen the light of day. Alistair's are like pipe cleaners and Craig has Kiwi cankles. But my legs are shapely, like Richard O'Brien's, only younger.

I put on my welding gloves to protect my actor's hands. Hassan explains that fishing without gloves allows him to feel every movement of the fish so he knows exactly when to pull the line up. (I guess it's a bit like a rider keeping a gentle contact with the horse's mouth to make small adjustments in speed and direction.) He confiscates the gloves – if I'm going to be a dhow fisherman I need to feel the fish and understand the technique.

We drop anchor at the edge of a reef, lowering bait to the bottom. A grouper fish tends to come out of its cave, take the bait and then try to swim back into the reef. You have to take a grouper quickly otherwise you'll lose it.

Mo gets a bite and heaves up a chakashangu, or a green job fish. I'm up next – at first I think it's a snapper but I've actually hooked a coral fish. I heave it up. Its colours are a stunning palate of purples, reds and yellows. It's part of the grouper family and it's the best-looking fish we catch all day, not that looks count.

Hand lining looks easy but it's a technique that takes time to master. The boys are pulling them up like they are going out of fashion and I am losing them at the same pace. They catch job fish, snapper and emperor fish. Hassan gives me a quick tutorial: 'If you lift [the line] quickly then [the fish] will know it's a trap, so you have to lift it slowly.' His words of wisdom work. I casually pull up the bait and bam! I get a second bite. As I wind in the line with my hands, the fish fights and the nylon tears into my skin. I think Hassan wants me to have 'dhow lines' on my hands as marks of honour so that I can look at the scars in years to come and remember this incredible day. I ignore the burning and concentrate on winning the battle.

'It's a grouper! I have always wanted to catch one of these!'

It's the biggest fish of the day and in my opinion the second-finest-tasting fish on the planet, after haddock. Its Ancient Greek name is *Epinephelus lanceolatus* (*epinephelos* meaning 'clouds') and its striking brown and grey markings do make it look as though it's reflecting the altocumulus clouds in the sky above. This fish with clouds on will bring a good price at the market, and in all we have eighteen of them. We later sell them on the beach to the locals for the going rate: 400 shillings a fish (under £3). It's a good day's work – my dad would be proud that I'd done at least one decent day's graft with scars to prove it.

Tana River Delta

I cannot believe the pilot of our plane, Gary Cullen, is best mates with the headmaster of my son's school! The clichés gush out of my mouth: 'It's such a small world, Gary. I mean, here we are on the way to the Tana Delta talking about people in Surrey! Unbelievable.'

The crew groan and stick their earplugs in. They think I'm such a twat today. Sod them. I natter away and Gary asks if I would like to have a go at flying. Would I? Would I? I smile from ear to ear: 'I have always wanted to be a pilot but I didn't have the aptitude skills or leadership qualities to join the Royal Air Force.' I once had to take five guys to a river with three planks and rope to build a bridge to cross it. The way I constructed the bridge ensured all five lads were swept away, with me standing on the bank wondering what to do next. We also had to lay a minefield, but first of all I didn't ask if any of the guys had done it before, which is a glaringly obvious mistake as one was an expert. Secondly, I didn't work out that it would be best to place all the mines on top of the ground before we dug them in and risked detonating them while trying to plant the others.

After a quick lesson, I take us to 11,000 feet. The Tana Delta is stunning from above: this is where the sea comes inland and forms an estuary and hundreds of little tributaries that bleed off it. I am reluctant to give the controls back to Gary but he insists on landing the plane, apparently because it's windy, we're landing on a sandy beach and, er, I've never done it before.

The crew still think I'm a twat: 'Oh, my God, I can't believe you know John Whatshisface. Such a small world,' they mimic.

We have dinner and go to bed. My room, a very smart colonial jungle tent, has no walls and 360 degrees of views and fresh air. There are only mosquito nets to protect me, which won't help against lions, hippos and other big beasts. I don't sleep a wink with all the wildlife noises, particularly the hippopotami feeding nearby. One of the most dangerous animals in the world, and the most dangerous mammal in Africa, it's not a beast you want to piss off – but in only a matter of hours I will be casting a small bait fish over a pod of hippos' heads and landing it into their dung in the hope of catching a larger fish. No, I haven't been drinking: that's my brief and I can hardly digest it myself and nor, from the sound of it, can the hippos. It's like a cacophony of dishwashers on drainage cycle.

As the sun rises we head off in a 4x4 with my guide, Keke, to a tiny village on Tana River. Here we're meeting the fishermen who risk their lives every day because of how and where they fish. It's the first time I've been on a fishing trip with a chap carrying a .303 rifle. Sporting an army green shirt, trousers and a kufi cap, this geezer looks the business. We walk in single file along the bank of one of the thousands of tributaries in the Delta and scramble down the sides to the water's edge. Five metres in front of me is a pod of hippos trying to wallow, snooze and defecate in peace. Bait fish like nothing more than chomping on hippo poo and where there are bait fish, there are predators. I cast a line as near to the pod as possible. This is extreme hippo-poo fishing. Only in Africa; only on this show.

I have to admit I am more than a little cynical, but as I bring the line in by hand I have a take. It's a small red snapper but I am happy. I ask Keke what 'beautiful fish' is in Swahili.

'Samaki Mazuri,' he says, grinning at the size of it.

Well, he can laugh but four hours later it's the only fish we have and I am more likely to be bored to death than gored to death. I spy a man in a dugout canoe catching loads, so I decide to ditch my two losers and hang out with him. Call me fickle.

Swab and his son take us upriver in their battered canoe to a secret location supposed to be full of fish, and most importantly away from hippos – the temperature is rising and they're becoming agitated. As we pass by, two of them scramble to their feet looking menacing, while the others scatter and dive under the water. I conclude that I'd prefer to watch them from the bank, not a canoe. The sun is baking and the chance of catching a fish remote. My gut instinct is to call it a day but Swab sets out crab lines – in my experience shrimp and crabs are always a last resort of a contributor. Well, after all the faffing about with poo and hippos we end up with one tiny crab, which looks like something I pulled out of a rock pool in Seahouses aged seven, a small bream and a red snapper. I cook them on the fire and eat them with all the other poo fishermen. It's a poo-tiful scene.

Lake Victoria

Gary's back and he's taking us inland to Lake Victoria, the second-largest freshwater lake in the world and bigger than Wales. However, this time I'm allowed nowhere near the controls of the plane. When the production company, IWC Media, found out I'd flown, they went ballistic.

'You are not insured. We are not amused,' said Hamish.

All the crew got into trouble so I am straightjacketed onto the plane and seated at the back, where I can't touch anything. The fact that I had always wanted to be a pilot isn't a good enough excuse to bend the health and safety rules in IWC's eyes, the killjoys.

After one aborted landing owing to a cow on the 'runway', we touchdown on a bumpy field where kids are playing football. When we've all coughed our tongues up, we head by boat to Mfangano Island in the middle of Lake Victoria.

Local fisherman Gilbert is waiting to meet us. He is a charming man with a kind manner. He welcomes us to his fishing village, which comprises square mud-and-wood huts with crude corrugated roofs. Children run around naked at the water's edge as mothers wash their clothes and cooking pots. Men busy themselves with carpentry and repairing boats ready for tonight's fishing. The lifeblood of the island is omena fish (think whitebait), which the locals catch and sell on the mainland.

As we set foot onto land, the little children rush over to greet us. Scores of them appear from nowhere and I high-five to greet them. It quickly becomes apparent that there are many more kids on the island than grown-ups, as many of these youngsters' parents have been casualties of the AIDS epidemic. According to Kenya's National AIDS Control Council, there are around 1.5–1.7 million people living with HIV out of a population of 43 million. It's eye-opening to see the effects of the disease so clearly here; in some cases grandparents are looking after twenty children.

I have a few hours to kill so I teach the kids the *Extreme Fishing* mime, where you cross your arms in an X, cast out a line and reel in the fish. It's become shorthand for the show and we are beginning to use it in the opening title sequences more and more.

Gilbert asks if I'm hungry and the crew nod their heads eagerly. He takes us to meet a lady called Paulina in the woods behind the village. She is dressed in a black and white patterned dress and a headscarf tied at the back to keep the sun off. She is waving a big cake bowl around her head, humming a tune, surrounded by a cloud of flies attracted by the resonance. Inside the bowl is a gloopy mixture that the flies stick to. These flies are the other main source of food on the island; they contain seven times more protein than steak. They might not taste as good as Aberdeen Angus but they will keep you alive. I have a go at catching some. Paulina giggles as I hum and do something akin to the 'Agadoo' dance – I could do a song from my own album but that might put them off. I have millions of flies in my face but none in the yellow bowl I'm waving around. I waft it about my head a bit more and look inside: 'I've got three!' But I need a plateful and it could take all night.

Luckily this is a TV show so, in the best tradition of TV chefs, Paulina produces a few thousand she's caught earlier. Who the hell discovered this technique and then decided to make fly burgers out of the paste? It's ingenious but all I can say is that they must have been really sick of fish. Paulina poaches the paste in milk – it looks like two mud balls and smells like acrid green meat. However, the kids love it. It's their version of M&Ms and they queue up excitedly for some.

It tastes like it smells but certain situations call for a swallow, especially in the presence of such a kind lady. Her love for the children is humbling. I discover that she is in her late fifties and is looking after sixteen kids on her own. Her selflessness, warmth and goodness make her a privilege to meet. We all fall in love with Paulina.

As we start to prepare to film the next sequence, night fishing for omena, a massive storm comes out of nowhere.

Gilbert says, 'We need to take cover – it's a bad storm.'

There is a bit of wind, the clouds turn black and within sixty seconds a hurricane hits. I've never experienced anything like it. It's quick, violent and like being mugged by Mother Nature. We run to a hut; the rain is pouring down, the wind thrashing us. We cover our heads and leg it. One by one we enter the hut. There is a thud, like a melon being split open with an axe. Alistair has smacked his head into the edge of the corrugated roof and is on the ground. We get him inside where we see the blood is pumping down his face like a waterfall. Everyone is panicking trying to keep the claret in the bottle. It's a deep diagonal gash across his skull – three inches long and an inch across. Alistair is in a blind panic; the more worked up he gets, the more blood he's losing. I want to slap him.

'Alistair, calm down. You're going to be fine.'

His eyes are haunted by an accident he had in 1991, when he was dragged under a car as it screeched to a stop over about fifty metres, subsequently trapping him under it. His bald head still bears the physical scars from that terrifying incident and now he's suffering the mental fallout. His heart rate is in overdrive. I use my shirt to stop the bleeding and pinch the wound together with my fingers. Craig finds a small first-aid kit in his camera bag and I grab the iodine.

'Right, Alistair, I need you to bring your breathing down. This is going to hurt but you need to breathe through it.'

Donning the latex gloves, I pour iodine into the wound. He whimpers and hums. I tell him to stop humming or he'll attract the flies and he raises a smile. We clean the wound with water and sterile dressings, then I cut a dozen thin strips of gaffer tape and begin to pull the wound together with the tape. It's a crude method of butterfly stitching but all I can say is thank God I played Jimmy the Porter in *Casualty*.

Alessandra gets on the satellite phone to Helen. She is amazing, and a flying doctor arrives within the hour. The doctor stitches Alistair up properly and he tells us that whoever taped the wound up was a genius who saved Alistair's life. I push past Craig and Peter and tell him it was me. He shakes my hand. Peter and Craig groan. The doctor tells Alistair he must rest and there is no way he can film the night sequence. Alistair is really upset and frustrated, and reluctantly we take him back to the hotel. On the way back, the Machiavelli in me rears his head – if Alistair's out of action this could be my directorial debut, my chance to be an actor/director like Tim Robbins, Kenneth Branagh or Mel Gibson. As Mel would say: 'If any of you have a bleeping problem with that I'll put you in a bleeping rose garden. But you have to bleep me first. I deserve to be bleeped first!'

All this megalomania is clouding my mind. I check on Alistair, like Macbeth on Duncan. He's in bed. He feels OK now and he wants to get up. I push him back down and put another pillow behind his head. He doesn't want to be mothered, he wants to direct.

'Alistair, you're badly injured. We'll be fine without you. Besides, I've been asked to direct before.'

'What?'

'*Doctors.*'

'*Doctors*? That shitty BBC excuse for a drama?'

Alistair sits up energetically. I push him down again firmly and walk over to the bathroom, returning with a hand mirror.

'Look at the size of your head!' I say dramatically. I show him the close-up.

'Oh, my God,' he whimpers.

'You look like one of the waiters in Cabbages and Condoms – you can't direct a night-fishing sequence looking like that, can you?'

'No,' he says, sinking under the duvet.

I tuck him in extra tightly so he can barely move. In my room I don a red cravat, select a Montecristo No. 2 from the thermidor, and I am ready for my directorial debut. I summon the crew together for a pep talk.

'OK, guys, this is how I see it.' I give them the vision. Four guys from the village are standing in front of me looking bewildered, while Gilbert translates. Peter thinks I've been chewing khat.

'The opening shot is of Gilbert, the fishermen and me heading off into the night. It's a beautiful balmy night and the stars are shining. Everything is perfect.'

Craig sets the camera up on the shore and I jump in the boat and we head out into the lake. We quickly lose sight of Craig and the crew. It's pitch-black on the lake and the only way the fishermen know where they are is by looking at where they've come from. It's Irish GPS. We wait for the crew to catch up and I call out their names, impatiently. Nothing. I get out my mobile.

'Craig? Where are you?'

'Waiting on the bank, watching you fuck off into the night.'

'You're meant to be following in the other boat.'

'You didn't say that.'

I apologise to Gilbert and the fishermen as we row back to shore. I'm well aware they have livings to make and, although we do pay all contributors, we like them to still carry on with their livelihoods where possible. I call a meeting but there is immediate dissent in the ranks.

'Let's talk to one another, work as a team and direct this sequence together,' says Craig.

I want to throw a boot at his head, like Ferguson did to Beckham, but I stay quiet. We row out again and crack on with the fishing. We're floating lamps on the water to attract flies that are snapped up as tasty snacks by the omena fish.

'Craig, I want you to film this sequence in a serendipitous way.'

'What the fuck does that mean?'

'Don't force it, just let it happen.'

'Where do you want me to point the camera, Robson?'

'At the fish, Craig.'

As we wait for the lamps to be surrounded by fish, the Kenyans sing a song, 'Naru naru'. I join in.

'Film it, Craig.'

'What does it mean?'

'I don't know, my Swahili's a bit rusty. How's your Maori?'

I sing the Northumberland folk song 'When the Boat Comes In'. It seems to go down well.

Fish begin to surround the first lamp. The throwers lower the nets off the side of the boat and the rowers, like me, paddle like crazy to encircle the fish. If our rowing is too slow the fish will escape. When we've rounded them up, we haul them in. It's back-breaking work and we won't know until the last moment if it's been worth it. We have a football-sized haul of omena, known as silver treasure by the islanders. They usually get thirty or forty times that in a ten-hour period and it's taken us five hours to film one cast. Not a big haul and worth about a quid.

We send the fishermen on their way so they can claw back some of the lost time. They will go from lamp to lamp for hours to catch enough to feed the village and make some money. Alistair is on the shore waiting for us. He is very irritable and feeling sorry for himself. We all tell him it went really well.

'One of the best sequences of the series,' adds Peter Prada.

Black Marlin

Alistair is much better the next day and there is no way on God's earth he is going to miss the black marlin sequence. We fly back to Watamu and are back on a big white flashy sports boat, with our new Kenyan fishing guide Jackson at the helm.

'Are you confident we'll catch today?'

'Why not?' he says in his rich-treacle voice.

'Exactly, why not?'

'Why not?'

The exchange continues thus for some time.

We're heading for Sailfish Alley, where I caught my dorado. Jackson and I set three rods, cast the lines and trawl them behind the boat. We're looking for bonitos with small squid lures, and within forty-five seconds a reel starts screaming like a small child: Waha! Waha! The line keeps going out and out and out. A bonito wouldn't take a line like that. Jackson and I look at each other. We've got a black marlin on forty-pound test line. No one's ready and the tackle's way too light: the density of a marlin leader line is 150 to 200 pounds breaking strain. I have to make a decision. Do I hard-play the fish and snap the line? (The problem being that the type of hook for bait fish isn't dissolvable – although the theory is that nature will take care of it and it will eventually come out like a splinter.) Or do I try to land this fish on tackle meant for a fish a third of the size? As I'm mulling it over the marlin blows out of the water like a missile. Craig misses the shot. We've all been caught on the back foot.

For the next two hours I play the fish and let the marlin run and run until he tires. I get the fish close to the boat for over an hour, but then it turns tail and I have to start all over again. It's a titanic battle that, slowly, I'm beginning to win. I bring the marlin back towards the boat while Craig puts the underwater camera beneath the waves to film the vast fish. It's a large male. Females are up to three times bigger.

To count as a catch I need to get as much tension on the line as possible so that Jackson is able to get hold of the leader (the last bit of line). I reel with all my might until the black marlin rises like a submarine. I can see the leader. Jackson puts a glove on and 'bills the fish', grabbing its lethal bill to make it safe. Just as he's about to get hold of the last bit of line to confirm a catch, the fish turns and bolts. The bill flicks Jackson into the air and he bombs into the water behind the boat.

'Jackson! Jackson!' We all shout helpful advice from the side: 'Don't thrash!' 'Get back on!' It is very telling that no one contemplates jumping in. He leaps back on board. I am freaking out but Jackson is calm.

'Let's carry on,' he says.

After nearly two hours he gets his hand on the leader again and I have caught a *Makaira indica*. Jackson tags the marlin to monitor migration patterns, removes the hook and then releases the giant, as heavy as a racehorse, back into the blue. He sends up the black flag so that everyone can see I caught a black marlin today.

My knees are buggered, my back's broken, but what a hit of pure adrenalin. I am in a state of manic elation. My pulse is racing, my breathing is short. I don't want it to end. I don't want to go back. But I have to.

'Hakuna Matata, Jackson.' I say, slapping him on the back. It loosely means 'Don't worry, be happy' in Swahili.

'Why not!' exclaims Jackson.

Chapter Nine

BRAZIL

The Big, the Bad and Arianna

November 2009, World Tour, Series 3

The Amazon River is so vast I can see it from 38,000 feet in the air. This freshwater system is home to over 5,600 known species of fish, possibly even accounting for 60 per cent of the fish reported to exist on the planet. Many species remain undiscovered, such is the complex network of tributaries that branch off the world's second-longest river, after the Nile. And I am going deep into the dense jungle in search of three legendary denizens – the piranha, the arowana and the arapaima. Coming with me are three other monsters of the deep: Craig, Peter and sadistic director Jamie.

We board a flight to Manaus and head deep into the planet's lungs, the Amazon rainforest. Amazonia comprises 40 per cent of the world's remaining rainforest, which filters carbon dioxide and pollutants out of the atmosphere. It's our medicine cabinet, and one of the most bio-diverse places on Earth, home to extraordinary creatures and plant life that we are only just beginning to discover. Scientists believe that less than 1 per cent of plant species have been identified. I am rattling with facts and swept up by the ecology, so it seems strange to be setting foot into a huge city slap-bang in the middle of the rainforest.

Manaus, which means 'Mother of Gods', is home to 1.5 million inhabitants and was created in the late 1800s by wealthy businessmen in the rubber boom. Latex was discovered in the sap of the rubber tree and you don't need me to tell you how revolutionary the natural material has been to all our lives: fewer babies and nicer cars. It's an ornate city and I only need to look at the opera house, Teatro Amazonas, to comprehend the opulence of the rubber magnates. It's quite beautiful in an over-the-top neo-Classical fashion. We walk into the main auditorium, where the Manaus Philharmonic Orchestra happens to be rehearsing the *Bolero* (think Torvill and Dean). It's hard to get my head round the fact I am in the middle of a theatre, in the middle of Manaus, in the middle of the Amazon rainforest.

Outside it's seriously hot and the humidity is 100 per cent. After looking round the opera house we drive to our hotel, which is again very ornate in its décor – even the tea-making kit in the room is very proper, with fine bone china cups and saucers and hand-painted tea caddies. It's a reminder of how things were during the boom times before the inevitable bust, when the British Flashman type Sir Henry Wickham smuggled rubber seeds out of the country and used them to cultivate plantations in Malaysia and Sri Lanka. Thus the British Empire took control of the rubber market and the barons in Manaus faced financial ruin.

I'm feeling rather Flashy today. Full of the yearning for adventure, full of bluster, and trying to keep the inner coward under lockdown until it's strictly necessary to run. The china teacup rattles in the saucer as I take it over to the window. I look out over the city and at the green canopy beyond but it's no good: I really don't feel in the mood for piranha fishing. Jamie bangs on my door. It's time.

Piranha 3D

Waiting for me at Lake Balbina, as well as the legendary shredding machines, is a man with a round face, grey hair, a handlebar moustache, not to mention moobs and a tummy to rival the average darts player. I choke when he says his name: 'Tarzan? Like the bronzed hunk who swung through the jungle?'

'Yes, Tarzan,' he beams.

He looks more like Bernie Winters to me.

I set out with Tarzan in his boat, and, no, he doesn't have a wife called Jane nor a chimpanzee – I did check. Balbina is an artificial lake created by flooding part of the forest in order to provide hydroelectric power to the city of Manaus. It's an eerie place. We quietly meander through lifeless trees sticking out of the water, haunting and rigid, as if marking the spot of a horrendous atrocity or meteoric event. The water is jet-black, and there is silence. The lack of wildlife or any life whatsoever makes what is below all the more menacing. We continue to gently motor in between the ghostly pale trees. It is a vast lake and I ask Tarzan how he finds his way back. He says he orientates by the trees – he knows and recognises them. Some look like pillars of salt.

We sail for forty-five minutes, more than enough time to let my imagination run away with me. We are after red-bellied piranha (*Pygocentrus nattereri*), the one species (out of approximately twenty in the region) that has a particularly vicious streak and has attacked humans on several well-documented occasions.

'If I swim naked, will they strip me to the bone, Tarzan?' I ask with wild eyes.

He tells me it's doubtful. Apparently, in order to attract the fish, you have to be bleeding profusely or have a chunk of flesh hanging off.

'Blood in the water excites them to madness,' wrote President Theodore Roosevelt in *Through the Brazilian Wilderness*, the account of his epic trip to Amazonia in 1913 with his son Kermit (I kid you not, he shared a name with the world's most famous frog). To test the theory, some local fisherman blocked off part of the river for several days to starve a school of piranha. They then pushed a cow into the river (quite possibly with an injury they inflicted beforehand) and observed as the ravenous piranhas tore the poor beast apart in a state of frenzy. I wonder what Roosevelt's holiday snaps looked like.

I certainly wasn't going to put my feet in to test the blood-excitement theory on the bunch of marauding meatheads below. I'd already tried a fish pedicure in the Philippines and I'm not up for trying the piranha version, particularly as I have athlete's foot. According to some experts, if the fish are hungry enough a fungal foot infection or a pimple on your leg is all it takes to become skeletal in seconds.

Tarzan places a big chunk of raw meat on a ruddy great hook, considering the size of the fish. The leader is wire. I've never used one before and it's bringing home how deadly their teeth are. These fish can grow to up to eight pounds with gnashers to match. They can cut through wood and leave bite marks in metal, so it's no wonder their teeth and jaws were used by Amazon tribesmen for hunting tools. I cast the bait by the side of the boat and lower the meat to twenty feet. Tarzan splashes the water to mimic the sound of a struggling fish … or actor. Bam! Thirty seconds and I think there's a take. It's a split-second sensation. I bring the hook up – all the meat is gone.

'That was like a hit and run!'

No fish comes close to the pace of the piranha so all I can do is hope that when the fish strikes the bait, it will take the hook with it. This is a matter of luck, not skill. Over the next ten minutes I experience some violent takes, the line twitches, the rod is yanked frequently up and down, up and down, in a matter of milliseconds, and each time there is neither meat nor a fish on the end of the line. After another strike I reel in half the bait; it looks as if it has been carefully sliced by a surgeon's hand. It must be terrifying to be a bait fish down there – like a permanent *Saw* movie. You pop out in morning to get the papers and wham! You're a toothpick in a matter of seconds.

Tarzan tells me I will catch a piranha after fifteen minutes. He's dead right: I carefully reel in the piscatorial pitbull and take a look. I let Mike hold the piranha first. The red-bellied fella is short, stubby and compressed with a jaw area packed with razor-wire teeth, the type that would keep trespassers out of a military camp or a top secret nuclear facility, all tightly packed and interlocking to puncture and shred their prey. I put a knife between the fish's teeth and it clamps down hard. I remove it and show the scratches to camera. It's my turn to hold this fish and it's a bit like trying to pet a rabid dog. I take hold of it by the caudal peduncle, the narrow part of the posterior end towards the tail fin, where there are fewer spines and more importantly fewer teeth. Its armoury is all at the anterior end (front).

We catch a total of four piranhas and grill them back on land. It's definitely a fish you don't associate with eating, more with *being* eaten, but they taste very good, with a surprisingly delicate white meat. I'm not sure if the taste measures up to the risk, however.

Fish Market

The next morning, at 4 a.m., we go to the bustling local fish market in Manaus to introduce ourselves to the other ferocious predators we are hoping to meet on this adventure. The market is on banks of the Rio Negro (Black River) and is alive with fish, fish sellers and the ugliest transvestites in the business, still plying their trade. It is a case of fish and very foul. Honestly, these two blokes are so hideous they look like Harry Redknapp and Avram Grant in wigs and thongs. Think about that for a moment, then add the smell of fish! It is wrong on so many levels. The gathering crowds jeer and shout as they pass through.

As well as the trannies on display, there are catfish, piranha, peacock bass, arowana and arapaima (like the one I caught at IT Lake in Thailand, known locally as pirarucu), one of the largest freshwater fish in the world and the largest in the Amazon basin. I examine the serpent-like fish. She is nightmarish in her looks and proportions but perversely I still want to pull one ... out of the river. She is an air-breather and has a lung-like labyrinth organ that allows her to survive in oxygen-deficient oxbow lakes or even in mud, in times of drought. A fearsome predator, she uses her bony tongue to crush her quarry against the roof of her mouth, be it fish or foul, she's not fussy.

And, by the looks of it, neither are some of the men from Manaus, as the trannies trot past again. They want to be on camera and start peering over my shoulder. Another bloke wants to sell me an armour-plated catfish. I don't want an armour-plated catfish but he's desperate to be on TV. We turn away from him and move off. Undeterred, he runs after us, sticks a live fish in his mouth and does a dance, the tail still swishing. He makes the cut in the final edit; it's too weird to miss. Perhaps he could be a contender for *Brazil's Got Talent*? It beats the dancing dog act.

Rainforest Digs

As if the market wasn't strange enough, we are booked into a Fawlty Towers, Amazon-style. To get there we head up the Rio Negro for two hours by boat. The Rio Negro is one of the biggest of the Amazonian tributaries and the largest blackwater river in the world. Blackwater rivers are coloured like strong Yorkshire tea by all the tannins leaching into the water from decaying vegetation. I look across to the horizon and cannot see the other side of the river. It looks like a dark, foreboding sea.

As we arrive at the rainforest hotel, we see pink river dolphins leaping alongside of the boat. It's a heart-warming sight and I wish Taylor could be here to see them. Maybe I'll take him swimming with them one day. I catch Jamie staring at me. His eyes flicker with the flame of a cunning plan. I shake my head – me and them in the drink together, no way. He nods with a sadistic smile. Thankfully we don't have time in the schedule.

We jump off the boat and hike our bags and equipment up to our mad eco-hotel on stilts. At the moment the river is really low but during the rainy season it can rise up to sixty feet. We march across the treetop platform to reception and there to greet us is a woman who could have been out of Papa Lazarou's circus. Except I don't want her to be 'my wife now', with her coconut-encased boobs, headdress made of green and purple crêpe paper, feathers and all sorts of nonsense going on around her lady parts. She howls 'Welcome!', puts a necklace on me and wants a photo. Bewildered, I am shown to my room. It's as I suspected: the accommodation is exactly like our coconut-clad hostess, a bit strange and definitely past its best.

Peacock Bass

The man who is taking me peacock bass fishing this afternoon is Mike Cartwright, who looks a bit like Tarzan, heavy-set with a grey moustache, except Mike's wearing specs on a cord and a crazy camo T-shirt with a metal chain around his neck. He could be the ageing MC Hammer in a *Never Mind the Buzzcocks* line-up.

We hop into a fifteen-foot fishing boat with a basic prop engine and head a couple of miles upriver to some deserted islands. My tummy begins to gurgle and churn. I inwardly hope it's not the prelude of some dire Amazonian tummy bug.

I ask Mike about his name: 'Mike Cartwright doesn't sound South American.'

'I'm from British Guiana,' he explains, referring to his country (now Guyana) by its old colonial name, as if to help me place it.

'What brought you to Brazil?'

'A messy divorce.'

My tummy growls again, but thankfully Mike can't hear it over the noise of the boat.

'Ah, divorce,' I say, knowing one or two things about the topic.

'The Latin word meaning "to rip out a man's genitals through his wallet".'

He chuckles, but his doleful eyes do not share the same merriment.

Mike tells me that, pound for pound, peacock bass is one the most powerful fighting fish in the world. The impact on the lure or bait is superlative.

'I heard that the greatest fighting fish is the Papua New Guinean black bass,' I say, my stomach making a loud noise like an industrial drain.

'No, the peacock bass is incredible,' Mike assures me.

Because the water level is low we are going to trawl for tucanaré, as peacock bass are known here in Brazil. Lower water levels mean the fish tend to congregate together in a much smaller area. We are using man-made lures (rapala) that replicate a distressed bait fish. Mike sets four rods. We trawl and cast for hours in the blistering heat and catch ... nothing. We've brought no umbrellas to shade us and my tummy is now spasming. I let a silent one go and realise that I'm about to follow through. Help!

'Jamie, I desperately need to go to the toilet!'

We head to the riverbank but nature doesn't wait and I am humiliatingly forced to let the hydrant gush over the side of the boat. The more I go, the more dehydrated I am becoming and I'm starting to get in a bad way. Jamie announces, in his typical tyrannical fashion, that we have to catch a peacock bass today because not only is it an iconic fish but also they have spent a great deal of money on the steamboat accommodation, which we are travelling on to Jaraua for our next assignment.

Hours later and I finally catch a very small peacock bass, but I return him to the water as he is too small. Jamie announces a new plan: 'We will stay another night at the crazy rainforest hotel and will fish again tomorrow morning, starting at four a.m.'

We are all pretty miserable about this but Mike's face looks like he's back in touch with his ex. Obviously not an early riser, then. On the positive side, at least we're going to call it a day: I need to get to my bathroom and fast. I am about to step out of the boat when Jamie puts his hand out to stop me: 'Wait. I know you're ill, stressed and in need of a little relaxation. I have a surprise for you.'

I immediately know it's not a spa treatment.

'It's the bloody dolphins, isn't it?'

'Yep.'

As luck would have it Mike knows just the place for me to swim with dolphins at sunset. And, what's more, his friend Igor Andradis is an expert who specialises in pink river dolphins and their behaviour. Igor tells me he has such an amazing way with these creatures that if he calls them they come to him. Well, most animals would if you wave a big bucket of sardines in their face. Unfortunately, I am blissfully unaware that Igor a) isn't a marine biologist and b) has been feeding the dolphins swimming in front of us. I hang off his every word.

'Are you sure it's safe to swim here? What about piranha, caiman or other predators?'

'Trust me, it's fine. No one has ever come to any harm,' he says.

'In you get,' says Jamie. My tummy groans, mimicking my emotions. I could really do with giving this experience a miss. I dive in wearing my pants and shirt. I wish I had worn trousers.

Everyone says swimming with dolphins is a once-in-a-lifetime experience and it probably is if you don't have Igor throwing sardines and sending them into a feeding frenzy with me in the middle. They thrash the water, violently butting me out of the way. One nuts me square on in the chest; it's like being at a Newcastle game with my dad. Another takes a bite at my leg. Referee! He nips my thigh and his friend leaps at me again, so I take a swing and bash him on the pecker. This is supposed to be a life-affirming experience with gentle creatures that heal your soul, but they're more like a bunch of Sunderland supporters. But then again, I can't entirely blame them for wanting to take a pop at me – it's like someone crashing your Sunday lunch and jumping up and down on your Yorkshires. If someone did that to me I'd butt them in the chest, too.

I am furious with Igor and Jamie. I want to kill both of them. What fucking expert puts someone in the water with a bunch of dolphins at feeding time? Haven't I learnt anything from making this show? Never trust a contributor who says they're 'an expert' when they blatantly are not. It's like a bloke who feeds ducks in the park sometimes calling himself an ornithologist. Jamie loves the commotion – 'It's TV gold, Robson. TV gold!' – and my vanity perks up. I waterboard her into submission and refocus on being angry. However, my ire doesn't last long – my bottom is in charge once more. I leg it back to the hotel.

Countless explosions later I drown my sorrows in a bottle of wine. It's going down so well that I have another few glasses. The crew joins me, then I remember I have to be up at 3 a.m. to film at 4 a.m. and it's now 11 p.m. I sink another glass and stagger to bed.

*

After three and half hours' sleep I feel like hell but the sunrise a few hours later is so spectacular that the lack of rest and the raging hangover evaporate. It's far better than the nitrous oxide I used to inhale on the set of *Casualty* most mornings before work. Everyone looks like a bag of shit. Mike is monosyllabic and stooped with morning grumpiness, like the troll under the bridge. We head out. We are going to find a peacock bass and we're not coming back until we have.

Three hours later we have nihil, nada, nichts. My patience is worn through, like my bottom, and the red mist starts to rise ... and wham! I get a bite, but I lose the fish. This happens several times. Finally, another flipping three hours later, I get a bite and this time I bring home the bass – it's a two-and-a-half-pound speckled peacock bass. Other subspecies include the three-bar, popoca and butterfly, which have different markings but they all share one detail in common: on their tail fin is the eye found on a peacock's feather. The theory is that predators think that's the front end and attack, and the bass is able to escape, perhaps with a damaged tail, but with his life. This speckled fish is eating size so we're going to keep him. Mike and I tuck in back at the hotel. The bass is seasoned and grilled and it tastes delicious. We're behind with the schedule, though, so after shovelling up lunch the crew and I need to get a move on to our next RV point.

Fitzcarraldo

I take one look at the steamboat and want to run. It's exactly like the one in Werner Herzog's epic movie *Fitzcarraldo*, where this mad Caruso-loving wannabe rubber baron with delusions of grandeur tries to get a steamboat over a mountain and everyone suffers or dies.

Goodspeed to all who sail in her

Jamie is morphing into Fitzcarraldo with the scale of his extreme ambition. He's not going to take me with him. This boat is meant to be our floating hotel for the next four days. I look around and it is immediately clear we have a major problem.

'Jamie, can I have a word?'

He comes over.

'I just want you to know that there is no way I am sleeping in this rat-infested, drug-smuggling, sailor-spunked-up gambling brothel on water. I wouldn't have a dog in it. It's disgusting. Even Craig agrees it's terrible and he's from New Zealand.'

Once again I get on the phone to the production manager and Helen Nightingale.

'I'm not travelling on this vessel. It's not river-worthy, for a start, and whatever's happened on this boat – let's just say I don't think they missed out a sin. The marks of all seven are here and some have been done to death.'

'But it's the only boat available in the area,' says Helen on the phone and Jamie in unison in my ear.

The captain comes to see what the commotion is about. He

couldn't look dodgier if he'd spent six hours in make-up, fraternising with Abu Hamza. And then there is Arianna. Dear, sweet Arianna, the cook who comes with the vessel – a podgy twenty-eight-year-old with a pretty face and an eagle eye for the fellas. She winks and smiles at me saucily and when that is ignored I find her staring at me, communicating with her twinkling eyes that she wants to ride me like Seabiscuit. I am not alone in this strange compliment – she wants Craig, Peter and Jamie as well. She wants us all.

Having no other choice, we set off on HMS *Shitpit*. I take the diary camera around the rooms of this floating hovel with its sweat-ridden beds, stained sheets and toilets to rival the one in *Trainspotting*. The engine is like an MRI scanner and we've got to sail five hours into the night to Jaraua. The sun is setting and I film a piece to camera: 'Well, this is as bad as it gets . . .'

Suddenly there is a klaxon. It sounds again. We all look panicked. What's happening? People are boarding the boat. Suddenly we are eyeballing half a dozen soldiers pointing large guns at us. We put our hands up and they want to know who we are, what we're doing. They want our paperwork. They arrest the captain of the boat, who is led away in handcuffs. The vessel is not seaworthy and they are not happy with his documents. We are ordered to leave the boat immediately so we grab our stuff as quickly as possible and start to pile it up on the bank. When the last of our bags are unloaded one of the soldiers pulls up the anchor and sails the boat away. Another smiles, waving.

'Welcome to Brazil!' he shouts.

We are left stranded on the riverbank, the sun setting, wondering what the hell we are going to do now.

A little way up the bank is Arianna, surrounded by all her pots, pans and utensils, which, by the way she's looking at us, she doesn't just like to use for cooking.

'I'm not going to leave you,' she says reassuringly.

She grabs my hand roughly and looks at it: 'Are you married?'

'Yes, happily.'

'Cabrão. Cabrão!'

'What?'

'I believe it's Portuguese for bastard,' says Peter coolly.

I can't confirm this as our translator, Alessandra, is tucked up in a hotel in Manaus because Helen Nightingale doesn't think a boat, with all us boys, is the right place for a young lady. Looking at Arianna we all strongly disagree – we need her here to protect us.

Jamie is straight on the satellite phone to Alessandra to work out a way of getting to our destination. But Craig, Peter and I have other ideas of getting the fuck back to Manaus and hitting the bar. Eventually we get the fixer to rustle up a tiny speedboat with a local from Manaus who can navigate us up the Amazon at night to our destination. So the whole team, along with psycho Arianna, who keeps asking me to take my wedding ring off, head into the night, embarking on a seven-hour journey to Jaraua.

São Raimundo do Jaraua, Mamirauá

We arrive at the Jaraua Reserve in the pitch-black. Our first concern is where are we going to sleep? A kind lady vacates her hut on stilts and the whole team piles in, proceeding to install hammocks so we can swing ourselves to sleep. This will be our abode for the next four nights. Five blokes snoring, farting, gurgling, dreaming, fidgeting, and all acutely aware that Arianna could jump us at any moment.

Arianna is really pissed off she can't share the same hut as us and she's not going to bed without a protest: 'She is cold and lonely in her hut.' We ignore her and slowly all drift off to sleep when suddenly I become aware of a warm sensation by my ear.

'I can't sleep. Can you?' Arianna whispers seductively.

'I could until you woke me up. Go back to your hut, Arianna.'

'Come with me, Robson.'

'No,' I say, turning my back on her as best I can in a swinging hammock. Silence descends once more.

'Jamie?' she mummers.

'Mmmn?'

'I can't sleep.'

The whole hut is now awake.

'Go away, Arianna – bugger off!' we grumble collectively.

The next morning, after little rest because of Arianna going bump in the night, we try to film our first sequence: my counterfeit arrival in the village. I step off a small boat looking like a sexually molested hobo in desperate need of lager and therapy.

'There's no one here. I wonder where everyone is?' I say.

Well, I know bloody well where all the men are: they've gone out fishing and we've missed them because we overslept. Unable to have the meet-and-greet he planned for, Jamie decides to see what the local Jaraua women are up to, and that's when we discover a scene given by God. They are playing football, of course, and Jamie asks me to join in their game. They are happy for me to do so and I need no encouragement. The girls are lovely and fit, with a kick like a frigging mule. I run round trying to play like a professional: I fall dramatically at tackles, call for the referee and run around with my shirt over my head – well, that's what the paid ones do. I pass the ball to a very cute Amazonian lass and she fucking belts it into the back of the net.

'GOAL!' I jump around hysterically inviting us all to hug and kiss but there are no takers and with the way I'm behaving there is no way I'm going to score! Arianna watches from a distant hut, arms folded like a jealous wife. She stomps inside and continues to poison our lunch.

Eventually a few guys return from their morning's fishing, including father-and-son team Fernando and Juma. Fernando, I'm told, is sixty-five but has the body of a ripped thirty-year-old gymnast. Juma is charismatic and good-looking and, I've heard, the best fisherman in the village. I hate him. Our objective is to catch tea for Fernando's wife Alija so she can cook and feed her family. Thank God Juma is with us, then, because by the way I look and feel there is no way I could catch supper on my own.

We set off in search of a Jaraua favourite: the silver arowana. The Japurà River channel is bustling with activity. The waters are alive with small fish feeding – I've never seen so many – and we all know that small fish signify predators. As we hum up the waterway, I see black caiman, alligators that can grow up to fifteen feet long. In front of us, a 500-strong congregation of white egrets takes flight, cormorants dive for fish, a barrel of squirrel monkeys call in the trees, and a wake of black vultures on the banks inter the remains of a dead animal into their lead-lined stomachs.

I am busy observing one snapshot of nature and missing the next – there is so much to see. In front of the boat there are thousands of small fish jumping out of the river, splashing back down like an ornate fountain. They are only a couple of inches long but can leap about five to ten feet and some land in the boat. I pick one up; it's iridescent silver and gold. Fernando suggests they are escaping predators but he doesn't know what they are called and neither do I. (Possibly marbled hatchetfish – answers on a postcard, please.) I go to put the little chap and the other fliers back in the water.

'No! For the soup!' says Fernando, preventing me.

However, these small acrobats pale into insignificance when compared to the mighty flying fish of the Amazon, the arowana. This fish loves to leap out of the water to devour insects. It is a long, silvery compressed fish with a strange oblique mouth and a large gape to swallow its prey. Fernando drops anchor and we start to roll out a gillnet, vertical walls of netting set across the Japurà. We are working in tandem with men in smaller boats a quarter of a mile upstream, who act as beaters, driving the fish down towards the nets like driven pheasant across the line of guns. When our net's in place they slam their paddles on the water to flush the fish towards our trap. Within minutes the gill-net starts twitching and I haul up half a dozen silver arowana. I pick one up; it's an extraordinary-looking fish with the power to fling itself two feet out of the water. And what a mouth! It's like the top of a pedal bin. It reminds me of Janet Street-Porter – only this must be her cute little sister!

The arowana is classified as *Osteoglossum bicirrhosum*. In Ancient Greek *osteoglossum* means 'bone-tongued' and *bicirrhosum* means 'two barbels', which are found under its lower lip like a couple of Rasta dreadlocks. These are thought to house the taste buds of the fish to help them search for food in the murky water. The arowana, like the arapaima, crushes its quarry with its bony tongue to eat it . . . I'm thinking Janet S-P again.

Fernando and Juma are working together in unspoken short-hand, gathering in the fish and re-laying the net. I help where I can but am conscious not to interrupt their synergy.

After a long and fruitful day out fishing, we return to the village. Aliga cooks the arowana over an open fire and Fernando, Juma and his younger brothers and sisters, the crew and I sit down to eat. The fish is placed in front of us, accompanied by manioc (cassava), which has been cultivated here since around 7,000 BC. The starch of this tuberous root produces tapioca. The manioc we are eating this evening is a dried powder that you stuff in your mouth, followed by a piece of fish. It has the consistency of small ball bearings in self-raising flour. I gave it a miss and delight my palate with Aliga's beautifully cooked arowana.

As the sun is setting I do a PTC explaining that the Amazon River system is not only where the villagers source their food but is also where they bathe and wash their clothes, as well as being their transport network. The river is a lifeline to these families and without it they would perish.

We finish for the evening and face another night in the hut-from-hell with an undeterred Arianna on the prowl. We take turns as lookout but we are useless: one by one we fall asleep on duty and the hut is left unguarded. Arianna makes a grab for Peter. There are swinging noises, creaking ropes, a frantic scrambling sound, followed by a primal scream.

'Get the fuck off me, you crazy woman!' yells Peter, falling out of his hammock.

He is in pain as well as shock. Arianna has squeezed both his testicles. She is frogmarched back to her shack and I am concerned: 'With all the cooking equipment she's got we could be murdered in our beds.'

'Shut up, Robson. Or I'll get the mad mare to cut yours off,' says a still-shaken Peter.

After a fitful night's sleep, disturbed mainly by a bloody cockerel that crowed from 2 a.m. onwards, we wait for breakfast. It doesn't come so we make our own. Arianna is on strike and is refusing to cook any more meals for us. What's more, she's copped off with a local Jaraua fisherman, the poor bloke. He'll need as much manioc and fish as he can physically digest to survive her wanton lust.

Pirarucu

I am determined to catch a pirarucu today to feed the village, and more importantly Arianna's poor sexually ravaged fisherman, so I set off with Jorge. One look at him and I know he's the business. He's dressed in pink trousers, a yellow cardie and a straw hat – only a tough guy could get away with that outfit. He has a kindly way about him and he finds me amusing. But I know he's thinking 'Who the hell is this guy? Bruce Parry was way better.'

This morning the village has received some good news. There is a sustainable fishing policy enforced across the reserve and a government official is here to tell the village their quota for pirarucu hasn't been caught; as a result, over the next ten days, they are allowed to catch 500. Although the government has banned commercial fishing of pirarucu, catch-and-release is permitted in certain areas of the Amazon basin and native tribes, like the Jaraua villagers, are allowed to harvest this giant on a strict quota system. Thanks to these restrictions the pirarucu's numbers are beginning to recover.

I ask Jorge, using my best mimes, where he stores the nets and fishing tackle? To my dismay I discover we are using a harpoon.

(Nets, rods and reels are just too expensive.) It's brutal but that's not why I am anxious – I was useless at javelin at school. I have never had any upper body strength. I was crap at shot put, rubbish at throwing the cricket ball but was very good as Captain Hook in the school production of *Peter Pan*. Armed with a couple of spears, Jorge and I head upriver looking for signs of the large serpent-like creature to surface and show itself. The pirarucu is an air breather and comes to the surface in a swishing motion every ten to fifteen minutes to take a gulp of air. The fish is only visible for a split second but it's enough to pinpoint and launch our harpoons. Well, that's the theory.

The temperature is nearing fifty degrees and there is no shelter. Remember, the heat is reflected off the water so it's a double whammy, and the sunscreen is applied and re-applied as it trickles off. We slowly glide along looking for signs of disturbances in the water.

SWOOSH! SWOOSH! Jorge raises his hand, indicating I need to and keep quiet as we are now in stealth mode: we have spotted our target. And there is more than one, so all we can do now is wait. Wait and stand, arm raised with the spear like a coiled spring. Waiting and standing and waiting. After three minutes my arm begins to ache.

(Loud whisper) 'Jorge, my arm is about to drop off.'

He looks at me, smiling. I see something move in the weeds so I raise my harpoon.

'Jorge, what's that?' I say dramatically, ready at any moment to deploy my weapon.

'Alligator,' he says.

'Oh.'

I'm sure poor Jorge has been told I'm an expert from Europe

and now he's discovered that I am in fact a puny, whingeing, mediocre harpoon-throwing lad from Newcastle upon Tyne. Actually he doesn't know I'm a crap harpoon thrower yet – but he will. Now I wish ex-Royal Marine Bruce Parry were here as well.

I need to lower my harpoon but Jorge signals for me to keep it raised – I only have a second to fire and if I'm not primed it'll be too late. Whoosh! To our right, about thirty yards from the boat, the fish takes a big breath like a drunk lass preparing to go into a stinky public lav, and Jorge fires his harpoon – he just misses. Seconds later after the fish has disappeared without trace, I fire. I miss, just. In fact, I'm short by about twenty-five yards. Jorge laughs. He's never seen anything so funny in his life.

'The thing is,' I try to explain in an elaborate system of arm gestures, 'I had no rehearsal for this and Jamie, that "cabrão" of a director, thought it would be a good idea not to tell me the method of fishing.'

In this moment I know for a fact that if I aimed the harpoon at Jamie I would get a flipping bullseye.

The scene of Jorge just missing and me throwing like Bridget Jones continues for hours and hours. The unrelenting heat is getting to me and so is Jorge's chuckling.

'You might be laughing at me, Jorge, and you may think my technique leaves a lot to be desired, but quite frankly, bonny lad, you've caught fuck-all as well!'

He smiles and ups the ante, starting to throw like Fatima Whitbread.

Seven hours go by and I am delirious. Jorge spots a distur- bance in the water twenty yards directly in front of the boat. He fires. It's a hit, and the rope attached to the spearhead tightens. We are in.

'You are amazing, Jorge. Simply amazing!'

Then the rope slackens and the fish is off.

'No! Jorge, no!'

The spearhead is retrieved and all that is on the end is a single scale of a giant pirarucu, equal in size to the palm of my hand. It would appear to belong to a 200-pound-plus fish. Morale is rock-bottom.

'Don't worry, Jorge. All we have to do is get the other part of the fish.' I suggest helpfully.

We spot the creature time and time again but I keep missing and finally, near to a swoon, my deltoids shot, I collapse and lie prostrate in the bottom of the boat. A passing fisherman takes pity on me and lends me his umbrella. So there I am, fanning myself like Helena Bonham Carter with a white parasol, while Hercules is primed and ready to take out the serpent. Splosh! Jorge strikes again and it's a hit! And this time the rope is running, the spearhead is secure and Jorge has a victorious expression. I can only stare in awe at the man's endurance, strength and skill.

'We did it, Jorge! We did it!'

Jorge throws me a look.

'*You* did it! *You* did it!'

The creature shows itself in the distance to be a 100-pound pirarucu. Jorge takes the rope and starts to fight the fish, trying to bring it to the side of boat. Unsure of what to do, I find a wooden club.

'Do you need this?' I enquire.

It's a veritable cardinal rather than the modest fishing priest I use to dispatch brown trout on the Coquet. He asks me to do the honours, so, raising the club, I bring it down on the fish's head with all my might. It's brutal but swift and efficient, and it's how these guys survive.

As I sail back to camp I have time to reflect on what an astonishing journey along the world's most iconic river this has been. It's been a great privileged. To top it off, the fixer has ferried in 140 cans of Skol and an electric piano out of nowhere – this river really is the giver of life. Our classically trained sound engineer, Prada, starts banging out the tunes. I sing 'Proud Mary' as Arianna gyrates in front of us, trying to show us what we've all been missing. And thank the Lord we missed it! Her fisherman beau takes her away by boat – now that truly *is* a great river.

Chapter Ten

CUBA

'The Land of the Lotus Eaters'

December 2009, World Tour, Series 3

As I lean out of the cab window taking in the sights, I am hit by the distinctive smell. It reminds me of when I was on holiday as a kid in Binibeca, Spain – the smell of baked terracotta in the warm air, only this time mixed with the savoury smoke of cigars. I inhale deeply. Havana is alive with colour: the faded colonial architecture, the fabulous 1950s cars, the women, the street musicians, and the vibrant blue ocean. I feel heady with excitement. Jamie, Peter and Craig are caught up, too. Cuba has an intoxicating flavour and I want to lap it up, bathe in it and lick the bowl.

We pull up at the iconic Hotel Nacional, where Sinatra, Marilyn, the Rat Pack, Rita Hayworth and Ant & Dec have stayed before me. We dump our kit and take a wander round Havana. Americans haven't been able to legitimately visit this Caribbean island since the Cuban Missile Crisis in 1962, and the embargo is still in place today. As a result of these tough sanctions, Cuba is a place that has remained unhomogenised by the outside world. Florida is only sixty miles away but the cultures couldn't be further apart. And even though the islanders have been held in an iron grip by Communist dictator Fidel Castro since he seized power in 1959, and are now ruled by Fidel's younger brother, Raúl, their sense of identity feels so defined, their self-worth defiant.

We walk past a cigar factory and pop in for a quick look around. I want to stay longer but there's no time to film – our schedule is so tight. Contrary to popular myth, Cuban cigars are not rolled on the thighs of virgins, but the factory girls do stretch the tobacco leaves on their laps as they sort and grade them. A professional storyteller reads to them as they work. Cuban women are like no other – beautiful, with classical features, healthy skin, no make-up and plenty of life in their eyes. I listen for a while before asking the name of the book. It's Harry Potter. The reader tells me she also reads Dickens and Hemingway. Cuba might have a terrible human rights record but it has one of the highest literacy levels in the world and most people speak English fluently.

Jamie has decided he wants to celebrate the Cuban clichés. Across the road is parked a blue open-top Cadillac in immaculate condition. The Cubans not only take great care of their vehicles, polishing and buffing like the average classic-car geek in Britain, they also engineer the parts themselves. I jump in the back of the Cadillac Eldorado and Jamie hands me a mojito. I'm liking this new non-sadistic style of directing. I sip my drink. Only a Cuban mojito tastes this fresh. My taste buds give the minty rum syrup a full-on snog while Jamie cuts a cigar and lights it. He hands over my Montecristo No.2 and I am taken for an elegant tour of the town. I feel like Sinatra.

Malecón Promenade

Before sunset we film a fishing sequence on the Malecón Promenade in Havana. Fidel Castro, worried his citizens would attempt to flee his regime, strictly controlled access to all boats. As a result of this, all fishing boats are owned by the state and use is only for the privileged few. This is bad news for Cubans, but good news for fish stocks, and better news for me. One of the only ways for people to catch fish is off the promenade. Hundreds of men and women line the sea wall, day and night, using rods and hand lines to catch bait fish, snapper and sardines, which they eat or sell to the government-owned restaurants, some of which are house-based. Basically you can go to people's houses and they will cook for you but the money earned has to go to the state, otherwise they will go to prison. This is enforced by the secret police, who, dressed in plain clothes, are indiscernible from regular citizens. We have been followed from the moment we arrived and I know that two men in a black Ford are watching us right now. It's a strange feeling.

There is a knack to fishing off the promenade but if you don't know what you're doing, like me, it's like casting a line into a washing machine! A wave smacks the sea wall and we all get drenched. *Ah, that's why everyone's wearing anoraks*, I think to myself. I had thought maybe it was going to rain. The trick is to put your line out in water, jump behind the wall and then jump back up. The waves bring the fish in. Lots of people are catching fish, except me, so I ask some guys across the way what bait they are using. Shrimp. We buy their whole supply. But it's not the bait that's getting fish, it's the spot they are fishing in. There are lots of sardines and small jacks and we're in the wrong place. But there's no room. I cast again in the same barren spot and vainly hope something might swim by. A wave slaps me in the face.

The sun is beginning to go down and the light starts to change. Out of the corner of my eye I see a pelican stealing one of the fishermen's bait. I chuckle. Then I realise the pelican is actually on the end of his line. *It must be an accident,* I think – it's not. This dude is purposely catching pelicans for a local restaurant to roast. Alessandra, our AP, gets deeply upset. The man yanks the pelican in, grabs it, closes its wings and binds its beak and feet. Alessandra is now beyond distressed.

I tackle him: 'That's not a fish!'

He looks at me as if to say 'So what? Mind your own business', and I begin to get upset myself. But then I start thinking *What's the difference between catching a fish or a bird? Am I being hypocritical?* I look at the pelican – his distress somehow seems more poignant, more dramatic. To ease Alessandra's inflamed sensibilities I offer to buy the pelican from the guy. He's over the moon. He'll just go and catch another one but I'm pleased with myself, thinking I've done a good turn. Alessandra hugs me and dries her eyes. And then the pelican attacks me. I untie the bird's beak first and it goes berserk. Now, I want to carefully explain my rationale here; I know what you're thinking 'Why didn't you unbind the feet and *then* the beak?' Well, I didn't want to untie the feet first in case it escaped with a taped beak destined for a slow death by starvation. I couldn't think of anything worse, so now I have to deal with this furious-feathered-fucker viciously pecking me on the arm. I'm bleeding. Bleeding! I hurriedly untie

the pelican's feet, deciding that all pelicans are inherently racist.
I yell at him in my head.

'I'm the good guy who rescued you from the bad guy, you
idiot! But you think we all look the same, don't you? You racist.'

He looks at me with his blue eyes as if to say, 'Yeah, like you
can really tell us pelicans apart, you asshole? I bet you probably
thought I was a fucking heron or a swan first of all, didn't you?'

'No, how dare you? Never in my life have I met such a rude . . .
pelican! I want you to know I only saved you because she,' I point
at Alessandra who is now crying again, '*she* wanted me to. I
should have let you roast.'

He pecks me on the arm again.

'Ow!'

I let him go and he flies off without so much as a kind look
behind. I wait for him to circle above or do a fly-past like animals
do in the movies but I get nada.

'Bloody pelicans.'

'Did you get that on camera?' Jamie asks Craig.

'No, it was too ridiculous,' he says.

Jamie is disappointed. As you know, he loves a good sequence
where I experience pain, especially at the hands of nature.

After more than enough excitement for one day we walk back to
the hotel. The Cuban Film Festival is on and there is a bustle of
activity with press and filmmakers. I try to do a bit of schmooz-
ing with a couple of directors but I soon tire of their company
and want to be back with my team. We decide to have 'welcome
to Cuba' mojitos and an early night . . . by 1 a.m. we are all shit-
faced, our speech slurring, like we're electing a new pope. We all
have a taste for the Cuban elixir.

Freshwater Tarpon

At breakfast we are all feeling like poo. Why do we do it to ourselves? We travel an hour and half by van southeast of Havana to
the River Hatiguanico National Park. I am freshwater tarpon
fishing with Lazuro Vinola, who, according to our fixer, is the
best tarpon fisherman in Cuba, if not the world. Philippe
Rodriguez, who is supposedly the best guide in Cuba, if not the
world, accompanies him. No pressure on them then.

We motor up the sparkling river on a state-owned boat, driven
by Lazuro, who is also the park's head ranger. I ask the guys to
give me one piece of advice for tarpon fishing.

'Patience,' they say in unison. 'You will need a lot of patience.
It's very difficult to catch tarpon. You will lose many fish today.
Take, take, take, off, off, off,' adds Philippe.

'Oh, ye of little faith,' I say, fronting it.

I mean, that's not to say I haven't had my bad days, I think to
myself. We all have. There was the time I lost the monster sturgeon in Canada but that was totally Randy's fault. Or what about
the dorado in the Philippines, which was gutting. The worst was
probably dropping another man's machaca in Costa Rica. That
was a real low moment. Lazuro and Philippe trade glances and
smile, knowing that, because of my fly-fishing background, I will
automatically set the rod incorrectly and the fish will come off.
They keep schtum.

Philippe slows the boat down and we come to a stop, and he
cuts the engine.

'Tarpon spook easily,' he tells me.

As we gently drift down the middle of the river I try a few
practice casts. The tarpon tend to hide in the root systems of
overhanging trees and Lazuro tells me I need to cast two feet

from the edge of the root. We travel downriver all day, perhaps twenty miles, and never see a single soul.

Lazuro practises his cast. Wham! A tarpon takes the lure and leaps three feet out of the water. It's a twenty-pound fish but it comes off and he's gutted. I commiserate with him: 'It's an awful feeling,' I say.

He speaks to Jamie in the boat across the way: 'Please don't show that.'

'No, of course not,' says Jamie, with his fingers crossed behind his back.

We drift to the spot where Lazuro says I'll catch my first tarpon. I'm using a popper – a weighted plastic lure in the shape of a sprat. I cast and I'm in range. I pop the floating line across the water a foot at a time to mimic a bait fish. Pop, rest, pop, rest. Wallop! A tarpon is on. I immediately set the rod up like a fly line. The fish comes off. Little do I know that it is impossible to set the hook in the upper part of the mouth because it's solid bone; the trick is to set the hook in the lower part of mouth. I lose seven tarpon before the guys let me in on this secret.

'You need to set the rod away from you, parallel to the water,' says Lazuro.

Set down, away and down again, tip to the surface of the water. Got it. On the eighth take I forget everything I have just been told and set the rod up. Of course I lose the fish and have the biggest hissy fit ever.

'I cannot lose EIGHT fish!'

One of them whispers in Spanish (picked up by Alessandra): 'What a drama queen.' It's true – today I am channelling Ava Gardner.

Nine, ten, eleven and twelve all stay on but come off during the fight. I set the hook correctly in the mouth, but the fish leaps and it's over. After fish number twelve Lazuro lets me in on the second crucial secret: 'Tarpon are known as the Silver King, and when a fish leaps you must bow to the king and drop the rod to the water.'

The fish are bigger than the leader on the line in terms of weight, so when they jump the dead weight will snap the line, hence needing to angle the rod downwards.

'Thanks for the top tip, guys,' I say, wishing they'd bloody told me this earlier.

Tarpon number thirteen is on. I set the rod away, bow to the king when he leaps and catch my first ever tarpon! I bring him aboard with the help of Lazuro. He is a bright, clean-looking fish with scales of sterling silver. His distinctive upturned mouth reminds me of the arowana's pedal-bin trap and, just like the Amazonian fish, the tarpon is an air-breather, extracting oxygen with the help of a modified swim bladder. These fellas are very adaptable fish and can reside in a variety of habitats, from low-oxygenated stagnant ditches or ponds as newly spawned tiddlers to freshwater rivers or brackish creeks as juveniles, to the saltwater of the ocean as adults. As long as the water's warm they don't care. They're a bit like me sister Joanne when it comes to the cold – they just can't stand it. Her house is like a sauna, I tell you.

When tarpon reach sexual maturity between the ages of seven and thirteen, they return to the ocean to join the other adults migrating. And at the end of this trip we are going after a Big Daddy tarpon that could be ten times the size of this youngster today and measure up to eight feet. I pop tarpon junior back into the river – apparently these guys aren't for eating, as they are too bony.

Strangely we feel similarly about the hookers who chat to us in a bar later that evening. Naïvely we think they are friendly locals who want to trade a bit of banter – that's before we meet their pimp, Scarface. We tell them firmly we're not interested and they scarper. Some things are not meant to be caught and taken home – they should be released very quickly or never fished for in the first place!

Bonefish

The anglers who have done it say it's the most exhilarating feeling in the world, and those anglers who haven't done it dream of the day they will try it. I'm talking about bone-fishing. It's the exotic aspiration of the fly-fishing fraternity and I just hope it lives up to the hype.

From our hotel we head 200 miles northeast to the island of Cayo Romano, via El Pedraplén, a thirty-mile-long causeway, which in places is treacherous. I had wondered what the planks in the back of the van were for and I soon discover they are for making ad hoc bridges where the road ceases to be. We make several of these temporary crossings where the waves from the ocean have taken great chunks out of the tarmac, like marzipan. At one point I get out of the 4x4, as there is a ruddy great drop to the sea below. I'm not staying on board taking bets as to whether the car is going to make it across or not. The driver negotiates across a crude wooden bridge that the locals have built. Castro might well have taught everyone to read but his roads are crap.

The island is empty, as is the sea. There's no one around because no one is allowed a boat. I meet Eddie who, my fixer says, is the best fisherman in Cuba, if not the world. He has a handsome face with a big moustache but unfortunately he doesn't speak a word of English. We muddle on with sign language.

Bonefish are notoriously difficult to catch because they are very skittish, reacting to every sound and vibration. One slip-up and the fish is gone. Known as the 'grey ghost', its silver design reflects everything around it, making it invisible, like a moving mirror. The best way to spot this pelagic phantom is by its shadow on the sea floor. I am using my own seven-weight fly rod I've brought with me. It's a Hardy Zenith with a Hardy Angel fly reel given to me by Val McDermid, the writer of *Wire in the Blood*. I show my rod to Eddie and he shakes his head and laughs.

I say, 'Hardy's is the best in the world!' but he shakes his head again. 'Listen, I have caught some big trout with this rod.'

It's our only conversation; from now on I have to be totally silent. This is the hardest part of fishing for me.

Eddie cuts the engine and begins to punt across the gentle lapping sea. The water is shallow and gin-clear as we head out to the salt flats, where the bonefish reside. They are powerful fish that take off at incredible speeds, which is extraordinary given that shallow saltwater contains little oxygen. These fish extract oxygen from the water in a hyper-efficient way in order to move like forks of lightning. Eddie stops punting and lets the boat float with the current. We are fishing from a platform boat, specifically designed for bone fishing, with a high umpire's chair for spotting fish. Eddie is sitting high in the chair and I am at the front of the boat, ready to cast. I need to be accurate – two feet off its mouth will spook it, but four feet away is too far. It's a windy day so it's not going to be easy.

*

Eddie puts his finger to his mouth, signalling to be quiet. He sees something and points.

'Cast,' he says softly.

'Cast at what?' I whisper back.

'Fish,' he hisses.

'I can't see it.'

I pull the line out from the reel, ready to load the rod, but the whir of the reel spooks the fish. Eddie puts his hands on his head in despair.

'It's gone,' he says.

'I never saw it anyway,' I say, grinning.

Using a mixture of English, Spanish and sign language he tells me, 'Pull the line out beforehand. You need to be prepared.'

After the first unsuccessful attempt I suggest Eddie uses the clock system to tell me where to cast. He understands and we are set. Five minutes pass.

'One o'clock,' whispers Eddie.

I see a shadow. I do two false casts that don't touch the water. Over, over, out, my first cast is on the money. He gives me the OK sign. A fish comes towards the lure. I have to keep a three-foot distance to replicate an insect moving jerkily along the water's surface. I do this using a figure of eight retrieve, winding the line gently around my fingers. It's a very effective method of pulling the line in. The fly I am using is like a bug-eyed nymph or caddisfly with large eyes, and it's weighted. Bonefish also like small fish, but they are particularly partial to their insects.

A six-pound bonefish gobbles my fly and WHOOSH! It shoots off like an underwater bullet, creating a bow wave in its wake. Faster and faster it turbocharges off in a straight line, zipping off right, straight again, and back to the right. It's taking the leader, fly line and backing line out to sea and I only have fifty metres of backing because I use this rod for trout and the odd salmon in Northumberland, and no fish has ever taken this much line this far out before! As it gets to the backing I start to panic. I am going to run out of line and – oh, holy mother of Jesus, son of God, no – I haven't tied the backing onto the reel with a fucking arbor knot! The fish is going to fuck off to the Bahamas with my entire line. I grab the line with my hand and put the brakes on. The line snaps and the fish is away.

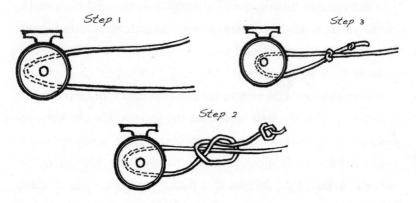

Arbor Knot

Step 1

Step 3

Step 2

Eddie is agog. He cannot believe what I have done. I didn't think I needed the extra backing or to tie it on with a knot. It's one of the most stupid mistakes of my career. Eddie continues staring at me with absolute incredulity, but on the plus side I realise now that bone-fishing really *is* as incredible as everyone said it was! This is no consolation for Eddie and he is still poleaxed.

'What an extraordinary fish! And the run – while it lasted – was out of this world. Unbelievable.'

I can't meet Eddie's eyes. He steps down from the umpire's chair, shaking his head. He silently takes my rod and winds in the line, then passes me his own. It's a 10-weight, built for the job with 150 metres of backing, fixed with an arbor knot . . .

I feel so ashamed of myself and wring my hands anxiously. Jamie, however, is all smiles. He fucking loves it. My catastrophes are his triumphs and I hate him like a Frenchman. Eddie punts over to a new spot but the water is so shallow that the draught of the boat is touching the bottom. We get off and wade in the turquoise water, like real hunter-gatherers in pursuit of our bony quarry. No one is about and the distressed trees of the salt flats look beautiful. Eddie is focused. He genuinely wants me to catch a phantom today. He also knows I hate myself enough for two people and gives me a kind look, willing me to succeed.

We gently wade out when I see a shadow. It's a huge bonefish.

'Eddie. Eddie!' I stage-whisper, wading towards the fish and pulling out the line.

The fish fucks off.

Eddie says, 'You have got to shush.' I upbraid myself internally. *Eddie is the spotter, yer numpty. You need to concentrate on being prepared for when he calls a fish.* But after the adrenalin rush of the first run I am way too excited. Seconds later he says, 'Two o'clock.' My first cast is short; my second cast is in the window. The fish takes it and flies. It penetrates the water like a Lockheed SR-71 Blackbird. I don't know what the equivalent of Mach 3 is in water but this baby's packing some Gs. Whoosh, it continues to run and I have enough line and now the experience to know how to slow it down – it's been a quick learning curve.

I start pulling the fish back in but it changes direction and bolts towards me. I strip the line to keep it tight and he keeps on coming. I wonder if he'll break my legs on impact. He darts away again taking out 150 metres of line at top speed. It's incredible. But this fish is built for short bursts of speed and not endurance. He's Usain Bolt, not Mo Farah, and his race is run. After a fifteen-minute battle I reel in the grey ghost. I look at him and can't believe he's not panting after that incredible run. What makes bonefish so spectacular is that they are so unassuming in appearance. His shallow slope at the head is more elliptical in design than other powerful fish and he has a proportionally larger forked tail to his body, which helps him move through the water, but he isn't solid muscle like a barracuda or jack. His power comes from within, somehow. A bonefish is, I guess, a bit like Bradley Wiggins: not much to look at, being so lean and almost gangly, but the power within him to win a Tour de France and then Olympic gold makes him magnificent.

I raise my silver medal – he is only four pounds in weight, relatively tiny for the race he has run, and as I pop him back I imagine what it must be like to catch a bonefish three or four times his size.

Supper and Salsa
We head back with Eddie across the causeway to the hillside town of Trinidad. It's a beautiful old place with cobbled streets, where old men and girls are dancing and laughing and there's not a single tourist. A band is performing in the square: twelve guys playing double bass, trumpet, maracas and guitars. People

have just come from work – they stop by to dance salsa and enjoy a drink. There is a raw beauty to the Cubans that does not require make-up or costumes.

A stunning woman dances with her friend, and when she sees us she asks me to dance. *My father was a champion ballroom dancer so I must have his genes*, I think. *I pray*. She grabs me and says, 'Uno, dos, tres, cuatro, cinco, seis.' She is doing salsa; I am doing Dad-dancing. Yet again I have brought shame on the family name. She counts again: 'Uno, dos, tres, cuatro, cinco, seis.' I am trying to keep up but it's a terrible situation. I'm the guy who doesn't know the dance, surrounded by people who do. I have an idea. I show her 'the lawnmower'. I pull the cord three times left to right, then dance forward pushing the lawnmower. She kisses me on the cheek and goes to dance with another man. I am stranded. Jamie is pissing himself laughing and decides that we need to film a sequence where I am taught how to salsa properly. He says, 'If you catch lots of fish tomorrow, I'll hire a seriously hot instructor.'

Barracuda

I spring out of my bed extra early the next morning.

'I need to catch me some fish,' I say, stretching.

I do my morning exercises, limbering up in preparation for another evening of salsa. But first the fishing ...

Guillermo Perez and Jorge are going to show me how plentiful the ocean is around here. They are government fishermen and have one of three boats in Trinidad Port, which are used as game-fishing charters for tourists. After shooting some meet-and-greet footage, we are marched off the boat by the police. They want to check our passports and documents, which we have to carry with us at all times. We are taken to an office nearby and after about an hour they are satisfied we aren't CIA spies and we head out to sea.

'Ha-ha! Fooled them again,' I chuckle.

Apparently fishing trips, birdwatching and charity work are classic forms of deep cover.

Barely out of the harbour, we start to trawl our Rapala lures, which are shaped like small bait fish and mimic them in the water. I film a piece to camera saying, 'Today we could catch grouper, jacks, barracuda . . .' – but as I'm speaking both lines go off simultaneously. Moments later we have two barracuda around four and a half pounds apiece. I pick up one of the ambushed predators and put it in front of the camera. I open its mouth for a close-up.

'It's equipped to kill,' I say. 'Remember, this is the guy who killed Nemo's mum.'

On board is a metal priest with a wooden handle. I haven't used one like this before – they are usually all wood. I hold up the fish and go to strike it but it twitches and I miss and smash the glass of a little gate at the back of the boat. Jamie can't breathe from laughing; tears are streaming down his face. Peter and Craig are bent double. Thankfully Guillermo and Jorge are up top and didn't hear the crack. I panic, trying to hide the cracked glass with my body. Peter finds a towel and I casually drape it over. IWC never broadcast the footage, afraid the Cubans would kick up a fuss and bill us for thousands of pounds, and I just want to say here and now I am truly sorry.

I dispatch both barracudas and dinner is on me. I am going to cook them back in Trinidad.

'How good-looking is this dance instructor going to be, Jamie?'

'If you catch some more fish, Eva Longoria level.'

This time I want to see if we can catch another type of fish for our supper. I set the lines again. Wham! Wham! It's barracuda again and they are everywhere. I pull them in.

In order to get another species, we anchor the boat and go in pursuit of bottom feeders. I am after grouper, with some squid on the hook, and before long I catch a beauty. The trick is to pull the bait in such a way that you do it very slowly. But when there is a take you need to yank up the line very fast. I'm not as quick off the mark as I should be and the grouper takes the bait back to its cave. Internally I start to panic, thinking the line will snap, but Jorge tells me to let it go slack and wait for the grouper to come out of his cave. I take the tension off the line and wait. The grouper swims out of his lair, the line goes tight and I pull him up. He's a brown-spotted grouper, covered in red and tan speckles. His dorsal and tailfins are jet-black with white edges and the first seven spines are iced with tartrazine, warning of their toxic nature.

I take the smorgasbord of barracuda and grouper to a restaurant in Trinidad and, in my best sign language, say we would like them cooked with chips. The chef tells me in Spanish how he will prepare them. I nod, not understanding a word. We sit out on the cobbled street, enjoying the warm evening. It's mojitos all round again. I've certainly got a taste for them and am beginning to get a little mojito belly.

Half an hour later the waiter returns with fried, poached and grilled grouper and barracuda, accompanied by a mountain of patatas fritas. I try the grouper first.

'It's sensational – a salsa on the senses,' I declare.

The crew groans. Surprisingly the barracuda is just as good. The poached fish is more succulent but I am a fan of all of it. A

Cuban band starts playing and everyone gets up to dance. Jamie has set the whole thing up and – surprise, surprise – no one wants to dance with me. Cue ravishing salsa instructor (Jamie's done well) who takes me by the hand and encourages me to go with her, and I really want to on so many levels. It's an intoxicating mixture – mojitos, salsa and Latin women. We glide to the music. Midway I say, 'Do you know the lawnmower?' I do the dance and she loves it. We do the lawnmower together.

'You are so funny,' she says. I completely charm her. She looks over my shoulder at Jamie as if to say, 'When am I getting paid?'

I drink another six mojitos and we dance the night away. This truly is the Land of the Lotus Eaters and I don't want to leave, ever.

Giant Tarpon

One man who came to Cuba fifteen years ago and never left is Fabrizio Barbassa. The charismatic Italian married a seriously red-hot smoking Cuban lady and is living the dream, taking tourists tarpon fishing in Cayo Las Brujas. Fabrizio wasn't always a fisherman; he used to be a Formula 1 driver until he suffered a terrible collision in 1995 in which he broke his legs and an arm and sustained severe chest and head injuries. After that he decided to get out of the fast lane for good, and I don't blame him.

Today we are in pursuit of giant grown-up tarpon, which can grow up to eight feet and leap their own height. That's like Lawrence Dallaglio doing the high jump. We are on a similar platform to the bonefish boat except this one has an F1 400 b.h.p. engine. We motor across the iron-flat ocean. Samuel Yeras

On its day, Ascension Island is the greatest fishing destination on the planet

The one that *didn't get away*

Honestly, it wa[s]
THIS BIG!

On this adventure I
have caught the weird,
the wonderful . . . and
the downright
dangerous

During this extreme
journey it was only a
matter of time before
I caught king crabs

Wouldn't a worm
be better?

WE.ARE.IN!

A bigger version of
something you might
see in a bowl at home

Some of the scenery on this trip can only be described as simply breathtaking

'Team Extreme' living the Dream in Patagonia

Not for the first (or indeed the last) time, we play the waiting game

Rarely a case of
'one man and his
boat' and barely
enough room to
swing a minnow,
you could cut the
atmosphere with
a cricket stump

There are so
many lovely folk
in the world, and
my philosophy is
you should try to
meet as many of
them as you can

Table for two, please

Travelling the globe and catching fish most anglers only dream of, where do I sign up?

Err... Erm... I think this is its head

One lean, mean, killing machine

The crew in Costa Rica

Pound for pound the Papuan black bass has to be the greatest fighting fish on the planet. Think of it as Muhammad Ali in fish form

Spot the guy who thinks the plan for today *isn't* a good one

My Uncle Matheson, the Obi-Wan Kenobi of fly-fishing and the man who taught me everything I needed to know about angling. Can you tell he's genuinely gutted I got the gig and he didn't?

My dad, Robson Senior, or Big Rob as he is known to his mates. My Rock, well, more a mountain

Pompa, Fabrizio's assistant, tells me what I can expect from today's trip.

'There are thousands of tarpon here. You will catch many,' he says.

I take it with a pinch of salt. I'm just happy to see what happens. However, after the bone-fishing and my earlier tarpon experience with Lazuro and Philippe, I am beginning to realise the Cubans don't bullshit.

We arrive at the spot where Fabrizio thinks the tarpon are. He cuts the engine. As we wait I wonder whether he can smell fish, like Steve Hall in the Azores.

'The fish will come to us,' he says presciently. 'There are giant shoals in the area that move around. They will come.'

If they are nearby and something spooks them they will leap out of the water. They also show themselves by rolling to the surface in order to breathe. This is when they are most vulnerable to predators and piscivorous fishermen.

We wait two hours for them to show.

'Any size will do, Samuel,' I say.

Jamie is starting to get irritable, but Fabrizio is super-cool with not a care in the world. All of a sudden the vast shoal of tarpon show themselves to us. They are running by the side of the boat, like the superpod of dolphins in Costa Rica. We start casting out fly lines forty yards from the boat. I use a 12-weight rod – not like a Spey rod; much shorter. I get a take. I set the rod parallel to my hip bone, keep it down and set the line as if pulling back a bow. I reel as quickly as I can. It leaps. Wow! It comes off. Bugger. What did I do wrong? I realise that I forgot to bow to the king when it leapt, that's what. I raised my rod up like a revolutionary and put two fingers up to the king. I'm a big fan of royalty – well, Elvis, Freddie Mercury's Queen and now the Silver King – and next time he leaps I'm going to kowtow, nay grovel like Uriah Heep at his feet.

Fabrizio senses my inner turmoil.

'Don't worry, it happens, Robson. In the moment you forget what to do,' he says generously. 'They're here. They're here. We will catch.'

I cast again, a tarpon takes the lure, the king leaps, I bow my rod and for the next hour Fabrizio and I take it in turns to bring this giant fish to the boat. The fish is running, leaping, and diving down to the bottom, which causes real stress on the body but my back is fine because I'm using a fly-line and not a harness. I slow down the barrel of the reel with the palm of my hand. Only a wuss would ask for a glove – real men do it with skin. I now have real calluses to prove my machismo. I used to be a hand model before this show.

I love fly-fishing and somehow this method seems a fairer fight than all the heavy-duty tackle used for game fishing. I feel closer to Santiago – after all he caught a marlin on a hand line in Hemingway's novel *The Old Man and the Sea*, which the author wrote and set here in Cuba. With the help of Samuel, we get the fish on board. It's breathtaking. Its silver scales are like elaborate chain mail. This is *Megalops atlanticus*, which loosely mean 'big eyes of the Atlantic'.

Nothing can top this extreme fish. Nothing can top Cuba. I found love here, not in a person, but in a culture and a place that I haven't experienced before, other than with Newcastle. Fabrizio fell in love, too, and he is now at peace with himself, he is serene. I look at him and think it must be a great feeling to be at peace with yourself. In the material world we have such high expectations of our lives and ourselves and sometimes our goals are impossible. Dissatisfaction and depression creep into the void between our expectations of how things should pan out and how they actually are. If we don't expect too much and we remember to get pleasure from the natural world and simple pleasures, we too can feel at peace. Especially in Cuba!

None of the team wants to leave the next morning; we all want to stay here forever. Maybe we could miss the plane and go another day? Where are we going next, anyway? I don't really care. In the distant recesses of my mind, Taylor and Vanya call to me. I snap out of my reverie; the spell is broken. I have to manhandle Jamie, Craig and Peter into the cab to the airport. Peter is worst of all.

'Go on without me. I'll only slow you down. There are others who have the gift of sound.'

'Well, none like you, Prada. You are a fucking one-off, my friend,' I say, booting him into the passenger seat.

Had I not had a beautiful wife and child to return to I would still be there to this day. Cuba is one of the most enchanting places I have visited on this fishing odyssey.

Chapter Eleven

PATAGONIA

Hostage of Fortune

January 2011, At the Ends of the Earth, Series 4

After what was a bit of a bumpy start, *Extreme Fishing* is becoming a veritable 'beast', a term we use in telly to denote a successful show. It's a case of 'be careful what you wish for', though, as there's little time for anything else work-wise and I can forget about a social life.

But everyone is talking about *Extreme Fishing*, and now in the street I am harangued thirty or forty times with, 'Caught any fish yet?' or: 'Off fishing?' I was even on the loo minding my own business when some guy popped his head over the stall wall and asked, 'Caught any extreme fish lately?' I bombarded him with toilet rolls until he left me alone. When I was Jimmy Porter in *Casualty*, I used to get 'Oi, Robson, I hurt my finger.' When I was Tucker – 'Where's Paddy?' And when I was the surgeon in *Reckless* I would have grannies winking at me, asking if I could do reconstructive bowel surgery. I definitely prefer the fishing questions.

In this latest series, our objective is to go to the ends of the earth, and there's no place further south than Patagonia. Patagonia is the tail region of South America, with territories shared between Chile and Argentina. The British Falklands Islands (Islas Malvinas) are just off the east coast of Patagonia on the Atlantic side, but it's best not to mention the war! It's even more important they don't know I was in *Soldier, Soldier*, for obvious reasons. Personally I don't know what all the fuss was about – some small rocks in the middle of the ocean. I mean, it's not like they found oil, minerals or gas there. Oh, they did, did they? Now, fancy that.

Torres del Paine

After a fourteen-hour flight to Buenos Aires and another internal flight, we are travelling eight hours by bus to Torres del Paine National Park in Chile. Our plan is to fly-fish for the king salmon, or chinook as it is also known, and then continue to Tierra del Fuego in Argentina, where I hope to land the biggest brown trout of my career.

The hitchhikers we have picked up along the way, one German and two American girls, think we have a great plan. They are all travelling alone in search of adventure and I am envious of their pluck. I don't think I could have done that at their age. They are impressive kids who can all speak three languages. They seem to hit it off with each other, crammed in like sardines in the small minivan, and they start to hatch a plan to travel together for a while.

We arrive in Torres del Paine around 3 a.m. It's pitch-black so

I can't get much of an idea of my surroundings. I'm too tired, anyway. My head hits the pillow and zzzz . . .

I pull back the curtains of my cosy log cabin and stare open-mouthed out of the window. The panorama is incredible, mountainous and dramatic. The name Torres del Paine (pronounced 'pie-nee') is from the Tehuelche Indian word for 'blue', and *torres* is Spanish for 'towers'. It refers to three jagged granite peaks that violently pierce the sky; they are magnificent and defiant. The largest horn, the Grande Paine, is over one and a half miles high. In front of the mountains is a lake, Lake Pehoe, perhaps five miles across; its bright azure colour indicates its icy temperature and mini icebergs float around in it. The frozen breeze ripples the water. In Patagonia the wind can be cruel and unrelenting. Locals call it 'the broom of God', as it can literally sweep everything away. As I walk outside to take some photographs I feel like I have been superimposed here by special effects.

Chinook Salmon

Patrick Marcos looks like a revolutionary. A young Fidel Castro, without the cigar and beret. We are standing next to the Serrano River, only minutes from the hotel. I am hoping to catch a hefty chinook (or king) today, the biggest of the species.

The chinook is thought to have made its home here some time in the twentieth century, after hundreds of non-endemic salmon were released by fishermen in the 1930s and again in the late 1970s, in the hope of establishing the species here. Only DNA tests can reveal their true mitochondrial heritage, but many are thought to have come from North America. But one thing is

for sure: they have set up home here and are thriving, making the
600-mile runs from the Pacific back to their new-found rivers
and tributaries. It's spring and we have arrived during this epic
journey, when thousands of them return from the sea to spawn
and then, as we discovered in Alaska, die.

Today Patrick is my ghillie, which is a combination of best
friend and fishing mentor in one. He will be there to give me
assistance on casting techniques, where the best pools are, where
the fish congregate and rest, and the best lures or flies to use.
Patrick knows this river like the back of his hand and he says he
knows the back of his hand really well. I'm not sure I could spot
mine in a line-up but he says he could. ('It was *that* hand that
stole the handbag, officer. I never forget a hand.')

I tell him the biggest salmon I ever caught weighed eighteen
pounds.

'You could triple that in this river,' he says. The biggest fish
Patrick caught here weighed sixty-four pounds!

'That would be a record in Britain, Patrick.' In fact, it would
match the enormous salmon caught by Georgina Ballantine in
1922, a UK record that remains unbeaten to this day.

We start casting at his favourite spot – the weather is slightly
overcast and it is about four degrees. We are using spoon lures,
which look nothing like spoons but instead like small silver fish
that replicate a distressed minnow. The salmon don't attack the
lures because they want to eat, and I ask Patrick why they go
after them – his theory is that you're trespassing on the fish's
property. My theory is that we are trespassing on their lovemaking.

I say, 'Imagine if I cast a spoon over you while you are making
love to your wife, Patrick.'

'I would kill you,' he says.

We wade out into the river. I am dressed up to the nines in technical fishing gear that keeps me cosy and, more importantly, dry. I dangle the spoons in the water and cast. As I am casting, a stranger appears to my right. He walks into the water and sidles up to me, within about five yards. He then starts to cast. I am incensed. Angling etiquette dictates you don't walk into another fisherman's beat. This guy is trying to nick my spot. Patrick very politely asks him to leave and suggests he find his own spot. If that had happened on the Coquet, I would have decked him. I know how the salmon feel about our lures. I want him to bugger off.

I carry on casting. Patrick's reel starts screaming.

'Robson, I have a present for you,' he says, and passes over his rod.

This is the first time this has ever happened on the show, as I always have to catch my own fish.

Patrick says, 'I want you to feel this fish. You think you have caught a big salmon – you have seen nothing yet!'

I take the rod off him and immediately the chinook becomes airborne, like the helicopter of the same name. Cameraman Keith Schofield keeps his lens on the fish as it leaps – it's the biggest 'springer' I have ever clapped eyes on. Bosch! It leaps again and flies across the river, jumping five or six times, left to right, showing itself.

'Oh, my God!'

Salmon: derived from the Latin *salmo*, and possibly the verb *salire*, meaning 'to leap'. And boy, can this fish leap. I can tell it's a male because of his large gib. When males become sexually mature, the bottom part of their lip passes over the upper lip –

it's like putting your bottom lip over your nose – and it looks extraordinarily phallic.

He's still fighting hard. I play him, and it's one of the most beautiful plays I have ever experienced. Finally I start to slowly reel him into the shallows. I am excited. Patrick is hysterical – he forgets he is the ghillie. He thinks it's one of the biggest fish he has ever seen. It's certainly the biggest I have ever seen. I bring it ten feet from the bank, and to my disbelief, Patrick goes over and tries to pick the fish up. It's a forty-five-pound-plus salmon. He kneels down in two feet of water and puts both arms underneath it. I'm not sure this fish is ready to bring in – it could run again – but I rush over to help Patrick. He drops it but manages to corral it with his legs and get hold of it again.

'Don't lose it. Don't lose it,' I say, trying to hold it by the caudal peduncle. (This is known as wristing a fish and it's the correct way to take hold of them.) But Patrick can't keep hold; the fish struggles one last time and is away, motoring with its powerful tail.

The silence is deafening. I stare at him. He stares into the water. The greatest salmon I have ever seen and he's let it slip away. He stands chest-high in the water and wipes his eyes as if hoping he might awake from a bad dream. He rubs his whole face with his hands, trying to take in what has just happened. He silently walks off and stands and stares into space. Alistair, however, is elated.

'That was brilliant! So many corridors of drama: elation, conflict and despair.'

We look over at the sad figure of Patrick.

'Go and console him, Robson,' says Alistair, never one to miss an opportunity. I go over.

'Robson, you cannot broadcast that. It will be the end of my career,' he says.

'No, it won't. Everyone in the area thinks you are the best. We are all fallible. Fishing is a battle: we lost and the fish won.'

There has been a paradigm shift. I am now the comforter rather than the comforted and it's a nice position to be in. Thank God it wasn't me that fucked up this time! Patrick is still glum. We sit on the bank together.

'To paraphrase Gene Wilder in *Young Frankenstein*, "If fishing teaches us anything, it teaches us to accept our failures, as well as our successes, with quiet dignity and grace."' I pretend to sob uncontrollably, then turn to him and say, 'But if we catch another fish like that and you lose it, I will wring your fucking neck!'

He smiles for the first time.

Back at the hotel I take Patrick for a beer. The bar is packed, news is breaking that the government has raised gas prices in the south by 50 per cent as an austerity measure. The people are very angry and there is going to be a general strike.

'Life is hard enough here, why are they doing this to us?' one lady says on the news.

With very few trees and little coal, gas is the only source for cooking and heating in the area. The unions announce that, unless the government backs down, they will go on strike and they call on all Chileans to support the cause. All roads will be blockaded – there will be no way in and no way out. Supply lines will be cut, tourism will cease and there will be a general standstill.

Patrick says, 'This will never happen. They can't implement these measures. They will sort it out.'

We call Helen to update her on the situation.

Daniel, our fixer, says, 'It should be OK. Governments do some stupid things but this would be suicide.'

He says, however, that it is up to the office whether we stay or leave. Alistair liaises with Helen and they agree we should stay put. Unbeknownst to us, this is a bad plan because the government goes ahead and implements the austerity measures overnight.

Inflatables and Escape

We have an early start with Patrick at Lago Sofia, about half an hour away. We do not get a chance to catch the news, and besides I'm trout fishing, which is far more important than politics. Today we are fly-fishing with a difference: it includes flippers, a pump and an inflatable. It looks like I'm getting ready for a Conservative Party Conference.

Rainbow and brown trout were introduced here more than a hundred years ago and they grow to sizes never seen back home. The biggest trout I ever caught was on the Coquet and weighed four and a half pounds, which is a decent fish for that particular stream. Here many grow closer to the size of the British record, which currently stands at thirty-one pounds. For many years the record was thought to be thirty-six pounds but it turned out the guy who took the title had actually found dead brown trout in a lake at Dever Springs. He held the record for seven years until he could no longer live with the guilt. His behaviour became erratic, his marriage broke up, and he never fished again. He was to fishing what Lance Armstrong is to cycling: a big fat cheat.

Patrick has blown up his inflatable and it's now my turn to

pump. I say to him, 'I know it gets lonely out here but this is ridiculous.' From a distance it would look very wrong!

Inflatables are used in the UK for trout fishing, but they tend to be a bit rustic – mainly the inner tubes of tractor tyres. It's never really appealed to me but it's time to give it a go. I finish pumping and behold my comfy chair, complete with a drinks holder – it can even recline! It's far more appealing than an old tractor tyre. An inflatable allows for a stealth approach and is powered by your flippers. I have my waders on and several layers of thermals, but I am already freezing my cojones off.

I stand on the edge of the natural lake, with my webbed feet, fly rod and inflatable, looking ridiculous. I feel like Ade Edmondson in *Bottom*. Patrick is alongside; he always looks cool. We paddle out together. It's quite breezy today – and inflatables and wind don't tend to mix. The broom of Patagonia starts to gently brush me across the lake, and I attempt to steer myself back on course, my flippers going ten to the dozen. It's not easy but trying to cast into the wind is nigh on impossible. I cast again and the fly drops a few metres away, nowhere near the point I was aiming for. I look over at Patrick. Where is he? What? He's now back on shore, chatting on the phone. Great, I am the butt of a Chilean practical joke.

I shout, 'Help, Patrick, help!' but he doesn't look round. Unbeknownst to me, he is on the phone to his wife, who is frantically telling him to 'get out now': they are closing all the roads and two protesters have been killed. (Two people have been knocked down by a car, which many think to have been an accident. However, others think it was done intentionally and it's causing a lot of friction.)

We stop filming immediately and Alistair yells over to me:

'You need to get back here. We have got to get over to Argentina.'

I paddle with all my might, but keep being swept away by the ubiquitous broom. It is pushing me further and further from the shore. I paddle as fast as I can, trying to use my hands to row, but it's no good. I am stranded. Eventually a boat is sent over and I am rescued. We jump in the van and scream off to the hotel. It's deserted. Everyone has left. The receptionist says, 'All the roads are blocked; you will never get out. You should have left earlier.'

My stomach lurches, not because of the unfolding crisis but because I am having a bout of badly timed bottom explosions. All the gear is packed up and everyone is ready to leave, but I have to use the toilet, urgently. I feel dreadful and I look ashen. I hang on tightly to the toilet seat, ready for the diarrhoea rollercoaster ride, humming the hymn 'Dear Lord and Father of Mankind', which seems to help relieve the burning pain in my tired bottom.

Each time I get to the van, I have to rush back to the hotel again and my bowels ultimately cost us forty-five minutes; a critical amount of time when trying to escape a country. We head to the border, where 200 protesters and three coaches block the road. It's the only way out. Several men stop the van. I jump out, run for the nearest private area, drop my trousers and make my own dirty protest. I peep at the protesters from behind a rock, thinking no one can see me. One looks back at me straight in the eye. He is full of aggression but I am too dehydrating and poorly to be alarmed. Daniel, our fixer, is trying to negotiate for us to be allowed across but it is no use: the protesters say the van has to stay here and we have to walk over. The border is twenty kilometres away and our gear weighs half a ton. It's impossible for us to continue on foot. We have to keep trying to get our vehicle through.

I do my paperwork and reappear from behind my rock. My bottom is so sore it takes my breath away. I mince over to speak to Daniel.

'Tell them what you are working on, Daniel. Tell them who you are with, but don't mention the singing – it could sway it.'

Daniel, Patrick and our driver, Nelson, go to talk to the pro-testers again. Keith continues filming covertly on GoPros, tiny hidden cameras, as we watch from the safety of the van. There is no way they will let us through the line. They shout at Nelson and tell him he has to join the protest. It is clear there will be consequences if he doesn't. Patrick is debriefed as well. He explains he is a fisherman and needs to take us back to the hotel. He says he is not working for us. They are furious that, as Chileans, they are not supporting the strike. Thankfully Daniel is Argentinian, and therefore not betraying the cause, so he tries to pacify the ringleaders. We watch as Nelson is taken away to help man the blockade. He waves at us, smiling but slightly shell-shocked. I'm not sure this is how he expected his day to turn out. Patrick jumps in the driver's side and Daniel climbs into the back.

'It's no good, they won't let our vehicle across and are keeping Nelson here as well. We've got no choice but to go back.'

'Have they taken Nelson hostage?' I ask.

'Yes, it's serious. Basically we had to swap drivers because they were angry with them as Chileans for not supporting the strike so they asked one of them to stay as a guarantee and only that way are we allowed to get back to the hotel.'

'So we could have been taken hostage,' I venture, as I take on the scale of the situation.

'Yes.' Patrick turns the minivan around and we skedaddle.

Daniel says, 'We really should have left earlier.'

I blanch. My diarrhoea has scuppered our *Extreme Fishing* adventure and we are stuck here indefinitely. This could go on for weeks. I berate my bottom.

'Well, at least we'll be safe at the hotel,' I say, noticing the petrol gauge. 'Patrick, I don't want to worry you but have we got enough fuel?'

'I hope so,' he says.

'And what if we haven't?'

He looks at me and shrugs. The hotel is about an hour and a half away and all the petrol stations are being picketed.

'Great, so I was nearly held hostage and now we're going to run out of fuel and we'll be stranded in the middle of nowhere, surrounded by llamas.'

Daniel chimes in: 'Gonachas.'

'Gonachas? Gonachas to you as well!'

The llamas, or gonachas, are everywhere. I start to make a mental plan of how we might kill and eat one if we do become stuck in the wilderness. *We'll be OK*, I think. *Patrick and I can fish; I can make a fire and I can make a bivouac, although if it's anything like the one in the Philippines we may perish, quickly. We could use the fat and skin of the llama to keep warm, like the natives used to. It'll be fine.* But after the Philippines experience I really don't want to try it. The winds are punishingly cold. I glance at the gauge again: 'It's on fucking empty!'

'We'll have to use the reserve tank,' says Daniel.

'Oh, good. Have we got a reserve tank?' I say, turning round.

'No,' says Daniel, pissing himself.

Oh, cojones.

The van makes it to the hotel but we glide in on no more than fumes. The hotel is empty – it's like *The Shining*. Alistair and Alessandra get on the phone to Helen and Hamish, who are looking at every option to get us out, including rescuing us by helicopter, Navy SEAL-style! Calls are made to the British Embassy. They send an email with the latest advice and as I read I become increasingly nervous. What started off as a mild inconvenience has turned into quite a serious situation: 'The mood is getting progressively ugly and there is a tendency to violence. The best advice is to stay where you are.'

This is not good news. I need to be back for Taylor's parent-teacher meeting and to film *Joe Maddison's War* with Kevin Whately and Derek Jacobi, but I can't think of that right now. I am so poorly and now it's gushing out of both ends. I take to my bed. Besides, I can think of worse places to be trapped. It suddenly hits me that we are stuck in the world's biggest open prison. For some reason I start thinking about Jeffrey Archer. He went to an open prison and could go home from time to time and work in a theatre, and he got to keep his title. That doesn't sound like punishment to me, but then I can't remember what he actually did. Was he charged with crimes against literature? OMG, I might be charged with crimes against music. But if I go down I'm taking Simon Cowell and Louis Walsh with me.

'Robson. Robson!'

'Yes?'

Alistair is staring at me. I realise I am delirious with dehydration.

Patrick fetches a doctor from the village. He checks me over and gives me a potion to get rid of a parasitic infection, most probably amoebic dysentery. Lord knows how I got it but somehow I did. That night I sleep soundly and so does my bottom.

Salmon Fishing Part Deux

We still can't leave Patagonia so it looks as if we're going to have to make the best of the situation. One thing the protesters can't stop us doing is fishing, especially with the Serrano River located right by the hotel. We have another chance of catching a giant chinook with Patrick. But before we start fishing, we start off by setting the mood. Patrick plays the guitar, I sing, and Alistair has written us a song to perform. We sit next to the Serrano on chairs, wearing shades, while Patrick strums his guitar and we perform the Chilean Blues.

I woke up this morning
I couldn't get out
I couldn't get about
Need to catch me a trout
It may be fate
It may be a fluke
But I need to catch me a chinook.

Patrick says, 'You have a lovely voice, Robson.'

I start to tell him about my time in the music industry: 'I had three number ones and kept Michael Jackson and Oasis off the top spot . . .'

Patrick gets up and leaves midway.

I turn to the camera: 'He'll be back – there's no fuel in the van!'

*

I spy a little boy fishing on the bank. I wander over.

'Please don't tell me you caught something.'

The little boy replies, 'Yes, I catch a trout.'

He takes me to his dad's car to inspect it. I'm about to be upstaged by a twelve-year-old. He opens up a plastic carrier bag. It's a decent size but thank God it's not the size of the chinook we – I mean Patrick – lost. I take it out to inspect it.

'That is a beautiful wild brown trout . . .' The fish twitches and I drop it! I try to pick it up. 'I'm sorry. Sorry. So sorry.'

It's all going to hell in a handcart. I have never felt so harassed as an angler – trapped and held captive in Chile. But if I'm feeling the extreme pressure, Patrick looks one seriously worried man. As we prepare our lines he confides in me, 'I have never felt so much pressure in my life; it's like my whole life depends on catching the salmon. That cannot be right – I'm not enjoying this.'

But this is Patrick's chance to redeem himself and he needs to show the world what an excellent angler and ghillie he truly is. We wade out and start casting. After five minutes, one of Patrick's beautiful casts gets a fish. He knows how to play the lure better than me, and lets it drop much deeper. I think my retrieve is too quick but it's sometimes hard to judge. Salmon will take at any depth and it's your job as an angler to find the right level; Patrick instinctively knows in these waters. It's important to take into consideration the weather, for example; with low pressure they stay down, while high pressure brings them up. When it's sunny they take lures below, when it's windy it keeps them down as well. If you can judge by sight, all the better – but this depends on the water clarity.

Patrick hands me the rod and, as I start to gently play the fish, it leaps. It's a glorious platinum chinook. She's not as big as the last one but her bright silver scales mean she has just come up from the sea. After a few days she will start to take on the colours of the terrain. As I begin to reel her in she turns towards the bank – I am the wrong side of her! I try to bring her round but at the moment she's in charge. She swims towards me.

'I am too close!'

The closer the angler is to the fish, the more likely the line will go slack and we'll lose her.

'Walk back slowly,' says Patrick. 'Slowly.'

I keep walking backwards. I'm on the bank, still pacing back. I fall down a rabbit hole and into the gorse. I get up, still bringing the line towards the bank.

'You did it! You're there. Perfecto!' Patrick lands the fish and we both go wild. I start to breathe; I didn't realise I had been holding my breath.

'You did it!' Patrick is jumping for joy and I am so happy. We hug.

'I have never been so scared in my life. Oh, my goodness!'

It's a thirty-pound king salmon, so healthy, so vibrant; it's a credit to the species, *Oncorhynchus tshawytscha*. And that's easy for me to say! She has come up to spawn and who am I to stop her? Well, I kind of did, temporarily. I release her into the icy waters saying, 'Go forth and create other king salmon of good health and size.'

I run around the hotel grounds naked to celebrate my victory. I feel liberated. They can keep me here against my will but my spirit will not be broken. During my victory lap, Alistair gets a call.

'Put your clothes on, Robson, we need to get across the border NOW! The British Embassy has negotiated us a two-hour window.'

The van is still packed up and we leap in, me dressed in full fishing gear, unable to locate my clothes at the bottom of the baggage mountain. We bid a fond farewell to Patrick and Torres del Paine. The British Embassy has played a blinder and we are waved on through the barricades. It is only thanks to the negotiations and tireless efforts of the British diplomats and Helen Nightingale that we got through, as the strike continues for many more days.

We cross the border into Argentina. Just like the salmon, we are free once more.

Chapter Twelve

ASCENSION ISLAND

Shark Back Mountain

October 2010, At the Ends of the Earth, Series 4

It's 2 a.m., I'm in a cab on my way to RAF Brize Norton, Oxfordshire. As we enter the military compound I see floodlit razor wire and men with attack dogs. My stomach lurches. I'm definitely outside my comfort zone.

After rigorous security checks by military personnel, including an iris scan, fingerprints and tabs in my passport, I enter the strange airport lounge. Three hundred servicemen are asleep on chairs, trying to get some last-minute shut-eye before journeying to far-flung places such as the Falklands Islands, Iraq, Afghanistan and Ascension Island, which is where I'm heading. The passport-control man looks at me steadily; he wants to know why I'm going to Ascension.

'I'm off to fish there,' I reply.

His face breaks into a smile: 'You'll enjoy yourself. On its day it's the greatest fishing destination in the world.'

Billed as the Jurassic Park of fishing, Ascension Island is a tiny dot seven miles wide and nine miles long in the middle of the vast Atlantic Ocean, about halfway between West Africa and South America, and because of the island's remote location I'm told it's home to some of the best game fish in the world, as well as many unique and strange species. The only way to get there is to catch a lift with the armed forces, who fly there once a week.

As I creep past the sleeping soldiers I'm keenly aware I'm out-numbered by people who get shot at or shoot at others for a living; they have been in some extreme situations in the real sense, not like Ross Kemp or me with a back-up team and a nice hotel to sleep in. These are the men in the arena who live life on the edge and have seen some frightening things, and they are paid a pittance to risk their necks. As my dad used to say, I just ponce around wearing make-up for a living.

Suddenly a soldier, who's spark out across a row of chairs, sits bolt upright and does a quadruple take: 'Fuck me, it's Tucker!' I automatically put my hands up in surrender. 'Is this heaven?'

'No, welcome to hell, my friend.'

The incident wakes up many of the lads; just what I didn't want to happen. Spot the odd one out. I can tell what they're all thinking: 'Here's a reet pansy who thinks he's a hard man.'

Come on, Robson, man the fuck up. You're a well-respected actor, singer and presenter – a pillar of the community.

Pillock of the community, more like.

I hate my internal monologue. Of course, I have nothing to worry about: all the guys and girls are brilliant and a lot of them turn out to be fans of *Extreme Fishing* – well, they're only human.

*

Things are getting weird. It's time to depart but not by military plane, as I'd assumed – no, by Air Seychelles. As I board the aircraft I discover it really is a completely normal plane with seats, overhead lockers and no leg room. Unthinkingly I ask the air hostess where business class is located and all the soldiers look at me like I've just burnt down their houses and peed on their children. I'm escorted to the front of the plane by the base commander and offered the best seat in the house – next to the pilot. I'm living the dream. Take-off is my favourite part. It's exciting, especially when you're near all the knobs. If I were eight I'd now be swinging my legs in my chair, humming in contentment.

I'm looking forward to the adventure ahead. The first time I ever heard of Ascension Island was during the Falklands War, when Britain used it as a military base to fight the Argentinians. I don't think many people knew it even existed until then. Well, apart from the Portuguese, who discovered it on Ascension Day back in 1501. They owned it until 1815, when the Brits stole it off them, and Ascension has remained a British territory ever since. Today the island is still used by the RAF and US Air Force as a strategic outpost and communications base.

As we land I swallow hard: the runway is only a mile long and is cut into a mountain that we're approaching very fast. World War II pilots named the airfield Wideawake because they had to be wide awake to find Ascension in the first place, and then seriously alert to land there safely. There's no second chance. Mercifully our pilot's a pro and I'm right behind him if he needs me. It's three o'clock in the afternoon by the time we land. It's been a thirteen-hour flight but there's no time difference from the UK, so at least I won't be hit between the eyes with jet lag. As we disembark, the base commander asks if I would like to sing for the people of Ascension. I pretend not to hear him.

My first thought as I step off the plane is *Shit, I'm tired*. My second is *I'm not fucking singing*. I'm scooped up by the welcoming committee, who think the Beatles have finally arrived, but instead it's some dog-tired Geordie they've never heard of. I follow them into the airport, if you can call it that – it's more a shed. The whole population of the island is out to greet me – all seven of them. Although the island has no indigenous population, it is home to 900 residents, who are a mixture of UK and US military personnel and St Helenians, known locally as the Saints. As I make my way through the 'crowd', I am honoured that the governor of the Falklands Islands and the garrison commander have come out to greet me.

On the way to the hotel, I survey the scene. Ascension is a cross between Thunderbird Island and Los Cristianos in Tenerife, albeit without drunken Brits doing 'The Birdie Song' or 'Agadoo' by that really annoying band. The strange volcanic landscape is littered with cutting-edge *Star Wars* technology: giant golf balls protrude like cysts out of mountain tops and spider webs of wires form listening devices to communicate with anything from space stations to nuclear submarines. NASA even tested their moon buggy here – I can see why: I think I've landed on a different planet.

I loved *Thunderbirds* as a kid. Those were the days before political correctness when puppets could drink and smoke as much as they goddamn liked. And they smoked ALL the time. Lady Penelope was a forty-a-day girl – she must have stunk like a bad kipper. Apparently when *Thunderbirds* was rebroadcast on the BBC ten years ago, Lady P was criticised for smoking, wearing furs and shagging in the back of her car without a seatbelt on. How times have changed.

I drop my luggage off at my accommodation, and I use the word 'accommodation' loosely. It's a horrid pre-fab building that reminds me of a place called Killingworth in Newcastle, now condemned. There is nothing starry about the aptly named Obsidian Hotel. *Bear Grylls would definitely complain*, I think to myself – it would be too much like camping for him. Not that complaining would do him any good; it's the only hotel on the island.

Spear Fishing

There are only two sports boats on Ascension; one is owned by a German called Olaf Grimkowski, the other by South African Colin Chester, who I'm spear-fishing with today. I'm going deeper than I've ever gone to get a fish. We head out in his boat, the *Wide Awake II*, to Boatswain Island, which is a bird sanctuary. It's also a major fish attractor. There's a funny smell in the air and I discover from Colin it's bird guano – that's bird poo to you and me. It smells bad up top but looks beautiful down below, as the water is gin-clear. According to Colin it's the most spectacular spear-fishing on earth, and he should know as he's a spear-fishing champion. I'll be starting with fish such as black trevally or black jack.

I'm actually very nervous about diving down so deep – we'll be going down a full fifty feet – and we have to prepare our bodies properly to be able to free dive in one breath. I start holding my breath for ten seconds, fifteen seconds and then twenty seconds. Then I repeat the exercise holding the spear gun. After an hour I manage thirty-three seconds, which doesn't sound a lot but when you're holding a spear gun, diving down and moving around you get through a lot of oxygen. If I were going down under any other circumstances I could hold my breath for two minutes.

We clean out our masks and get ready to dive down. I watch Colin, who makes it look effortless, but it's deeper than I've ever dived before and with the adrenalin pumping it feels like your lungs could burst. The waters are choppy, which doesn't make it any easier. I'm bricking it.

Colin explains what I should do when I spot my target: 'Take a few deep breaths, go down and approach the fish. Your natural instinct will kick in. You point the spear where you want to shoot it and your finger will do the rest.' Simples.

No sooner have I put my head under the water than I spot a black jack – my heart is thundering in my ears. I hesitate. I'm so glad Colin's with me as he's such a relaxing influence.

'Take it easy, Robson, just dive down and fire,' he says.

The spear gun is heavy and the recoil great. The trick is to aim at a fish ten metres away or nearer. I take three big breaths and follow Colin's advice. He's right: my hunting instincts kick in and I quickly pursue the grey pocket torpedo. A black jack's turn of speed is phenomenal, so the secret is to get close and hover, like a kestrel over a vole. The knack is to let the fish come to you, and to my astonishment it glides towards me, then turns profile on and I fire. To my utter amazement it's a direct hit.

Even though I train hard every day, running and resistance training to keep fit for this job, I can't believe how truly exhausting this is. However, I feel very comfortable in Colin's company. Psychologically he is a safety net and somehow any sense of fear melts away. The breathing definitely helps, too – when you breathe in and out properly or concentrate on your breathing for an extended time you achieve a Zen-like state. Omm ...

Colin spots a fish – three breaths and he's down. His lungs are champion-sized, he is a natural hunter and is totally in tune with the ocean environment and his prey. He brings a healthy-sized black jack to the surface. Colin is doing something he was born to do. When I watch Rooney play football, I never worry what he's going to do with the ball; I'm always excited. Many other players are scared and unsure in the arena whereas Rooney belongs there; he was born to play football. I feel the same about Colin and fishing. I really envy his inner contentment with who he is and what he is doing. Too many people leave this life with a bewildered look on their face, unfulfilled and having done something they hate for too long. Colin's one of the lucky ones.

Colin's down again. I watch through my goggles as he strikes a medium-sized blue fish. Suddenly, his catch attracts a Galapagos shark. It propels itself towards Colin and from where I'm positioned it looks as if the shark is trying to remove his hands.

I start yelling: 'There's a shark eating Colin, there's a shark eating Colin!'

I splash around like a lunatic and, like the true coward that I am, hurl myself into the boat, leaving Colin for dead. I gingerly peer over the edge before Colin emerges without his blue fish but with both hands. Hooray! He thought it was wise to give that particular fish away.

After twenty minutes the sharks have vanished and I'm back in the water. I'm ready for my next fish and this time I've got something bigger in my sights – much bigger. One, two, three, I suck as much air into my lungs as possible and propel myself down after the fish like an ancient hunter. I shoot, I strike, I score. The speared fish bolts for the rocks, followed by dozens of hungry trigger fish after a meal. Colin dives deep to bring up my prize. I'm exhausted and gasping for air but I can barely believe what I've caught. It's a dog snapper – named because of its extraordinary canine gnashers. These fish are ambush predators that lie in wait for their prey to glide by and BAM! Their iridescent blood-orange colouring is surprisingly perfect camouflage, as the colour red is taken out of the white light spectrum as it hits water, so they appear almost invisible to unsuspecting bait fish. Rather like Jean Reno in the movie *Leon*, dog snappers are silent assassins.

At twenty-two pounds, my beautiful fish is easily the biggest I've hunted with a spear. Colin is thrilled and convinced I've smashed a spear-fishing record.

'Now, that's a fantastic fish. A winning catch, Robson!' he says.

It's all down to my tutor. Colin has the experience and knowledge of a true expert; he is a special person who cares deeply about what he's doing and wants to do it as well as he can. Some people have a notion that we don't belong down there in the world below, but I think as a species we are naturally drawn to water. It's not so much the need to escape or get away from it all, but perhaps more a need to get back to how it was. My father swam in the North Sea most of his life. Maybe he was subconsciously freeing himself from chains of oppression. But one thing I know is that when you enter water you cross a border, one that is mysterious, sometimes dangerous, but in the end always magical. Whatever it was he was always happy and now I'm ecstatic.

*

As we head back we are in agreement that there's no harm in casting a line. Immediately we're in – it's a yellowfin tuna *and* it's a ninety-pound monster. It's the biggest yellowfin I've ever seen, let alone caught. The lack of pollution and water temperature, which is about 17 degrees, makes conditions perfect for pelagic species, such as tuna, dorado and marlin, to thrive. I give the yellowfin to Colin's deckhand – at that size it should last him and his family a couple of years!

What better way to end the day than by eating what we caught? Our piscatorial smorgasbord comprises blue fish, black jack and dog snapper – it's an anglers' version of a Renaissance feast.

Kenny G

Today I'm taking part in a 'fish fry', which is basically a local knees-up disguised as a fishing competition. We meet at the Saints Club in town – the Saints (St Helenians) love to fish. My team-mates are Justin Wade and Adrian Henry, known as Kenny G. Not the cheesy 1980s sax player, but hopefully a great fisherman. They are both sullen-faced and kicking their heels; as it turns out they have been reluctantly shoved into something they really don't want to do. To them, fishing with me is worse than national service, being made to dress up as women or being sent to Rochdale.

I say, 'You guys really don't want to be here, do you?'

They shake their heads miserably. OK, so I've got my work cut out today to jolly along two kids who don't want to play with me. I tell them that losing is NOT an option. We are Team Extreme, living the dream – yes, I am as cheesy as my pop career and Kenny G suggest. Cue 1980s sax music as we walk down towards the ocean as Team Extreme.

As the ice starts to thaw between us – and believe me, I expelled a lot of hot air to achieve the melt – I realise their initial reluctance was actually a case of shyness. They were both completely star-struck ... No, not really, but incidentally I am well known on the island of Saint Helena. Many women approached me (yes, they were older; they're always older) and showed me their VHS recordings of *Soldier, Soldier* and Catherine Cookson's *The Gambling Man*. DVD players haven't quite made it to these parts, but I have.

We head down to the coast. We've got three hours to fish for our target: grouper. There is a prize for the biggest, smallest and largest number of fish caught.

'I see we're using snapper as bait, Justin.'

'No,' he says. 'They're squirrel fish.'

'What have you been smoking? They're snapper, matey.'

These boys may have highly qualified jobs as marine engineers but they just make things up as they go along. As we arrive at Justin's favourite fishing spot there's a problem as we discover another team has nabbed it. One of them is Justin's girlfriend, and seeing as she's no stranger to the sweet trolley there's no arguing. We are left with a small pier to fish off. The boys handline and I have a rod. I've never won a competition before. I'm not the competitive type, but today I'll make an exception.

Our neighbours appear to be catching but Justin's mind doesn't seem entirely on the game. In fact he's far more interested in his girlfriend than he is in grouper. Luckily Kenny G's all over it – fishing like a man possessed. He pulls up a medium-sized grouper and it's beautiful, with its speckled patterning and sharp fins. I handle it up carefully as the dorsal spines can do some serious damage. It's well equipped to defend itself but it's also equipped to attack, with its cavernous mouth, powerful jaws and razor-sharp teeth. Kenny pulls out another beauty – a three-pound rock hind grouper. This guy may be a moody bastard in the morning but he can certainly fish.

Justin and I have so far caught bog-all. But just when I think all hope has disappeared, something explodes onto my bait. Sadly it's a jack trevally – I've never been so sad to see a fish. I put it back and start again. Soon Kenny G has another fish on the end of his line – a seven-pound grouper. He may not have the other Kenny G's blonde highlights but this man has a magic all of his own. I feel sure Team Extreme is going to romp to victory. It's all about teamwork. Kenny G's not so sure.

As we gather at the Saints Club for the weigh-in it becomes crystal-clear we're up against some stiff competition, so I try to find out from organiser Suzie how Team Extreme is doing. I hypnotise her with my signature blue eyes – she wobbles for a moment, before giving me a look that could freeze my chestnuts and hides the figures. I'm asked to hand out the prizes and guess what? We didn't catch the most fish. We didn't get the smallest or the biggest. But the runner-up for largest grouper goes to Mr Robson Green, and being the narcissist that I am I go completely wild. I take the award and accept it but then I see Kenny G back-lit and hazy and I have to confess to everyone that I didn't catch any of the fish – it was all down to him.

The Old Geordie and the Sea

I'm slightly apprehensive this morning. I'm back with my mate Colin Chester and we're going marlin fishing. A *Makaira nigricans* would be a huge catch and we've got an unnervingly small boat; the giants out there could do a lot of damage to it and, more importantly, me. I'll be hiding behind burly Colin if a marlin jumps on the boat. I've left him for dead with a Galapagos shark once before, and I'll gladly do it again.

The topography of the island is also the reason fishing is unbelievably good here. Ascension Island is situated on the Mid-Atlantic Range, a divergent tectonic plate boundary located along the floor of the Atlantic Ocean. Part of the longest mountain range in the world, Ascension is essentially a mountain peak that rises 10,000 feet up from the sea bed. Because of this you don't have to go too far out to find deep-sea fish.

Here in the rich Atlantic waters, blue marlin grow to record-breaking sizes and are among the fastest and most powerful fish in the ocean. If anyone can catch one, my new buddy and I can, as we are the angling equivalent of Starsky and Hutch, Butch and Sundance – or is it Laurel and Hardy? To my amusement, Colin decides to remove the fighting chair: 'It's a wonderful way to fish for marlin as you're in direct contact with the fish. It brings us back to our roots, fishing like the old boys did in the frontier days,' he says.

Colin shows me what the pressure will be like on my body when we hook a marlin; as he pulls the rod down, my back groans. It's a lot of pressure. So we are going back to the days when men were men and fish were frightened. Colin tells me I need to 'man up' and I say, 'That's going to be difficult – I wear make-up for a living.' Our banter continues and the morning disappears. Soon we've been trawling for three hours but haven't caught a thing. Once again I feel like Santiago in *The Old Man and the Sea*, waiting and waiting. OK, he did it for eighty-four days, but we live in a far more impatient age nowadays. Maybe the waters off Ascension Island are fallible?

After what feels like an eternity there's a sign: dolphins. These beautiful mammals always bring luck, and suddenly something attacks the lure. Colin and the deckhand signal the driver to speed up the boat. I know I'm into something big by the sound of the reel – it's an angling symphony – and on the end of the line is the Holy Grail of game fish.

'It's a marlin!'

Colin holds on to me to stop me disappearing overboard. I'm hooked on to one of the largest and fastest ocean-going predators – if you want to know what it feels like, cast your line of 150 pounds and test it at full tension on a high-speed train. I have never done this and neither should you, but you get the idea.

As I tighten the line, the marlin explodes out of the water 200 yards ahead of me. It's ten feet long and 450 pounds of dynamic power. His bill alone, which he uses to slash through dense schools of fish like a carnivorous gladiator, is at least three feet in length. No superlative can accurately describe the sight of this creature other than 'awesome'. He takes off sideways at about 50 m.p.h. – I can't even travel at 5 m.p.h. in water and I'm a bloody good swimmer! I'm reeling in with everything I've got – I shout for Justin to turn the boat to the left.

'Quickly!'

It's enormously powerful so I dig deep and turn the reel with all my might. I am instantly reminded of Santiago again – it wasn't so long ago that guys would fight a marlin on a hand line. If I did that I think this beast would dislocate both my arms from their sockets. The one thing you can do when hooked into such a predator is: nothing. It becomes a test of strength and endurance between hunter and quarry. We both try to exhaust each other. He starts to tire and the retrieve begins. If I let this line go slack for even a split second the fish is off.

After thirty-five minutes there's colour. In the next thirty seconds I will be up close and personal with the greatest fighting fish on the planet, but at this precise second my rod whiplashes and I'm sent reeling back. He's off. Gone. And I am totally and utterly empty. The feeling is an overpowering sense of loss and failure, an emotion that I am sure is rooted in the hunter not being able to provide food for his family and the pending disappointment it will bring. I can't believe it: twenty metres away and we lost him. It's hard to take but this marlin has got the better of us today.

Colin says sagely, 'There's always another marlin out there to catch, Robson.'

And he's right: there are plenty more fish in the sea, especially around here. I go to bed early and dream of the mystical creature that got away.

Green Mountain

Ascension Island is mostly dry and volcanic but rising up in its centre is something very different: a green mountain called, er ... Green Mountain. It's where I'm heading today.

The mountain is a man-made forest in the clouds that generates rain. When the early explorers first found the island they discovered they couldn't live here because there is no natural source of water. It's is thought that, in the nineteenth century, some bright sparks, possibly Charles Darwin himself, conjured up the idea of the forest, with vegetation from around the globe, in a grand experiment to see if they could create an environment conducive to habitation. It truly is a miraculous place.

I'm meeting the conservationist who looks after Green Mountain, Stedson Stroud. Stroud, as well as having an extensive knowledge of botanical life, also knows a thing or two about fish, particularly moray eels. So off we trot to a weird landscape of volcanic rocks by the sea.

Our bait is rotting tuna heads, which eels have a penchant for. As I dangle my stinky bait in the water – waiving it around a bit to get maximum blood in the water – I'm thinking this is hardly the poetry of fly-fishing. Robert Redford would definitely have turned down directing the moray eel version of *A River Runs Through It*. I'd do it. I'd do anything. But it's not long before we get some interest in the form of a spotted moray eel. Quickly I bring the gaff down and try to hook it, but he gets away. They're slippery sods. I see another one and pull it out the water; Stedson hooks it up onto a rock and then rather surprisingly lands some thundering blows to stop it going back in. Yep, that's stopped it right in its tracks – Stedson isn't the hippy I thought he was. But blows to the head are the only way to dispatch a moray eel. It isn't pretty but if their teeth get hold of you they will sink right in and they won't come out. They use the same principle as a fishing hook: they hook around the prey and have barbs that you can't pull out. These eels are vicious, but in spite of that I still think they are beautiful. And apparently very tasty.

Later, as Stedson cooks the eel over a fire on the beach, he explains that moray eel tastes like Dover sole and the skin is the equivalent of pork scratchings. He uses the berries, wild rocket and other salad leaves we picked earlier on the mountain as delicious accompaniment. Eels are common fish around the world but not usually served for dinner. I think we'll have to change that. I try the eel. It's sensational and, you know what, it tastes just like chicken. No, Stedson's spot on: it has the delicate succulence of Dover sole. He's way off the mark with the pork scratchings, though.

German Shark Fishing

Tonight I'm going shark fishing and I'm apprehensive. In fact, I feel sick. A fucking cello plays over and over in my head as it did when I went mako fishing off Cape Cod. Dur-nur, dur-nur, dur-nur . . . I feel worried because I have a sixth sense that we're going to hook one tonight.

I really don't want to see a shark, let alone catch one, but paradoxically I'm compelled to find out more about what lies beneath these waters, however frightening. I need to discover if Ascension Island really *is* the Jurassic Park of fishing. And the only way to find out is to catch one of its most fearsome prehistoric creatures. Luckily the man who is going to help me catch a monster is no lightweight. He's big, he's German and his name is Olaf. He's quite frankly built like a brick scheisshaus. Olaf owns *Harmattan*, the only other sports boat on Ascension. He fires up the engine. Oh, God – this is really happening.

As we head to a shark feeding ground about a mile out, I try to appear casual, nonchalant even.

'The biggest fish I ever caught was a 500-pound blue marlin off the Azores,' I say, and Olaf nods, seemingly with angling approval – we're bonding.

'On a good night,' he replies, 'I would catch a fish four times that size.'

I nod with angling approval, disguising the fact in my mind I've plucked a pistol out of thin air and just shot myself.

'The largest shark I've seen up close was an eleven-foot, four-

hundred-pound reef shark in the Gulf of Mexico,' I say, beginning to hate the sound of my own voice. *For pity's sake, Robson,
put the spade down and step away from the hole.*

'Really? Wow!' says Olaf. 'Well, tonight, my friend, you are
going to see something three or four times the size of that.'

Shit. The. Bed.

According to Olaf there are some very ancient species in this
part of the ocean: mako sharks, thresher sharks, and Galapagos
sharks – like the one who tried to eat Colin's hands the other day.
But also under these inky waters lurks a true dinosaur whose
design hasn't changed for nearly 200 million years. The particular monster we're looking for is a sixgill shark, or cow shark.

Like many deep-sea creatures, the rarely-seen sixgill is known
to take daily vertical migrations, moving up to the epipelagic
zone (the surface) at night and returning to the mesopelagic
zone (the middle) of the ocean before dawn. The sixgill, which
has six gill slits instead of the usual five, is one of the few surviving members of the Hexanchidae family. All its other relatives,
apart from the dog tooth and Greenland shark, are only found in
fossils. Sixgill sharks get up to around twenty feet here, which is
too big to land (can you imagine?), but if we get it to the side of
the boat and set it free it counts as a catch. That said, getting it to
the side is down to me, and the impending sense of dread is suf-
focating. At this moment in time all I can think about is the
bloke on the Discovery Channel who had his calf bitten off in an
attack. This really isn't a safe situation.

Olaf hands me some of the most extreme gear I've ever seen.
There are buckles, ropes and a codpiece to rest the rod. So, just to
recap, I'm on a boat in the pitch-dark in the middle of the

Atlantic Ocean, wearing some seriously kinky fishing gear with a hulk of a German – we all know what they're like – and to make things worse I'm about to invite Jaws to the party. Olaf manhandles me again: 'I'm testing the pressure, ready for you to reel in a sixgill,' he says. But it feels more like he's giving me a heart attack and a hernia all at the same time.

'Please be gentle with me, Olaf,' I whimper.

I'm only a five-foot-nine actor weighing ten and a half stone (I know, I know, there are girls heavier than me). He's a bear of a man, six-foot-four and probably nineteen stone of pure muscle. There's no way I'm messing with this SOB; he could break me in two with his little finger. Forget Popeye and spinach, I think it's all the prehistoric fish he's been eating – he's pumped up with Omega-3.

Olaf places a massive piece of yellowfin tuna on the hook. I throw it in. There is total silence as the bait descends into the dark depths. The tension is set. Olaf ties an extra knot at the small of my back just in case. I wait. I wait. I wait. The only sound is of the water lapping gently against the boat's hull – click, click, click. I look into the night beneath. How many sea-monsters are lurking down there? I'm reminded of scary stories from my childhood in the north of England, like the Loch Ness Monster or Jenny Greenteeth, who stole people's children and drowned them. I think that's partly why we're so fascinated by this other world, all the myths and legends that surround lakes, rivers and oceans are as important as what we scientifically know. Fishermen are very superstitious people, you know. In fact, fishermen and sailors both believe that bananas on boats bring bad luck. It's true, because bananas give off spores that spoil other fruit, which would have been a disaster on board ship back in the 1700s: your whole fruit and veggie supply would perish. That's why you should never put bananas with other fruit but instead place them in a separate bowl. I'm dead useful, aren't I?

Bananas to one side for a minute, I feel a very distinct and sharp yank on the line.

'We have an enquiry,' says Olaf. He continues ominously: 'It's time.'

I put on the instruments of torture: an S&M harness from Herr Flick and Helga's fun cupboard, and immediately the pressure is absolute hell. The reel is on full tension. The rod starts to bend and keeps bending until I think it will snap. I am straining, gurning, sweating, but Olaf calmly holds me steady from behind.

Suddenly I get the full force of this gigantic fish going through my body like a pickaxe in my spine, tearing my spinal cord. I knew it would be tough but nothing prepared me for this. I'm jerked forward. Shit. I head for the inky water but manage to wedge my feet on the side of the boat. One more yank from the creature and I'll topple over. I'm attached – if the reel goes in, so do I – but Olaf keeps me upright and holds on to the reel. Whatever it is down there I've now really pissed it off. Another deckhand joins in the group hug. I've never been so pleased to have two men hugging me from behind before in my life. They're so close I can feel their conkers brushing against the backs of my thighs, but there's no time to be squeamish. I've got a shark to wrestle. I'm yanked violently forward again. This seems impossible – I'm suppose to get this fish to the surface but it seems more likely to pull me down to the depths. My harness and reel are re-connected again. I've got to bring this beast up more than 300 feet and I'm already losing my nerve.

The shark yanks again and I feel something explode in my back. I scream. I have a terrible sinking feeling – I know I've injured myself badly but I have to continue fighting the monster. The pain in my back starts shooting down the backs of my legs. Why didn't I do that TV drama instead? At this point I'd present *Daybreak*. I'd even go on *Strictly*, it's that bad.

I whine to Olaf, 'It's just too heavy – I can't do anything.'

Olaf says, 'Try and use a bit of fishing technique. Lift it slowly.'

His advice gets right on my wick: what does he think I'm bloody doing?

'I'm *trying* to lift it slowly,' I snarl.

As I finally get into a rhythm I start to get somewhere.

'Ja, Robson, I like the way you do it.'

I say, 'Liking your accent at the moment, Olaf; it's very Germanic.'

My muscles and head feel like they are going to pop, my face burns and I have a big hairy German standing behind me, watching my every move.

Olaf shouts, 'Faster!'

I dig deep. *Come on!* I get angry with whatever that thing is out there that's sapping my strength and has prolapsed a disc in my back (as I later find out). One–nil to the big guy – it's my turn. Robson's coming back for more.

Unfortunately my success pisses off the creature more and he swims down, yanking the heart out of my chest. Olaf tells me it's all OK and puts a big arm around me again – I'm so not happy now. *Dad, I know you didn't want me to be an actor, I should have listened to you – this is punishment. Or maybe it's poetic justice for* Unchained Melody. *Don't punish me; it was all Simon Cowell's idea. We didn't even make that much money out of it. He took the lot! Feed* him *to the sharks. Actually, he's quite a strong guy,* I think to myself, *he could do this. I'm not sure who would be the bigger shark though, the sixgill or him? It would be an interesting fight. Perhaps it could be a new programme format:* The Fishing Factor? *Maybe not.*

I mute my inner monologue and try to stop thinking of Cowell in a harness.

'Are we nearly there yet, Dad?' I ask Olaf.

'You have another eighty metres to go,' he replies. 'Lift slowly, go fast forward and wind at the same time.'

But just as I'm making progress the pressure on my body starts to tell in a completely unexpected way. I let out a ripper. Well, something had to blow – I'm just pleased it was my bottom. I apologise to Olaf, who is still holding me from behind – he must have felt the rumble: 'It appears my belly retired and my bum backfired.' I need the costume department and fast. Well, that's what happens when you've been wrestling with a shark for thirty minutes. But the change of cacks will have to wait. Slowly but surely I'm starting to win.

Suddenly the shark breaks the surface right by the side of the boat. Whoosh! Only swear words can describe my reaction. I instinctively move to the other side of the boat – it's an enormous sixgill, just what we were after. Its head is almost a metre wide, its mouth gaping open exposing a set of ragged brutal teeth almost two inches in length. And the eyes, oh, the eyes – in them is only death. They are two green fluorescent holes that flash menacingly in the torchlight; it really is a true dinosaur of the deep. The creature is about fourteen feet long and a massive 1,100 pounds. I tell Olaf I want to let it go now. I know it's an amazing fish and incredible to think he and his relatives have been lurking on the ocean floors for 200 million years, but it really is time to say goodbye.

When I get back to the hotel I take some painkillers and sleep like the dead.

Noddy

I wake up in searing pain and feel mortified. Not only have I done my back in, I also farted on camera. Oh, the shame of it. As I try to get out of bed, I find I can't, and when I move the shooting pains in my legs are now like red-hot pokers.

A month later I have an MRI scan back in the UK, which shows the shark has prolapsed discs in five of my vertebrae. Some of the extreme fishing I have done over the course of the show has put such an incredible load on my lower back, and my consultant says that if I haven't engaged my core correctly, even for one moment, damage will have occurred. He says I will need an operation in the future but for now all I have are painkillers and a vague idea that something's wrong with my body. Suddenly I'm reminded of Chelsea Charms, the woman with the biggest boobs in world. She was on *This Morning* with Fern and Philip and I shared a green room with her. Imagine what her back must be like, having to hold up double-Xs every day. She must be in permanent agony, poor thing.

The man I'm meeting today would like Chelsea Charms a lot, in fact he's got tattoos of big busty ladies all over his arms. His name is Noddy and not only does Noddy have proper seafaring tattoos, but he also actually looks like a proper sea fisherman, suitably weathered. Completely desiccated, to be honest. I'm told this fishing Saint can turn a short boat trip into a fishing extravaganza, so I jump at the chance of spending the day with him.

Noddy has been fishing these waters for twenty-six years and is *the* Ascension Island fisherman. He is the only one who provides a daily catch for the locals to eat. His boat might not be the biggest (it's not much bigger than a dinghy) but Noddy is the real deal. Today we're looking for fish with a market value. With the rods we're going for tuna and wahoo, and with the hand lines we'll be fishing for deepwater fish like snapper, jack and our main target: deepwater bullseye.

But we've also got to keep a keen eye on the local boobies. These naughty seabirds are well practised at stealing a fisherman's catch. Boobies hunt fish by diving into the sea and chasing their prey underwater – they have facial air sacs under the skin that cushion the impact as they dive-bomb the water from a significant height. 'Booby' is possibly derived from the Spanish slang *bubie*, meaning 'dunce', as they are not the cleverest of birds and indeed were often captured and eaten when they landed on the decks of sailing ships, Captain Bligh and his companions most notably living off them after being set adrift by Fletcher Christian following the mutiny on the *Bounty*.

Only moments after putting out our hand lines there is a tug on the other end of one and I start to pull it up through the water. I pull and pull and pull.

'How far is this line down?' I ask.

Noddy tells me 400 feet – I'm going to be here for a while. You could make a cuppa, run a bath and probably have a good night's kip in the time I'm still yanking this line up from the depths. I didn't know I was going to get a full-body workout. It's taking an eternity but at last it's exactly what we hoped for: a bullseye. It is the most amazing fish I've seen and it's the first time I've ever seen one in the flesh. Its orange colour is so vibrant it's like a giant prehistoric goldfish. The bullseye has massive eyes, which is how we can tell it's a deepwater fish, as it needs large pupils to let as much light in as possible in order to see anything at all down below.

'What a great start, Noddy!' I yell.

He smiles and nods, calmly reeling in another fish at the back of the boat. He hands the rod to me and I take over. Thanks to him I just have to bring it in the last few metres. It's a beautiful yellowfin tuna and Noddy tells me it's twenty-five pounds. The unspoiled ocean is teeming with tuna. Shockingly Noddy will only get £15 for such a beautiful fish. I tell him that in a British supermarket it would be worth over £150. It seems crazy. The Latin name for yellowfin tuna is *Thunnus albacares*. And if you remember, *Thunnus* derives from the word meaning 'to dart away quickly' and these fellas can accelerate from 0 to 50 m.p.h. in the blink of an eye.

Suddenly fish start coming from all directions, throwing themselves at the boat. I'm back on the hand line trying to bring another fish up from 400 feet – I'm certainly earning my boat ride. Noddy is at the back of the boat playing his rod like Jimi Hendrix – he is a fishing virtuoso. Noddy's tuna comes in and there's a black jack, too. My line is feeling strangely heavy so I keep hauling it up. At last the reason I'm done in becomes clear: it's a double whammy of amberjacks.

I'm back on the rod again, tackling another Ascension predator, and it's pulling like a train. It could be the biggest tuna of the day but it's going to be a long fight to get this one up and I'm feeling every bit of it. However, this time I remember to keep my sphincter under control. Paddy and Noddy laugh as I have to put a harness on to keep hold and help me pull up the large fish.

Well, little do they know that I'm actually suffering from serious spinal injuries. It hasn't gone away and still bloody hurts. I'm here carrying on like a brave soldier but all the while I'm in terrible pain, you know, especially with a giant tuna yanking me about. I know I'm a weakling compared to those guys but eventually I land the tuna. It's a whopper and in just an hour and a quarter we have caught a ridiculous amount of fish. Back on land, they use a crane to bring in the haul. We've never needed one of those before. It's some catch, including seven beautiful tuna, which would make about £1,000 back home. After every trip Noddy fillets the fish with the help of his friend Paddy. I have a go but it's not easy. They are like surgeons and I'm more like a butcher – a bad butcher. The job is to remove the fillets as neatly as possible. Mine are rubbish so I give up. Sometimes it's better to let the masters do their work.

I throw the discarded tuna heads down from the pier head to the triggerfish fifty feet below. They turn the water into a frenzied whirlpool as they drag the carcass down and devour it. It's such a fantastically healthy ecosystem. Everything is in perfect harmony.

So it's time to leave. I really hope I can bring my son, Taylor, to Ascension one day and meet up with Colin and his kids. I want to take Taylor free diving and let him experience Ascension life before it changes. I hope it doesn't. I'll keep in touch with Colin on email and Skype. It's amazing that in such a short space of time I have found a new friend.

Sadly Noddy passed away in the summer of 2011. He was a very special man and I feel privileged to have met him. I hope he's catching marlin and massive tuna up there in the sky. I'll keep in touch with Noddy in my thoughts and perhaps through a medium, but not the Boston stalker!

As the plane lands at Wideawake Airport, suddenly there's an almighty bang. Seeing as this is the aircraft we are due to fly back on I take quite an interest. It turns out the undercarriage has collapsed in on itself! Now I'm not an aeronautical engineering expert or anything, but I believe the undercarriage of a plane is rather important. It turns out I'm correct. We are delayed for several hours as they try to stick the plane back together again. Oh well. I don't want to leave anyway.

When I was first asked to join *Extreme Fishing* they said, 'Robson, would you like to venture the world in search of the ultimate fishing experience?', and on Ascension I think I discovered it.

Chapter Thirteen

PAPUA NEW GUINEA

The Lost World

December 2010, At the Ends of the Earth, Series 4

Papua New Guinea (PNG) is exactly like the land described in Sir Arthur Conan Doyle's *The Lost World*: lush rainforests, virgin waters and smouldering volcanoes. It's not hard to imagine a passing stegosaurus tearing the tender leaves off a tree or a leathery pterodactyl gliding over the cerulean bay. It's home to 800 tribes with legendary tales of witchdoctors and other folklore. I am excited – this is the start of a strange and thrilling adventure.

The journey has been epic and we are all done in. We have travelled 13,000 miles, on five planes, over three days, and now, finally, we are heading by boat to Kimbe, the capital of West New Britain. The island was 'discovered' in 1699 by William Dampier, a celebrated British explorer, and it's incredible to think that it probably hasn't changed much since he came here all those years ago. Even though PNG is situated ninety miles from the northeastern coast of Australia, there was little contact with the West until after World War II. In 1942 New Britain was invaded by the Japanese, who established it as a key military base, and the territory was crucial to their proposed invasion of Australia. The plan never came to fruition and the Japanese forces surrendered in 1945, but they left a lot of their kit behind. Strewn across the rainforests are Japanese fighter planes and other military hardware, abandoned and decaying. It makes the prehistoric landscape seem all the more curious – like a deserted movie set. Underneath the ocean lie unexploded bombs and torpedoes, above it smoking volcanoes and steaming seas. It is a place full of obscure dangers, ancient secrets and hopefully many exotic species of fish.

I have followed Jamie's instructions not to shave whilst travelling and I have the beginnings of a beard. I can see my reflection in Peter's sunglasses: it's grey and ginger and I am devastated. What throwback gene is this? There are no gingers in my family. I think about phoning my mum. Hang on a minute, the man from the Providence loan company – he was a ginger! I start to dial but there's no mobile phone signal out here.

We head to the hotel and drop our bags off. As always we're on a tight schedule and need to crack on with filming shots of the landscape, culture and people to establish our setting. The streets are lined with poverty and the banks guarded by ten armed guards with attack dogs. But what is most strange about this place is that everyone has red mouths and red teeth.

I discover that the red in the people's mouths isn't blood but dye from chewing 'betel nut', areca nuts wrapped in betel leaves with a sprinkle of crushed seashells, which act as a lime alkaline to release the stimulant properties of the leaves. They produce a feeling of mild euphoria and alertness but the downside is everyone knows you're 'off your nut' because your mouth turns a vibrant shade of scarlet. I look at the men, women and children all chewing it – it's like a national drug. I suppose it's a bit like alcohol in Britain – after all, red wine stains your lips and teeth.

Our hotel is a beautiful paradise retreat with a wooden reception area and thatched huts overlooking the ocean. The chambermaid is still preparing my room as we arrive and she flashes me a crimson smile. She is blatantly 'on the nut' and is rather friendly, to say the least. I am not sure if she wants an extra tip but let's just say I think she's suffering from desert disease – a bad case of wandering palms. Still, she's only human. I'd want to paw me all over, too.

That evening we head to the bar. There is nothing quite like a cold beer after days of travelling. We are all in good spirits and clink our glasses, toasting to this 'ends of the earth' experience. We dine on steamed Papuan black bass, perfectly cooked by the hotel chef. It's the taste of things to come.

Papuan Black Bass

'Pound for pound the black bass is the world's toughest fish,' says Riccard Reimann, my fishing guide and black bass guru.

He's intelligent, at ease with himself and good-looking – we instantly have a lot in common. It's early morning and we are at the Kulu River in search of this legendary game fish. Indigenous to only this part of the world, the Papuan black bass is a prize fighter, explosive on the line, and has been known to snap many fishermen's lines by the way it takes the bait. I am coiled with anticipation. We stand on the edge of the crocodile-infested river and Riccard tells me that so far this year three guys have been taken from the banks while baiting their hooks. They were never seen again. Well, bits of them were. The crocs here are exactly like the ones found in Australia and they look for routines before they attack. If patterns of behaviour are the same, they remember them, then like serial killers they will watch and wait in the shadows before they strike. If there is a group, they will attack the smallest. I am a lot smaller than Riccard! I look around me in panic but Peter is smaller than me and with his shiny swede has a lot more skin on display. I think I am safe.

We set off in a small boat with Riccard's assistant, Chris, and I keep one eye on the vicious archosaurs as we drift along the slow-moving brackish water. We are using torpedo lures with propellers to make disturbance on top of the water – creating a wake with small pops of the line. Riccard points to some tree roots in the river.

'This is where the bass are hiding. They will be sitting deep in the snags or at the top. You have to get your lure as close as possible,' he says in hushed tones.

'So accuracy is an important factor today?' I ask, casting straight into the trees.

'Yes,' he smiles.

I am snagged and I can't get the hook off – it's a terrible cast with no sense of distance or height. I am yanking and yanking, desperately trying to untangle the line. Craig is filming, grinning.

'Will you just pan off while I get my five-a-day?'

Jamie is loving my failure. As a director, he brings out the worst in me.

I am jet-lagged, freaked out about crocodiles and for some

reason I can't get 'She Drives Me Crazy' by the Fine Young Cannibals out of my head. I hum it over and over, still trying to untangle my line, but it snaps and the lure is left dangling in the tree. There's no way I can get it. It's a twenty-pound leader attached to a forty-pound braid line – an expensive mistake. Riccard is so patient: 'Don't worry. It happens all the time.'

He casts his line out and places the lure perfectly by a floating log. Wham! Riccard lifts his rod up and starts wrestling the fish.

'As soon as he hits the lure he's turning and it's just like a steam train. If it's a big one you just have to hold on,' he says, reeling.

It's only a four-pound black bass but it's a massive fight for such a small fish. Many black bass come in at around fifteen to twenty pounds here, but several have been seen over thirty pounds in size. I imagine it would be like hooking a charging herd of mammoths.

The black bass is a fine-looking fish with shimmering silver, pink and gold scales the size of shirt buttons, and a spiky dorsal fin. The Latin name is *Lutjanus goldiei* and it's actually part of the snapper family, which inhabits fresh and brackish water. The two canines on its upper jaw and smaller teeth below allow this fish to feed on whatever comes his way: small fish, mammals, crabs, baby crocs … he's not fussy. He is the biggest predator in this river, save the reptilian rippers.

After setting up again, I cast out my line. I need to be between three and six inches from the edge of the structure, in this case a fallen tree trunk. *Come on, Robson, don't mess this up.* I get vegetation again.

'Can you please stop filming me doing stupid casts?'

Or maybe I could just stop doing stupid casts in the first place.

I am annoying myself intensely. I want to become a troll on my own Twitter page. Jamie grins: 'Just take a deep breath and relax. Calm down,' he says, knowing this will wind me up even more. Thankfully, I get the lure back this time and save Riccard £12. I cast again, this time three inches off my target. It's a cast that deserves a fish and I get one.

'Hold on, Robson,' says Riccard.

Just as he predicted the bass is fighting like a commuter train in full motion. And I lose it.

'I did everything right, Riccard! I did everything you told me!'

God, I hate myself today. I want to swap bodies and be Riccard – or even Prada – but not me. I exhale loudly. There is a way to fight a black bass and I put too much bloody tension on the reel – when the fish runs, you need to let the line go a little slacker and put just enough tension on, but not too much. This comes with experience and, as usual, I'm learning the hard way.

Riccard casts effortlessly with one hand. It's beautiful to watch and he is so precise. I need two hands and two minutes to get myself sorted; I'm all fingers and thumbs. Riccard's in. The one thing you must do with a black bass is move it away from the structure as quickly as possible because the fish wants to go back into his hiding place. In fact, as he attacks the lure, he is already turning for home.

'They bolt so quickly,' says Riccard. 'He's taken me into the snags.'

'What do you do when he's returned to his lair?'

'Give a bit of slack but not a loose line, and watch him.'

He swims out but the line is caught about ten feet down. The fish can't get off the hook and Riccard can't bring him in. It's stalemate – someone has to go in and retrieve the fish.

'In you go, Robson,' says Jamie.

'What about the crocodiles, Jamie?'

'I can't see any. It's fine,' he snorts.

'They are stealth hunters – they are not saying "Here I am, over here!"'

'Well, you've got a head start.'

Jamie would secretly love me to be attacked by crocodiles – to him it would be TV gold. I can imagine him shouting, 'No! Don't rescue him yet, don't rescue him yet! Let him have a little bite of your leg, Robson, just a nibble. You'll get a BAFTA! Maybe an MBE! It'll be worth it.' I fold my arms. I'm not going anywhere. So Chris puts his goggles on and dives in, holding his breath for nearly two minutes. He comes up and says the line is well and truly snagged and then suddenly he is yanked down. A nine-pound fish has just pulled a 170-pound man back into the water. He emerges victorious with the bass on a lip grip and passes it to Riccard. It's an amazing fish: solid, healthy and powerful.

That evening we eat the two black bass Riccard caught, garnished with my vegetation. I need to up my game.

Good Head

The next day we are in Rabaul in East New Britain – well, what's left of it after a twenty-foot blanket of ash buried the town in 1994. As with the World War II military hardware in the forest, they haven't quite got round to tidying up yet. The volcano erupted, the ash fell and everyone fled, and that's how parts of the area have remained. It's a tropical Pompeii. Mount Tavurvur smoulders ominously in the background, a sinister reminder of the red-hot bubbling danger beneath. Tavurvur is part of a horse-shoe of volcanoes – active and potentially deadly – surrounding an aquamarine bay. The water is beautiful and serene, like a lagoon, but it is in fact Rabaul Caldera – the eye of a supervolcano – and if this baby blows, the town won't be the only place in trouble. They will feel the effects in Newcastle. No wonder people are 'on the nut' here. It's a case of 'live for today, because tomorrow you could be covered in boiling hot lava'.

The topography is terrible news for Rabaul, bad news for the planet, but great news for fishermen. The area is alive with billfish and I am hoping to catch a Pacific blue marlin. It's been over two years since I caught my first marlin, an Atlantic blue, off the Azores. Today game fishing enthusiast and pervy lure maker John Lau is going to help me.

I meet him at his workshop, where he is busy working on a lathe. John's lures are known in game fishing circles throughout the world. We shake hands and he presents me with a lure he's made especially. 'It's called a "good head",' he says with a twinkle. His other lures are the Linda Lovelace and his personal favourite, the Monica Lure-insky. We walk down the private jetty to his gleaming white yacht, the *Stephanie*. After the saucy lures I can't help wondering how Stephanie, whoever she is, got a whole boat named after her. The mind boggles.

Soon we are powering through the waves and immediately we can see there are billfish feeding at every turn. There are sailfish circling a bait ball of rainbow runners, lashing into them just 100 yards from the boat. On the starboard side a marlin is tucking in to another shoal of bait fish. There is activity all around.

I tell John that I am changing the name of my lure to Marlon Brando.

'Why?' he asks.

'Marlin Brando – geddit?'

'No,' he says, looking blank.

'I'm gonna make that fish an offer it can't refuse.'

He looks at me, bewildered. It wasn't funny to start with and by the time I've explained it five times I want to stick an orange in my mouth, wind my head in electrical tape and jump off the side. Maybe that's the sort of stuff Stephanie was into? I want a boat named after me. I'm game.

We trawl through the feeding area with our lures but after thirty minutes we have no takers. There are tuna feeding as well, but none of them are bothered about Marlin Brando when they have the real thing, and the heat is starting to become unbearable.

'Let's give them fresh bait,' I say.

We send out Rapala lures for rainbow runners. The deckhand pulls them up with ease. After half an hour I finally catch one. We slowly trawl the live bait but after three hours we get nothing. A tuna goes by, looks at our bait and turns away at the last minute. These billfish are well fed and ready for an afternoon nap. I tempt them like Mr Creosote: 'Surely, Mr Marlin, you have room for one more wafer-thin rainbow runner?' Nope. They are positive.

I have never seen so many billfish in my life. We must have spotted about twenty-five in total, as well as porpoises, whales and dolphins all wading into the fray to enjoy a good old buffet. John Lau points at the leaping dolphins: 'Such beautiful creatures.'

'Yes,' I say, looking at Jamie. 'But have you ever swum with them? There is a dark side to dolphins.'

'Oh, you're not still going on about the pink river dolphins?' says Jamie. 'So what, one nipped your leg and butted you in the chest.'

'I have been doing some research, Jamie. Dolphins are rapists and are even into gang attacks – you look it up.'

'Really?'

'Yes, really. And it's the same with moles.'

'Moles? What the fuck have moles got to do with anything?'

'There's a dark side to them, too. Moles are misogynists. Ask David Attenborough.'

'Ah, it's funny you should mention him. Do you like bird-watching? Because I've just signed you up for some this evening.'

We jump off the boat and thank John for an enjoyable day at sea. After a quick wash and brush-up it's time for me to fall on the grenade and judge the annual Miss Billfish Competition, a beauty pageant for game-fishing enthusiasts.

I loathe and despise Jamie as I'm really not feeling this event. I stand next to John, the event's compère, curl my toes and fix a grin. There are about fifty people crammed into a makeshift marquee with plastic chairs, a dodgy red carpet and a table where judges sit. I'm one of four. It's thundering and lightning outside and the rain is cascading down. Kids and dogs are running around, screaming and pissing on the carpet. It's a shambles. John taps the microphone loudly and everyone has a mini heart attack.

'Good evening' – the feedback is excruciating – 'tonight we have a movie star all the way from England. I would like to extend a huge welcome to Robson Green.'

One person claps.

'Thank you. I'm still available for panto.'

My job is to interview the contestants, who are wearing a variety of costumes this evening. I come up with a great Miss Billfish question: 'If you were a fish, what kind of fish would you be?'

'I'd be a marlin so I could travel the world, as I've heard they migrate a lot,' says one shy young woman.

One lass says: 'I don't want to be a fish. Why are you asking me that question?'

Question two: 'Do you like working with children?'

'Yes, because I've got a lot to offer and I am a kind and giving person.'

'Do *you* like working with children?' I ask another hopeful.

'No,' she says flatly. Come on, that's beauty queen basics – you have to love kids and want world peace.

Question three: 'Who's your favourite actor? By the way, I'm an actor.'

'Tom Cruise. Never heard of you.'

I ask a girl in blue. 'Heath Ledger,' she says.

'Oh boy, do I have some bad news for you.' She hasn't got a clue he's just died.

'He's so talented and handsome.'

'Not any more, he's not.'

'What?'

I tell her. She puts her hands to her face. I have turned into Larry David from *Curb Your Enthusiasm*; my humour is becoming as dark as the atmosphere. I really don't want to be here.

The fashion parade begins, to the soundtrack of the dodgiest 1970s soft-porno music. It's all a bit surreal. The women are judged on their interviews, personality and their outfits, and the other judges are taking it very seriously. There is a female Aussie tourist guide, a young guy who fancies all of them, and some pervy old guy. I give them all maximum points for each category.

One model has a Naomi Campbell-style fall as she hits the catwalk. She gets back up and bravely continues. A dog jumps up at her and barks and kids run round in deranged circles. The next two models walk down the runway wearing only very small bikinis. Suddenly the generator fuses and the lights go out. About ten minutes later the problem is fixed and the parade continues. How much longer can this go on?

Finally the girls line up and the announcement is made: 'And the winner is . . .' – cue drum roll – 'Miss Billfish, winning by a nose, the girl in blue.' I put a ribbon over her and a tiara on her head. She is very chuffed.

We escape back to the hotel, sharpish. It's after midnight. I'm about to put my light out when there's a knock at my door. It's Jamie. He's had his bag stolen.

'With all my money, cards and my bloody passport, Robson.'

We call the police.

The day before, Jamie had gone to do a quick recce in Kimbe. He'd heard there was something called 'condom fishing' so he had driven to a pharmacy to see if they stocked prophylactics (it's an unlikely story but absolutely true!). He jumped out of the van, leaving his bag on the front seat. The pharmacy did indeed stock an array of condoms and the owners were happy for us to film in their shop. Having organised this set-up, he jumped back in the van and joined us at breakfast. Only now has it dawned on him that his bag had been nicked out of the van, which he admits he didn't lock. I shake my head disappointedly.

'Basics, my sadistic friend, basics.'

The police arrive at the hotel. They are the picture definition of 'dodgy' but couldn't be more helpful. They think they know exactly who has his bag.

'Leave it with us and we'll get your bag back,' they say.

Jamie calls IWC in Glasgow. He is very concerned about the next shoot in New Caledonia. Without his passport he won't be allowed in. Helen says if he goes back to the UK within the next two days they can issue him a new passport straight away and he can be back in time for the New Caledonia shoot, but it's a logistical nightmare. Jamie is stressed. It's nice to watch. Usually I'm the one sweating.

Eggs and Fish

Meanwhile we have a show to make, and this morning I am going hunting for eggs and hand lining with the Tolai tribe. We head by boat across the Rabaul Caldera, straight for the ACTIVE volcano, Mount Tavurvur. The lava has turned into metallic grey rocks of pumice. Every tree is a scorched post and the volcanic heat turns the waves to steam as they lap against the black shore. We navigate through a channel in thirty- to forty-degree heat. Local man Robot and three friends are waiting to greet me. They are dressed in sarongs and bare-chested like my dad, which, given what we're about to do today, feels particularly apt. I'm going to be mining. But not for minerals under the earth: for megapode eggs buried deep in the ash.

The native bird, which looks like a rooster-sized moorhen with massive feet, uses the heat of the volcanic ash to incubate its eggs, and apparently they're very tasty. Robot and his guys are going to help me find them. It's really not that hard – you just start digging where the footprints stop! I start burrowing and soon am grey with ash. Dad would be proud of my newly discovered mining capabilities. *It's in the genes,* I think, as I dig like a champion. He used to say: 'You graft? Your skin wouldn't bloody graft!'

Bloody hell, these birds certainly bury their eggs deep. I've been slogging away for two hours and I have ash in my eyes, ears, mouth and nose, but about four feet down I'm getting close. The air is hot and dry and so is the ash. I start to shovel and part the grey slag with my hands. I reach down into the hole and find an egg. It's like a large duck egg. I find another. I am triumphant but Jamie and Craig now want more footage on a different side of the ACTIVE volcano and I want to go before it starts to spew molten lava at us. Robot takes me to another spot and we start digging. The ash is acrid in my eyes and Jamie, all clean and Lynx-fresh, is sadistically enjoying my transformation into an ashen spectre of my former self. I dig for another *four hours*, finding half a dozen more eggs. Finally Jamie's happy he's got the footage he needs.

I pass the eggs to Robot and his team who will sell them for the equivalent of about 40p each; with all the eggs I've helped them find, they should make about four quid. They give me five to take for dinner. I thank them, hurriedly leaving the dry, dusty, ACTIVE volcano, and head by boat to a beautiful island paradise, home to the Tolai tribe. As I arrive, kids are diving off a tree into the turquoise-blue waters and playing tag on the sand. On the shore I am greeted by tribal leader Kevung, who reminds me of Nelson Mandela. He beams a wide smile. I shake hands with two other guys wearing very random T-shirts.

'Are there some big fish out there? What kind of big ones?' I ask.

'Breams,' replies one of them.

'Big bream? They're very tasty fish. Do they go well with eggs?'

'No,' he says bluntly.

'Oh, right.'

He gazes out to sea. I read his thoughts: 'Who is this guy? Who the hell eats fish and eggs?' *Note to self, Robson, next time just bring a nice Chardonnay.*

We go out in canoes with an outrigger on one side, a bit like the bancas in the Philippines. I'm sharing with Kevung. Out here the water gets very deep, very quickly. Even in these tiny hand-made canoes, we'll be fishing depths of more than 500 feet and using a hand line will be a test of endurance. Luckily I've brought my trusty chamois gloves. I'm not stupid. Besides, Kevung wears a glove too so I'm just copying the locals.

We send down weighted hooks with squid as bait. Anything more than ten pounds in size at this depth will take hours. And bingo! I've got a fish. I start pulling up the line, which I predict will take about fifteen minutes. The line winds against a carved-out tree branch.

'Pull,' says Kevung. 'Pull. Pull. Pull. Pull,' he says, getting me into a rhythm like a fishing coxswain.

The fish is fighting and my arms are aching. I start dreaming about electric reels. I'm usually not a fan of them. What's the point? Hard work is all part of it but now I'm beginning to think they are one of the best inventions of the modern age, along with penicillin and the Pill.

'Pull it faster,' says Kevung.

'I am pulling it fast. I can't pull it any faster, Kevung.'

My arms are a blur with motion.

Kevung gets a fish, and across the way so has George, but mine's nearly at the surface. It's a four-pound mandara, or perch, but the line gets caught around the side rigger of the boat and becomes taut. The fish flicks its tail and is off.

'Shit!'

I am so upset. That fish has just taken me fifteen minutes to pull up and now I've lost it.

All the guys pull up lovely fish. They wind in the line with ease. Kevung is about twenty years older than me but he is so strong he pulls the line up like a man taking it easy on a Sunday afternoon. These guys don't have any fancy boats or equipment; they are using what nature gave them. The only expense is the nylon line and a hook. And I've just lost one. Later, when we arrive back on shore, I give them one of mine and they are so grateful. Out here, it makes a difference. I think about Riccard's lure, still in the tree. Maybe I could tell them about that one, too. Poor Riccard – I need to give him one of my lures. Luckily I'm seeing him tomorrow and I might be directing myself, because it looks like Jamie will have to fly back to London after all.

George pulls up a six-pound mandara and he paddles over for me to inspect it. It will make a great meal for the villagers. I congratulate him and pass it back but I didn't travel 13,000 miles to hold another man's fish; I need to catch one of my own and I'm staying out here all night if necessary – and Jamie says it is necessary. Me eating eggs on camera with the Tolai tribe won't really cut it with the producers back in the UK. *Extreme Egg Hunting With Robson Green* might not get another series.

I drop the line and hope the fish are hungry. I wait. Nothing. I am impatient. I want a fish. I can't face the villagers without catching anything. I'm in. *Please, please stay on, otherwise it's boiled eggs and soldiers for me and I don't want that. Come on. Use your core, Robson. Straight back . . .*

'Oh . . . I'm fucked.'

Kevung laughs. He tries to improve my technique but I am in a rhythm. *Nearly there, come on. Oh, for fuck's sake, where's the bloody fish?* I keep pulling and pulling. It's never-ending. And finally I pull up the smallest fish ever. It must be no more that a pound and I haven't got a clue what it is. It's definitely not the bream I was dreaming of. I've lost more weight pulling in this blinking fish than I'll gain from eating it. Kevung informs me that it's a loueer – it's a sweet little thing with bright yellow markings. I knock it on the head. He's my contribution to the feast tonight, as well as the megapode eggs, of course.

Between us we have caught three large mandara, two decent-sized bream and my loueer, which, placed next to the other fish, looks like a rotten banana. That night we eat with the tribe, cooking the fish and megapode eggs over an open fire. I tell the children how I found the eggs, digging in the ash. They don't understand a word I'm saying but are transfixed by my mimes. The megapode eggs are delicious, all yolk and no white but do you know what, George was right: eggs and fish really don't go well together.

Giant Goldfish

Early the next morning Jamie calls the police to see if they have made any progress, and they have. They turn up at the hotel holding his bag. They've got the culprits. Jamie is so relieved – we all are. Everything is there save the cash. He kisses his burgundy passport and shakes the hands of the policemen. He has just narrowly avoided six days of the most arduous travelling imaginable.

The police tell us the story of how they got his bag back. They battered down the door of the suspects, who made a run for it, so they shot them in the legs and went after another guy with a machete. Jamie and I look at one another out of the corner of our eyes. What? Did we just hear right? The senior officer invites Jamie to go with them to the hospital to see that justice has been done. In fact, we can all go. Strangely we unanimously decide to give that particular treat a miss. Jamie shakes their hands again and they are on their way. All I can say is don't nick anything in PNG because they don't mess around like they do in Britain, where you'd get three meals a day, a telly and an endless supply of narcotics.

After a spot of snorkelling we drive back to Kimbe in West New Britain. Riccard's taking me out on his big boat. We are reef fishing about 600 feet down, and in answer to my prayers we are using electric reels! Riccard takes us to spot where he has caught unknown monsters.

'There are some big things down there that we haven't managed to pull up. I've had this reel here smoking sometimes,' he says in a light Aussie drawl. 'There's actual smoke coming out of it because it's going backwards and you know they straighten these big hooks.'

We send the squid hooks down and no sooner have they hit the bottom than both reels go off. They whine like distant sirens. Suddenly mine stops: the fish is off. I take the other rod port side: 600, 590, 580, 570 . . . kick gears click on. With forty feet to go the alarm sounds to alert you to the fact that the fish is near to the surface and it's time to reel in by hand. As I start winding, the rod bends acutely. I wind with all my might and what comes into view is astonishing. It's a giant goldfish! Like something Gulliver would have won at the fair. I am so astonished that all I can manage on camera is a load of 'wows' and platitudes.

It's called a ruby snapper and the Latin name is *Etelis carbunculus*, which means 'ancient stone' – hence ruby. It is a vibrant orange with a shimmer of gold and massive black eyes, because it's dark down there in the benthic zone where it resides.

Wow! It's a forty-five-pound goldfish! All I can say is we're going to need a bigger bowl. I mean, imagine flushing this one down the loo when it's dead. But we're not going to do that today, we're going to eat it.

The goldfish has whetted my appetite. What else is down there? What about one of the monsters Riccard was speaking about? One of the lines beeps. The electric reels perform their magic.

'We've got something very, very large on the end here,' I say. 'OK, we're at forty feet. We're at thirty feet, Riccard. We're at twenty feet, we're at ten, nine, eight, seven . . .' I start winding with all my might. 'Oh, that's a weird-looking fish – look at that. What *is* that?'

Neither Riccard nor I know. In fact, we don't find out for a couple of days and begin to think we've discovered a new species. I am hell-bent on calling it a Robson – even though it's as ugly as sin, I want a fish named after me. But, God, it's a minger – a cross between a barracuda, an oilfish and a gar with a black sail, like a ghostly pirate ship. I think of names that actually suit it, like the Cowell. Yes, that works. Or maybe the Mandelson, or even better the Janet Street-Porter, although the mouth's not big enough.

Three days later we find out from a marine biologist that it is a barracouta, or black snoek. Identifying fish can at times be very difficult, particularly as they're known by different names around the world, which is why the Latin term in the universal language of classification is so helpful. This is a *Thyrsites atun* – it's a versatile, oily, bony fish that can be grilled, fried and tinned. It was hated in Britain during World War II because canned snoek was associated with deprivation and rationing. Ask your Great Aunt Margaret, or anyone of that generation, if they remember tinned snoek. Just from the look of it Riccard and I don't fancy a bite, so we pop it back to go and frighten the other fish.

We decide to try our luck one more time and immediately something enormous fights with the reels. We pull it up and it takes the line back down. This happens again and again, until the reels are screaming under the pressure. The motors whir. Is it a shark? Riccard says it's not fighting like one but whatever it is it's enormous. The reels pull the fish to forty feet, thirty feet, ten feet, and then the creature takes the line back down to fifty.

'It's going to burn the engine out,' says Riccard.

'What the hell is it?' I say, imagining the undiscovered and mysterious creatures down there, like the one Riccard's never been able to land. Perhaps it's a world-record-breaking giant goldfish over 100 pounds? But, then again, it's more likely to be a bull or tiger shark holding on to the fish I've just caught, desperately trying to steal my prize for himself. The motor continues to struggle, until crack! The line snaps – it's over and the fish is gone without a glimpse or even a clue. But whatever it was has just broken a line built to take 250 pounds! I look at the rod.

'It's busted the whole rig. I'm kind of glad that we didn't bring it up,' I say. 'As I have come to realise on this journey, some fish aren't meant to be caught.'

We put the ruby snapper I caught on the barbecue and cook it until the flesh is succulent. I scoop up the meaty white flakes with my fingers and, as I chew, wonder if I'll ever discover 'the Robson'.

'You will have to come back and fish for longer with me next time,' says Riccard. Then maybe, just maybe, we will land one of the undiscovered monsters of this strange but incredible lost world.

Chapter Fourteen

RUSSIA

Crime and Punishment

November 2010, At the Ends of the Earth, Series 4

Arriving in Moscow sets the tone for the rest of the trip. It's cold, grey and not one person is smiling. At our hotel, the reception has no reference of our booking. The middle-aged shot-putter behind the desk is a thoroughly unpleasant individual who grudgingly finds us a few rooms for the night. It's a dour place and it's so bloody cold as we carry our stuff up the rickety stairs to our rooms. I open the door to reveal my threadbare bed with a minimum of battered 1950s furniture. This hotel is so bad, even Lenny Henry wouldn't advertise it.

I look out of the window onto the streets below. It's snowing. Everyone is wearing Cossack hats and furs and walking with their heads down. It's like a Norman Cornish painting. Norman, who is still going strong at the time of writing this book, is a pitman painter from the northeast who captured the factory workers and miners, their heads lowered as they trudged to work.

They probably had stoops a bit like my dad from being cramped in unnaturally small spaces underground. But there's no mining here: people have their heads bowed because of the biting cold and probably a good old dose of Russian melancholy. Have you ever read a cheery Russian novel? I haven't, but then again I'm not sure I've managed to finish one.

The rest of the crew go to bed but Peter, our indefatigable soundman, and I stay up and drink vodka for medicinal purposes. I take a sip and immediately choke – it's like rocket fuel. An old boiler, wearing the dress she was buried in, bangs some cold sliced beef in gravy on the table. This is accompanied by cold peas and potatoes (all tinned), pickled fish and boiled eggs. Everything is cold – it reminds me of a trip to East Germany before the Wall came down. The vodka dulls our senses and anaesthetises our taste buds, and we are slowly able to ingest the food. We take another shot of the firewater and retire to bed. It is so cold I get under the covers fully clothed and watch my breath make steam. As I drift to sleep I decide *not* drinking vodka is more of a risk than drinking too much here. I vow to top up for the rest of the trip in order to keep out the chill.

In the morning the same woman, wearing that same sage-green dress, slams our breakfast down. It's not much of an improvement on dinner. Today we're heading for Eastern Siberia. The new director, Matt Richards, is an energetic, affable guy, full of ideas. Sadly Jamie is booked up with other work so can't join the gang back on tour this time. I miss Jamie but am warming to Matt's ideas on how he wants to expand on the humour side of the show. I smile at Peter and Craig Herd, back behind the camera, and say, 'Yeah, Siberia's going to be rich territory for gags. The land of hundreds of Soviet forced-labour camps, where millions perished under Stalin's rule. There was a reason why he sent people to Siberia, you know?'

'Why?'

'Because there was no chance of them coming back. It'll be a laugh a minute, this episode.'

Matt smiles. He remains upbeat and ever the optimist.

Khabarovsk Krai

On the plane to Khabarovsk, I have never seen such a bunch of glum people in my life.. The pilot makes an announcement that sounds almost cheery: 'There is a technical problem with the plane. I will keep you informed.' Twenty minutes later he comes on the intercom again. This time he sounds like his dog has just been intentionally run over by the men who burgled his house and killed his wife: 'The technical problem is now fixed so we can take off.' The passengers' faces fall further and as the engines start they go from glum to looking like members of a funeral cortège. We must be heading to a really bad place.

The atmosphere gets worse as we come in to land. The mood goes from funereal – the dipped heads of Norman Cornish paintings – to Edvard Munch's *The Scream*. If I thought people in Moscow were miserable, the Khabarovskians are suffering from chronic depression. I am now seven time zones away from Moscow and 3,000 miles away from home. Even the gulags didn't make it this far. Right now I would give my left testicle to be back in Britain, drinking a pint (of Sauv Blanc) in my local, standing by a warm fire and hearing laughter again.

On the way to meet the fixer, Isabella, the Khabarovsk landscape is barren, lonely and grey. The winter is brutal in the far east of Russia, and the temperature drops below –30 degrees. I look across the Amur River and it's like the face of the moon: a rocky field of ice. Only the middle is still flowing. People pick their way across looking for a spot to dig a hole and perhaps, if they are lucky, find a fish.

We get out of the van. It is so cold that it almost burns. In spite of this, however, Isabella is dressed in a blue skirt, thin tights, flat summer shoes, a pink headscarf and a cardie, complete with a white handbag. She stands there shivering. I am not sure she's built for the job. We introduce ourselves and quickly discover she also doesn't speak a great deal of English. As a fixer you have to be a translator – it is part of the job spec. Matt looks panicked. It's as if the real fixer has double-booked and his mum's agreed to stand in. ('Your fixing job is easy. I shall make you proud. Go to your other job, Josef.' 'But you don't speak good English, Mother.' 'No, but I will learn. Nothing is as hard as Russian.')

As I prepare to film a PTC dressed in full Arctic gear, five layers of thermals and Arctic boots, I glance over at Isabella, still shivering, looking like she's just popped down to Tesco on a mild spring day. I smile. Maybe Matt is right about finding the humour on this trip.

. . . And action!

'Khabarovsk sits at the edge of Russia, less than twenty miles from the Chinese border. It's on one of the world's longest rivers, the Amur – and apparently because of its spectacular beach and similar latitude to the French city – it's known as the Nice of the Far East.'

Yes, it's guinea-a-minute here. I look at the moon rocks. It's not a beach, it's more like a coastline, because it's –20 and everything is frozen over. And it's on the same latitude as Nice?

So what! I've been to Nice and it's nowt like this bloody place. I've spent many a day on the Beau Rivage Plage, in my Speedos, doing my Daniel Craig impression. If I did that here, my testicles would retract to my ears and you'd have to call me Susan. I don't think the French Riviera is in trouble yet.

Nanai, Sikachi-Alyan

Isabella comes with us in the van to meet the Nanai tribe in our first filming sequence. The roads are treacherous with ice but that doesn't seem to bother our driver, who is motoring along at an enthusiastic pace, talking all the while on his mobile phone. In fact he's never off the damn thing. We begin to slow and turn off onto a beaten track leading into the forest. As we climb, the trees become denser and denser, and the snow gets deeper. At 1,000 metres up we hit a three-foot bank of snow. The fixer's job, during the recce before the shoot, is to let the director know that they can get from A to B safely. But it is now obvious that Isabella has never fixed anything in her life. She encourages the driver to keep pushing through. He tries, revving the engine and putting the tyres in a spin, but we slip backwards. We are stuck deep in the forest, halfway up a hill, trying to explain to Isabella that there is no way we can make it through. She finally agrees and says, 'Yes, it's terrible, isn't it?'

Not quite the response we are after.

'What shall we do?' says Matt.

'I don't know,' says Isabella.

Matt takes charge. The driver is still glued to his bloody phone. We get his attention. In my mind, I imagine slapping the back of his head and throwing his phone out the window but instead Matt puts a firm hand on his shoulder and suggests he hangs up.

The driver turns his head to look into Matt's black, angry eyes. He cuts the call and starts to turn the van around. But we have no snow chains, no snow tyres, and we're in a little minivan like a Bedford Cruiser, full to the gunnels; like the fixer, it just isn't built for the job. The driver is ignoring our protestations. He will do things his way. He tries to go forward again, then back. It's like *Austin Powers* in the snow. The engine whirs as he tries to get traction; he puts the steering wheel in full lock; he tries the same in reverse until smoke billows from the back. Finally he puts his hands in the air.

'We are stuck,' he declares in Russian.

Yeah, well done, mate, we told you that half an hour ago. We all look at Isabella for a solution. She looks back at us and starts to cry.

'I worried we are in the middle of woods with much snow. My cat? How will she eat?'

She meows and mimes eating, to get the importance of her message across. We are all agog. From that moment on, it's not about the show any more, it's about her hungry ginger tom.

After an animated discussion it is decided that Isabella and the driver should remain with the van. We leave her to organise a 4×4 to pull the van out of the snow and solve her pussy problem. The debacle reminds me of a time when I had just set up Coastal Productions and we were filming *Come Snow, Come Blow* with Tim Healy and Rodney Bewes from *The Likely Lads*. The crew and I were on our way to a recce when I said to the driver, 'Hang on, we're going in the wrong direction.' He said, 'No, I am late for my trumpet lesson.'

'What? But we need to be in Ashington.'

'Well, I need to be in Newcastle – my band's in the National Brass Band Championships.'

'Well, why the hell did you agree to drive us?' I said, infuriated.
'I thought it would work out but it didn't.'

It was of course his first, and last, driving job, and the band didn't even make the finals.

The crew and I unpack the van. We now have to lug our stuff half a mile up the hill, through three foot of snow, to a wooden shack where the Nanai are waiting to do a dance – well, they do! Peter and I bemoan the fact that we have no vodka with us. Everything is slowly coming apart at the seams. Matt's blood pressure is rising but veteran Craig tells him to keep on filming the story and it will be OK. I am carrying the least, as usual, so I bound on ahead to act as crevice spotter.

'If I disappear, then it's deep!' I shout.

I start throwing snowballs at the crew. None of them thinks it is funny. I get Peter slap-bang on his baldy head.

'Stop it, Robson!'

'I am just trying to boost morale,' I say, throwing more.

At the top I am pelted in a revenge attack. Snowball fights always improve spirits.

At the top of the hill we find the Nanai people. There are two women wearing traditional purple embroidered tunics and holding long sticks, and a larger lady in a red outfit with a woolly hat, who's on drums. They couldn't be less pleased to see us. We are an hour late, and because of that the men have buggered off. A dog bounds out of the woods and runs at Prada. It looks like a Rottweiler. Prada, carrying his heavy sound pack and boom, legs it through the snow like John Cleese. This dog is obsessed with him; it snarls and barks as Peter runs in the opposite direction, knees high. It's comedy genius but Peter is genuinely scared. We look to the women to stop the dog. They look over vacantly and do nothing.

Without anyone to translate, Matt is using sign language to communicate to the tribeswomen. There is a ten-foot square of space next to the hut. The large lady hits a Mike Oldfield-style drum with a stick: boom, boom, boom, boom. She is bored and looks as if she is waiting for a bus. The other two girls move their sticks side to side, up and down, and stomp the ground. There is no moving, no singing – that's it.

Matt wants me to react. I say, 'That has to be the worst dance I have ever seen, and if this is a blessing, we are not going to catch anything.'

It's like bad Morris dancing without beards and bells.

The drumming and stick twizzling stops. 'Thank goodness for that,' I say.

It starts again, only this time with one of the girls wafting cotton wool around. Craig is shaking with laughter, Matt is despairing and Peter is still dealing with a growling dog. We can't find the two Nanai guys, Alexei and Andrei, who are meant to be taking us fishing. After the stunning musical and dance performance that could rival the Bolshoi, we finally find them out on the frozen Amur River. There is no meet-and-greet, no hole to be dug – they are on stools, already fishing. I walk over and they don't even flick me a look.

The Amur River is half a mile across and not totally frozen. The middle is still flowing, but where we are is solid ice. There are huge blocks of ice floating down the centre. The theory is that pike, frightened by the ice blocks rubbing together, flee from the vibrations and take shelter under the ice. Well, now I am going to drill a couple of holes into that shelter with my corkscrew drill. To maximise their chances, the experienced fishermen here use two rods and two holes. I set up my fishing camp midway between Alexei and Andrei. I am piggy in the middle. They sit stock-still and expressionless, and they stay like this for hours.

It's painfully clear I'm not going to learn anything from these two today so I get on with the task in hand. I've got my two twelve-inch rods, which are two sticks with line tied to them, and my lure. I am using a brass circle an inch across with legs like a little crab. These brass crabs bounce off the bottom six to seven feet down. Pike have a voracious appetite and will eat almost anything, so hopefully one will come along, take a look, and wallop. Pike are vicious and strike fast so there won't be any doubt about a nibble.

I look over hopefully at Alexei. I've been proactive and am all set up for fishing; maybe now he'll acknowledge me. Nope. After an hour in the sub-zero temperatures the blokes still haven't said a word to me; talk about being sent to social Siberia. I jabber away to camera: 'I am so glad I am with these guys. I am having so much fun. Since the moment we got here we haven't stopped chatting. Alexei just doesn't shut up. Such fun. Such a bond.'

Even though I am mentioning their names loudly, neither of them moves. Finally Andrei moves his arm. I say, 'Thank God for that. I thought you had frozen to death.'

He looks at me like I am a Chechen separatist. Still, it's significant progress. Andrei suddenly gets up and silently walks across the ice to drill a hole somewhere else. The crew are wetting themselves.

'I don't think he likes you,' says Prada.

'I'll set the dog on you again,' I warn him.

I look over at Alexei and say in Russian, 'Where are the fish?'

He grunts an inaudible 'dunno', but I am happy. At last I have got him to speak. My objective this week is not landing an extreme fish, it is getting two fishermen to say anything at all. But of course I know why these guys are not up for talking: the secret to this method of fishing is total silence. It's the vibrations of my voice that are quite possibly frightening the fish. I shut up and it does the trick – Alexei and Andrei both catch an Arctic pike. I am thrilled and run over to Alexei, lauding praise on him. I want to go in for a hug and pick him up but I know that might end in violence so instead I hold his fish forth and say, '*Esox lucius*, from the Ancient Greek *lucus*, meaning "wolf", which refers to the fish's predatory skills.'

It's been five hours, it's dark and I haven't got a fish because I have been talking all the time. Alexei and Andrei are either side of me holding their pike up for the camera and I say, 'There you have it: Alexei caught a fish, Andrei caught a fish, and as you can see, they are over the moon, not only to have caught two lovely pike but also to have met me.'

They look stony-faced, not even a flicker of a smile or even a glower, just total and absolute indifference.

Deflated and tired, we trudge through the snow back to the van. Isabella has had the van pulled out of the snow by a 4×4. However, instead of transferring us into the 4×4, she has sent it away again. The shitty van makes its way down the hill, through the snow and ice, slipping sideways. Isabella is not speaking to us either; she is still obsessing about her cat. Louise Allen, our assistant producer, has been trying to organise another fixer with the office in Glasgow. When we arrive in Khabarovsk Matt and Louise take Isabella off for a word. She is paid and free to get back to feed her hungry ginger Tom.

Peter, Craig and I all trudge off to bed while Matt and Louise head to a bar. Matt needs a stiff drink. As luck would have it they bump into some students who are studying media studies in Russia. One girl called Anna has particularly good English and agrees to help us. She turns out to be a wonderful breath of fresh air.

Khabarovsk City

'Are you Red Fox?' I ask a random man. 'The seagull flies high tonight,' I say to another. I have on a large Russian hat and am hamming it up. I whisper to an old lady, 'Are you Red Fox?' She hits me with her handbag.

Matt wants to set up a thread of espionage and my mission is to find the agent who will help me succeed on my latest fishing assignment. I sit by the Amur River waiting for a signal, any signal. I get a tap on the shoulder. It's Anna; she is Red Fox and she has come to rescue me from this fishing debacle. She takes me to a tackle shop in town. We're fishing on the Amur in the centre of the city today, so I need to buy a rod and variety of lures. We are going for lennock, char, grayling and catfish. In the shop there is a wide variety of lures, many of which I have never seen before. There is a mouse lure the size of a field mouse, a hamster lure, and a squirrel lure the size of an actual bloody squirrel with a hook hanging out of its bum.

'What kind of a fish would go for these?' I say.

I ask the shopkeeper if it is a joke but he assures me it isn't. Apparently Amur catfish love squirrels. I nod but know he's talking out of his bottom. I get loaded up with a variety of lures, including a squirrel lure for fun (honest).

Anna takes me to the river, where supposedly a contributor is waiting for me. We scan the lunar landscape and indeed there is a fat Russian sitting on a seat. He raises his hand and then immediately lets us know that he doesn't want to be filmed. Anna translates, 'He thought he was just here for advice.'

He has the same depressive demeanour as many others I have met on this journey. Matt is overwhelmed with frustration but just when I think this episode has hit rock-bottom, enter a larger-than-life old guy called Victor, who saves the day. He has a bag of swag on his back full of fish. And he is *smiling*. He talks to us in front of camera and says, 'You have got the wrong equipment, it's the wrong time of day . . .' He inspects my luminous green rod.

'Ohhh. I have no words,' he says.

He picks up the rod and mimes throwing it away. He looks at my corkscrew drill with contempt and starts digging a hole with his spear. It's a wooden branch with a metal end, which gouges out the ice. I have just paid the equivalent of £75 for the drill and it's no use. He tells me the hole will be too small to get the fish out. With a spear he can make a hole four times the size.

I show him the squirrel lure. He chuckles, his whole body shaking visibly, and he agrees it must be some kind of joke. He tells me to use the crab lures. The temperature is plummeting to −20 but Victor has warmed our hearts. He shows us his haul, around twenty small Amur catfish, then bids me good luck and walks off across the frozen river. I am now on my own. I say to camera, 'It's hard to make friends in this part of the world. Victor has gone and I miss him.'

Off camera we tried to keep him. We offered him money, fame, friendship, but he said, 'No, no', and went about his business. In this place people wander on and off the stage when they want to – it's like being in a perpetual Beckett play.

The temperature has now plummeted to −25 and my line is frozen. There are no fish here – Victor must have taken them all.

The guy who sold me the squirrel lure saw me coming and the drill is as much use as a chocolate fireguard. I throw it down in disgust and walk off. I need a drink and a strong one. *No wonder there are so many alcoholics here,* I think.

That night all the crew, save Craig, who's the sensible one, go to the pub with the one sole mission of getting mullered with the locals. An AC/DC tribute band is singing 'Highway to Hell' in heavy Russian accents. The band are all overweight and drinking beer as they play. It's a brilliant atmosphere. We go long and we go wrong. It's a 'Whole Lotta Rosie' and a whole lot of Vodka. My face hits the pillow at 4 a.m.

Petropavlovsk, Kamchatka Peninsula

I wake up an hour and a half later at 5.30 a.m., fully clothed – but then that's normal in Siberia. We are meant to be flying to the Kamchatka Peninsula. I am so hung-over and the flight is at seven. Craig pops his head around the door.

'Don't ask. You have no idea what these eyes have seen,' I groan.

He shakes his head. Louise helps me pack by shoving everything into bin bags. She's in the hurt locker, too, but as the AP it's her job to grip the situation. At the airport, I hold Peter's hand.

He says, 'Shall we go upstairs to the café?'

I say, 'Please don't leave me.'

I am so vague and frightened. Peter is florid and I am concerned about his blood pressure. I squeeze his hand. I am on the verge of a theatrical breakdown and think I am going to die. I keep telling myself that it's just a hangover, but it is the mother and father of them all.

*

We fly to Petropavlovsk, the capital of Kamchatka, situated between the Bering Sea and the Sea of Okhotsk. The salmon-shaped peninsula is twice the size of Britain but with a population the size of Cardiff. The facts rattle around in my head as I throw litres of water down my neck; it feels like sand. My raging thirst is unquenchable. As I wave to the air hostess to bring me more, she huffs like Kevin the Teenager and flounces back with another cup. I drink. The prospect of going out to sea today is increasing my mania. Matt has arranged for us to go out on a trawler. My stomach knots a bit tighter.

We pile into a van and head to the coast. By the side of the road, someone has fashioned several snowmen and -women. They are really good with sculpted noses and detailed boobs, and all of them are smiling and waving. They are some of the most cheerful people I have come across on this journey, save Anna, Victor and the people at the bar last night. Louise's phone rings. It's the office. There are no trawlers going out today because the sea is too rough, too cold and parts of it have iced over. My colour returns but Matt goes grey. It's day four and we still haven't caught a single fish.

We go to various landmarks and film some GVs (General View shots), which help the viewer establish where the hell in the world we are. However, the weather's closed in overnight and what is meant be a spectacular view, a view to end all views on a clear day, is obscured by monochrome cloud and mizzle.

Matt says, 'Just say something about the view, Robson. Anything.'

'But we can't see a bloody thing!'

The facts spin in my head and I feel sick again. The Red Bull is beginning to repeat.

'Err ... Kamchatka is in the Ring of Fire and the bay that you can't see behind me is surrounded by a chain of volcanoes. There are more than a hundred and sixty volcanoes here, twenty-eight of which are active, but if one erupted today you'd only hear it; you wouldn't see it. Lava could be spewing out but nature's fireworks would be completely wasted. I've travelled five thousand miles for this stunning, breathtaking view. I could be at Whitley Bay, Northumberland.'

Poor Matt is now looking terrified. We need to get out of Petropavlovsk and fish in the Siberian wilderness, fast. We meet up with Sergei and Tatiana, who are descended from the Itelman tribe, Kamchadal natives who have lived here for hundreds, if not thousands, of years. We are hoping – no, praying – that they might help us catch a fish. Any fish will do, we're not fussy!

Tatiana comes up with a brilliant idea – she suggests we visit the fish market (!) to buy the ingredients for a traditional Itelman soup called Uuka. The main ingredients are crab, Arctic char and whole salmon, including its eyes and head. I'm not sure about the eyes, I don't like my food staring back at me, but some of the best meat is found in the cheeks and under the gill plate of a fish. It's always worth using in a soup or adding to a meal. At the market we look at the various fish. I spot Stalin crab, introduced to the area as a source of cheap crabmeat. Like king crab, they can grow to huge sizes and are very deadly predators. Everything is frozen and nothing is fresh, as it has been caught in the warmer months. I buy the salmon, and know to my core that we are not going to catch anything today – that's why Tatiana is getting us to buy all the ingredients. In spite of my deep-down reservations I say to Tatiana, 'Leave the final ingredient to me.' I am determined to catch an Arctic char – or at least try my damnedest.

We head straight to the fishing location on the Kamchatka River at a place called Pinchoseheeva (*pinch* means 'fire' in Russian). Here the river is the same size as the Coquet, but it's –20 by midday and will plummet to –42 at night. Despite this, the river has not frozen over and that's because of the hot springs heated by the molten lava of the volcano, which keeps the water flowing. We don't need to ice fish here, I can cast a spinner. First of all I build a fire for Tatiana at the edge of the river, and get it going.

I tell her, 'Stay here, it's going to take a real man to catch a fish today ... [pause] ... and here he is, Sergei Lukiv.'

Sergei crumbles in front of the lens, staring at Craig as if he is pointing a Kalashnikov. We try to warm him up but he is not one for small talk. Sergei would also rather stand by the fire and watch me fish than have a conversation.

The river is freezing and I need to wade in to get a decent cast. Almost immediately I can't feel my toes. In order to cast I use bare hands, which I need to warm up every few minutes. I'm using Tatiana's old tights filled with salmon eggs as bait, which I trot along the river and let the current take downstream. It's an unusual method and an unusual use of tights. I like to keep my wife's hosiery to buff up my brogues or polish the car. It comes up lovely.

The cold is perishing, my fingers are painful and the whole experience is far from enjoyable. Everyone is by the fire, including the crew. Craig is using a long lens and Peter has good signal – they are nice and toasty. There are no fish in this bloody river. Off in the distance to my right is a half-formed oxbow lake. Water is still flowing in and there are fish in there. We go and inspect. I can see dozens of char, but it's difficult to cast into and impossible to wade.

Luckily Sergei has a plan. I dangle my line into the lake while he runs upriver to scare the fish towards my balls of eggs. Slightly surprisingly he starts throwing snowballs at the fish, pounding lumps of snow into the water. Splosh! Sure enough the fish head in my direction, but the last thing anyone being pelted with snowballs wants to do is *eat*. When I smacked Prada on the bonce with one on the hill up to the Nanai, he didn't react by saying, 'Do you know what, I really fancy a steak sandwich now.' God help us! However, we are so up a frozen Shit Creek that all ideas, however bonkers, are being considered. Suddenly I feel a faint nibble on my line. I reel in a small parr (baby salmon) about three inches long. Sergei smiles; he's delighted for me.

'Wow, I feel so butch now.'

I pop it back in the water quickly and feel seriously depressed. This is getting ridiculous but then if the producers had wanted to make it easy they would have sent us here in the summer. That bastard Hamish Barbour has a lot to answer for.

Desperate times mean desperate measures but it turns out that Tatiana has an amazing plan. She announces she knows an old Itelman method, used for centuries to feed the tribe over difficult winter months. She makes two little fish lures out of reeds. I look at them.

'Are they meant to be fish-shaped?'

'Yes,' she smiles.

I smile back. They are truly rubbish. I am utterly sceptical but willing to give anything a go. She wades into the river and, on very short lines, she bends over and drags them backwards through about six inches of water. As she 'trawls' the lures she says, 'Here, fishy-fishy. Here, fishy-fishy.'

I've seen it all now, but she is determined this method is going to work. But it doesn't take an Oxford don to work out – it does not. I tell her if she catches a fish I will eat my own head. Only the most academically challenged salmon would go for this method. I can't stop laughing and she is genuinely offended.

'Here you fish for subsistence, not just for fun,' she explains.

'Well, the philosophy of what we do, you know, on this journey is that we eat what we catch, which I think will be pretty difficult today. But I tell you what, I'm really glad you're here. Do you know why? Because you brought a bit of glamour to the show. You smile, you're a lovely person, and you've cheered me up,' I say, gushing.

She blushes. 'You're very enthusiastic, too.'

'Very enthusiastic and handsome, right?'

'Of course,' she giggles coyly.

'Thank you, Tatiana.'

And that's how we end the sequence – me lamely fishing for compliments. It's the best we can do.

Having caught nothing, we return to Tatiana's village, where her mother and family are sitting down ready to eat the Uuka soup, without the Arctic char. They are not happy about it and neither am I. I feel like a failure. Imagine all those years ago, that sinking feeling of the hunter-gather returning from days of hunting, the expectant look on his wife and children's faces.

'What you got, Dad?'

'Nowt.'

I'd have gone AWOL for days rather than face that.

'Could you apologise to the chefs that I haven't brought any arctic char?' I ask Tatiana.

'Of course,' she says.

An exchange starts in Russian. The mother says, sarcastically, 'How did our butch friend get on?'

Tatiana says, 'Our butch friend took the piss out of our straw lures and caught bog-all.' (to paraphrase)

'Stupid Geordie pillock!' says Mum, or words to that effect. I don't care – it's the butch comment that cut deep. I'm not *that* scrawny.

The Uuka soup is delightful and really tasty. We eat in their wooden log cabin, which is basic but rather like a Swiss chalet. The family is very close and unified. In order to survive out here you all need to work together and be made of stern stuff. It strikes me as quite a matriarchal society. I have always said there would be no more war if women were in charge; just twenty-eight days of serious negotiations.

That night I am staying with the family in the Village of the Damned. The house is a kind of granny flat with a definite granny smell, depressing pictures of Tsars and religious icons all over the walls and some very worn and basic furniture. I am staying here without the rest of the team, who are all in different houses. I've lucked out with a vodka-juggling trio. I think the old fella's Sergei's grandfather but I can't be sure. He offers me vodka but I politely decline. He takes umbrage. The younger man passes me a plate of cubed horsemeat – *he obviously shops at Tesco*, I think. I politely decline again. He too takes umbrage. He clunks the plate down on a side table and we sit in silence, in the dark, with only the glow and crackle of the fire to warm the atmosphere. The old lady in the corner gurgles and dribbles in her chair. I think she's had a stroke, poor dear. The old man kindly wipes away her drool with his hand and takes another cube of horsemeat, *with the same hand*! He offers me the plate again. I smile, swallowing a gag reflex and, once again, politely refuse. I wasn't keen on the horsemeat to start with but now I'm defiant.

I am already sitting on my bed, a worn leather settee with a crocheted blanket and a cushion as a pillow, by the fire. The family soon melts away into the dark and I am left to a fitful night's sleep. The young man wakes to stoke the fire throughout the night – three o'clock, four o'clock, five o'clock, he puts logs on to keep it burning. Obviously word has got round that Butch would probably freeze to death without the fire. I thank him for his kindness.

Dolinovka

'To misquote a US president: "We don't do this extreme fishing because it is easy – we do it because it is hard." And one of the most insidious crimes an angler commits is when his ambition falters and he accepts his fishing limitations. I will triumph over adversity. I will catch a fish and put an end to this fishing debacle.'

'Hoorah!' Sergei and my band of brothers cheer, and we get in the truck and travel 300 miles north to Dolinovka. Matt said it was only four hours away – more like nine in our piece-of-shit army truck.

Oh my God, it has to be the most uncomfortable journey of my life and a bit like travelling in a freezer, only a freezer would have been warmer as it's only −18 degrees. The condensation on the windows has turned to ice. I am shivering and I am wearing an Arctic coat and trousers, two layers of thermals and another five layers under the coat. But the views are astonishing. The vast wilderness of Siberia is like nothing I have seen before. It is the most untouched, unspoiled and unpopulated place on the planet. We stop and take pictures at every turn. And in the villages there are massive murals of Yuri Gagarin on the sides of buildings, as well as other national heroes of the space race. Time, too, is on ice here.

We jump out of our *Apocalypse Now* truck at a place on the Kamchatka River, near Dolinovka. It's frozen over, and the ice is about four feet thick in places. Matt decides to have an ice-fishing competition to catch steelhead, Arctic char or grayling.

It's me versus Sergei, who is wearing some curious-looking camo ski gear that looks like it is from World War II – and it probably is. We have four hours and the winner is the one who catches the greatest number of fish. Sergei has already beaten me at poker on the bus, and we are pretending that I need to win back my watch. But this is a serious competition, not a TV set-up, and we are both VERY competitive. He is the Russian Bear, I am the British Lion and this is our very own Cold War. He stares at me with a steely gaze but I am strangely confident. I have learnt enough to ice-fish alone from Victor, the old man at the Amur River who taught me how to present the lure to the fish, how to dig a hole with a spear and what size, and from Alexei and Andrei, who taught me to shut up.

I keep my distance from Sergei, who is making a racket using his drill. I dig my hole with a spear made from a branch with a knife tied to the end of it. I have gone for thinner ice, and I feel there might be a feeding channel below. It's just a hunch but I'm going with it. I don't say a word, I just slowly bring up the bait, just as the dhow fisherman taught me in Kenya and Howard showed me when fishing for pike in Alaska.

After five minutes I get my first bite and I pull up a one-and-a-half-pound stone char. It's a pure char, indigenous to the area. The signature of char compared to a trout is they have a light background and dark spots, whereas trout have a dark background with light spots. Char also have brilliant white leading edges on their pectoral, pelvic and anal fins. The char is part of the salmonid family and it is its adipose fin that distinguishes it as game fish. No one's totally sure what this mysterious fatty fin is for but it is thought to help with swimming function. This turns out to be the first of many, and very quickly it's 7–0 to me.

I say, 'It's like Man-U playing Accrington Stanley. It's a battering, Sergei.'

Sergei has a fit.

'Why are you doing this to me? Why are you making fun of me? I don't understand. I have done everything you have asked.'

With ten minutes to spare, Sergei catches a grayling. I have never seen one before and am genuinely excited – it's an extraordinary fish with a dorsal fin like an angel's wing. Sergei is a good fisherman and has helped us a lot – I hug him and concede that he has caught the best fish of the day. I recite an anonymous quotation: 'She is sometimes called the silver lady of the stream and in the pure water, essential for her existence, she is as graceful and as clever as any of her rivals.'

As we enjoy the tender, delicate meat of the grayling and Arctic char by a makeshift fire, Matt turns to me and says, 'There is something in this competition lark.'

I agree. It's like the missing element of the show – the Higgs boson. Men behave in an entertaining way when they compete – the rivalry, history, preparation, winning and failing, and the struggle. As it turns out, when Hamish sees the cut he agrees, and picks up the phone to Channel 5 to pitch the new idea. They commission a fifth series almost immediately.

In spite of all the trials and tribulations of this final journey, the *Extreme Fishing* show is really beginning to work, and what a privilege it has been to work alongside and meet some of the most talented and amazing people on the planet. My dad always said, 'There are lots of wonderful folk in the world and you have to meet as many of them as you can.' I've done that against the backdrop of truly astonishing locations and connected with people of all nations through the universal passion for fishing. Except with Andrei and Alexei here in Russia – they were difficult nuts to crack – but everywhere else I've experienced nothing but kindness and enthusiasm, like from my old friend Sergei here. Long may the show continue.

And now it's time to drink vodka! Sergei and I clink glasses and the firewater blows my head off again.

Fade to black.

ACKNOWLEDGEMENTS

Thank you to Team Extreme (you know who you are) for allowing me to not look like a jerk at one end of the line waiting for a jerk at the other. Special thanks to Directors Jamie Goold and Alistair Smith who 'got it', along with the irrepressible Sound Supremo Peter Prada ... thank you for staying with me guys ... millions wouldn't! I can't leave out Hamish Barbour, Helen Nightingale and Gerry Costello, not only for giving me the dream gig but for throwing me a life line every time I was drowning in front of the lens, which was quite often. Sandra Jobling and her Husband Ken for being there when it mattered most, especially the phone call which went along the lines of 'Get me off this F****** Island!' The unending support of my mother Anne, two sisters Dawn and Joanna, along with my kid brother David. My Uncle Matheson for teaching me everything I know about fishing (yes it was his fault everyone). Briony Gowlett and the gang at Simon & Schuster, and my co-author Charlotte Reather for turning my notes, diaries and this extraordinary, extreme and sometimes absurd adventure into a beautiful and entertaining story. I miss our daily six-hour Skype calls. Thank you to Vanya for being a wonderful mother to our beautiful son Taylor. If I have forgotten anyone it's because I'm heading towards fifty and even though the wheel is still turning in my memory the hamster is well and truly dead.

Charlotte would like to thank High Tower for his unwavering support, love and belief, Mom and Pops for being there throughout my rakish journey for backing, supporting me and loving me without limits (even when the rozzers were involved). Maurice Gran for being the best confidante and chief cheerleader a girl could have, and Robson for his belief, integrity and friendship. You are amazing people and so are all my wonderful friends who have always known I am a star in waiting. Is this Kate Winslet enough?

About the Authors

Born in Northumberland on 18 December 1964, **Robson Green** is one of the best known faces on British Television. He has been associated with a number of the most celebrated television dramas of recent times including *Soldier Soldier, Reckless, Touching Evil* and *Wire in the Blood*. Robson still lives in Northumberland and spends whatever spare time he has seeing his son Taylor, reading, walking, going to the gym and fishing.

Charlotte Reather first spied Robson Green across a sea of meatheads and spray-tanned strippers at a cage-fight at the Radisson Edwardian, Heathrow, and asked if she could interview the actor for a magazine.

Robson says, 'It was fate and when I read the article I instantly knew Charlotte was the only person who could write this book. She is a serious talent, hilarious, gifted and inspired.'

Charlotte writes comedy scripts for TV and film. She is a columnist and contributor to several magazines and newspapers including *NFU Countryside, The Field, Country Life* and the *Telegraph.* Originally from the Cotswolds, she lives with her husband in Washington DC. This is her first book.

www.charlottereather.com

'Charlotte is incredibly funny, fearless and terrifyingly ambitious. Look out world!' Maurice Gran, co-creator of *Birds of a Feather.*